THE
VILLA TABLE
300 CLASSIC ITALIAN RECIPES

D1344862

THE
VILLA TABLE

300 CLASSIC ITALIAN RECIPES

LORENZA DE'MEDICI

PHOTOGRAPHS BY MICHAEL BOYS

PAVILION

This edition published in Great Britain in 1995 by
PAVILION BOOKS LIMITED
26 Upper Ground, London SE1 9PD

Originally published in hardback in 1993

Text copyright © 1993 Lorenza de' Medici
Photographs copyright © 1993 by Michael Boys

Designed by Peter Luff
Jacket designed by Bernard Higton

A CIP catalogue record for this book is available from the
British Library

ISBN: 1–85793–698–1

Printed and bound in Spain

2 4 6 8 10 9 7 5 3 1

This book may be ordered by post direct from the publisher.
Please contact the Marketing Department.
But try your bookshop first.

Title page picture:
Spaghetti with Oil and Rosemary
● **(p. 56), Rice and Spinach Mould (p. 61),** ●
Winter Salad (p. 138)

CONTENTS

Introduction 6

Introduction

I am not a professional cook. I do not even cook every day and when I do cook, I try to spend as little time in the kitchen as possible. For me cooking, however enjoyable it might be, is simply a means to an end: the pleasure of a satisfying meal in good company.

Whether I am cooking for my family or a group of guests I want to be able to enjoy the occasion. I do not want to be confined to the kitchen while my friends are enjoying good conversation in the drawing room. Since I have always worked as well as raised four children, I have never had the time to spend hours standing over the stove preparing a meal for company. If I thought it were necessary to do so in order to entertain, I would have ended up either denying myself one of my great pleasures – eating at home with friends – or would always be going out to restaurants. In Italy restaurants are considered suitable for certain occasions, but I think most Italians prefer eating at home. I certainly do. And home cooking ought to be superior.

As a result I have developed a repertoire of recipes over the years that are uncomplicated and take a minimum of last-minute fuss. My ideal is the dish that can be assembled beforehand and cooked while I am visiting with my guests. I also favour recipes that facilitate impromptu, improvised meals, the kind I can cook when friends drop by.

*E*ven when I have help for the large dinner parties we often give at the family winery, Badia a Coltibuono in Chianti, I want to have a hand in what is going on in the kitchen as well as receive my guests. On these occasions, too, I serve dishes that are simple, tasty and elegant.

When I am preparing new recipes to teach in my cooking classes or have some leisure time for experimenting in the kitchen, I enjoy challenging myself by cooking more elaborate dishes. I have also included these recipes in this book.

My mother was a great recipe collector and I take after her in this. These are mostly jottings on scraps of paper or written in little notebooks. The ingredients are given as they are needed but only with the most general idea of proportion – a pinch of this, a little of that. These recipes really tell a story about how the dish should be made to taste rather than give dry, technical information. They are also an expression of a certain attitude towards cooking. It is a skill that requires, above all, sensory judgements – touching, observing, smelling and tasting – rather than knowledge that can be found in a book.

*W*hen I began teaching cooking classes at Coltibuono and writing cookbooks for non-Italians, I found that this approach created problems. It presupposed that the one cooking the recipe not only had experience but also a refined palate, both acquired, like mother's milk, from childhood. I soon realized that this was often not the case when you are dealing with foods and tastes that are foreign to your students and readers. Now I write my recipes with as precise measurements as possible and include the necessary technical information. It should be remembered, however, that measurements are always an approximation. Cups and grams, for example, cannot be converted exactly and I have discovered that every food editor has her preferred conversion table.

I never cease to remind those who really want to learn Italian cooking that a recipe is no substitute for taste and by taste I simply mean what tastes right to you. We can all agree when some dish does not taste quite right, but there will always be different opinions about when it tastes JUST right – a little more of this, a little less of that. And that is how it should be. This is a matter of taste. My goal is to give my students the confidence they need to put the recipe aside and to start cooking with all of their senses instead, including a generous portion of their common sense too.

During my classes I especially enjoy proving my point when we make dough for pasta and bread. I tell the students to heap a generous amount of flour on to our large work surface without any regard to measurement, three times as much as I know will be necessary. They make a well in the centre and break the eggs into it. Then they begin to mix the eggs with the flour, little by little absorbing the surrounding flour. I leave it to their eyes and fingers to judge when they have worked the mixture into a paste of the right consistency to begin kneading it into dough. This always turns out to be a most satisfying and successful experiment both for me and for them. And the leftover flour is not wasted, simply sifted and used again.

*A*ll the recipes in this book have been tried and tested by my non-Italian students and I have written them keeping in mind that they will be used outside of Italy. The required ingredients and equipment are easily found, at least in delicatessens and speciality stores that now exist practically everywhere.

With regard to kitchen equipment I suppose most cooks would consider me a minimalist. I believe in investing in good pots and pans, some fine quality earthenware and excellent knives. Beyond these, all you need to make these recipes is a pasta machine for stretching and cutting the dough and a food processor for sauces and vegetable moulds. You will not need a thermometer. I indicate, where necessary, natural ways you can use for measuring the temperature.

A balanced composition of the menu is as essential for a satisfying and successful meal as the combination of ingredients for the dishes. This is another area where acquired taste plays a decisive role. It has often been remarked that not every Italian may know how to cook but they all know how to eat. Rather than composing set menus, I suggest dishes that go well with one another and indicate how I might combine them at my meals. Today an important dinner will be composed of three or four courses, whereas our daily meals consist of a single dish, with salad and fruit to follow.

Along with the kitchen, the other focal point of the Italian home is the dining table, much more than the drawing room. It is here the family gathers and we receive our friends, not only to eat but to spend time together. It has been observed that Italians eat quickly but stay at the table for a long time. Because eating is not merely a matter of nourishment, it is important not only that the food be satisfying and appealing to the eye but also that everything having to do with the table – linen, china and silver – be attractive. During the course of these chapters I have insisted on these points and have included what I hope will be helpful suggestions.

*A*s the title of this book I have chosen the same name that I use for my cooking classes, THE VILLA TABLE. To me these words speak of a tradition of eating and hospitality that has developed over the centuries in the homes and kitchens of the great families of Italy. Our cuisine is both uncomplicated and refined and its clean, finely balanced tastes depend on high quality fresh ingredients simply and sagely prepared.

For the past decade I have tried to reinterpret this tradition according to the necessities of a contemporary life-style. I note with satisfaction that the finest creative cooking in Italy today is going back to this same source. The recipes I have brought together in this book represent my most comprehensive attempt to transmit this heritage. I hope they provide enjoyment in the kitchen and satisfaction at your table.

Important Notes

In the recipes, two and sometimes three sets of measurements are given for ingredients. These are metric weights and measures followed by their nearest equivalent in pounds, ounces, inches and so on, and then, where required, a third measurement in American cups and spoons. Whenever preparing a recipe, follow only one set of measurements because they are not exact equivalents and cannot be used interchangeably with any success.

American cooks should always use the final measurement in sequence except in the case of oven temperatures. For these, American cooks should follow the Fahrenheit temperature.

Where ingredient names and terms in the method differ for the U.S., the American equivalent is given in parentheses.

Where a recipe calls for sugar, this is granulated sugar. Other types of sugar are specified. Please note that British granulated sugar is coarser than American granulated sugar, and in some cases British cooks are advised to use the finer caster sugar where American cooks can use their granulated.

Where a recipe calls for flour, this is British plain flour and American all-purpose flour. Other types of flour are specified. Please note than the appropriate British or American flour for each recipe is given if necessary, and that these may differ from recipe to recipe. For example, British strong plain flour is best to use for all bread and pizza doughs, where American bread flour is needed for some and all-purpose flour can be used for others.

Where a recipe calls for eggs, these are size-3 eggs (U.S. large eggs). Any other egg sizes required are specified.

Oven temperatures are given as °Centigrade, followed by their nearest equivalent °Fahrenheit, and then, for older British ovens, the gas mark.

Spoon measures used in the recipes are equivalent to metric spoons:
1 tbsp = 15 ml 1 tsp = 5 ml

Gli Antipasti

STARTERS

*C*ontrary to popular opinion, great platters of antipasti brought to the table to begin the meal are not a staple of Italian dining. They were never served in my family while I was growing up — not even at my wedding — nor in the families of my friends, and I don't serve them in my home. The first time I ever saw them was in a restaurant, where to some extent they still survive. Antipasti had their origin as banquet food and were served before a series of several courses — and then everyone went to bed for a long nap to sleep it all off. Who wants to be weighed down by all that food today?

Instead, I put to good use the various and tempting recipes from the vast repertoire of traditional antipasti dishes in other ways. Frequently I offer them to my guests with a glass of white wine as an APERITIVO, something to tease the appetite rather than to dull it. In this case I select finger-foods, titbits that I can serve without the additional work of plates, knives and forks, and that my guests can enjoy while standing up. These STUZZICHINI, or 'teasers', are especially useful for luncheon and dinner parties when guests tend to arrive over a certain span of time, especially in Italy where punctuality is not a national virtue.

*A*nother advantage to serving the antipasti in this way is that it provides me with a few leisurely minutes to spend with my guests before returning to the kitchen to put the final touches on the courses to follow. I find it very uncivilized to be obliged to stand over the stove until the last minute. So I choose antipasti that can be served cold. Ideal for this purpose are traditional Tuscan CROSTINI, little rounds of toasts that can be served with various herbal or meat spreads, or topped with a couple of slices of fresh porcini mushrooms, or perhaps a few pieces of Parmesan cheese sprinkled with balsamic vinegar. The classic BRUSCHETTA, grilled bread rubbed with garlic and soaked with extra virgin olive oil, reduced to a handy size, is always a favourite.

I take care that these APERITIVI are not only pleasing to the taste but also to the eye. When I am entertaining in the country I serve them in flat, hand-woven baskets with a white linen cloth beneath. For a colourful and very easy presentation, arrange little cubes

• Prosciutto and Figs •

of fontina cheese and salami alternately on small wooden sticks and fix them in a grapefruit or a plump apple. In any case, don't confuse the appetite of your dinner guests with too many choices. Two antipasti will usually do nicely.

*O*n the other hand, a generous assortment of antipasti is the perfect solution for cocktail parties. This form of entertaining is not as popular in Italy as it once was. Still, at least a couple of times a year when I want to entertain a large group of guests, even up to a hundred or so, I give a 'cocktail', as we say in Italy. Obviously, for these occasions I have help, both in the kitchen and for serving, so I can offer my guests as many as 15 different kinds of antipasti, both cold and hot. For hot antipasti I favour fresh greens dipped in a light batter, deep-fried and brought from the kitchen while still warm. Sage leaves and courgette (zucchini) blossoms are particularly good prepared in this way. Also delicious are rice croquettes. Then there are numerous shellfish recipes that are both delectable and elegant, such as breaded, baked mussels served on their half shell. These parties are not meant to take the place of a meal so you may want to regulate the flow of food in such a way so as not to encourage your guests to spend the entire evening. When most have departed, however, I usually serve a big bowl of risotto to nourish the ones who have persevered to the end.

Perhaps one of the most pleasant and relaxing moments during my cooking classes, both for me and my students, is our late-morning break. This usually occurs around noontime, when the day's dishes have been prepared and we are waiting for them to finish cooking. I use this opportunity to serve the antipasto, out in the garden with a glass of wine or just sitting around the kitchen discussing the luncheon menu. Even this pause is instructive, I hope. I intend it as a demonstration of how helpful and enjoyable it can be for the hostess-cook to take an antipasto break with her guests. I can also imagine other similar situations, social and committee meetings, club events and the like when you might be able to put to good use some of these antipasti recipes that follow.

Bomboline al Formaggio

CHEESE PUFFS

For cocktail parties present these on a platter garnished with parsley and lemon wedges. Accompanied by a light tomato sauce such as that on page 157, they are also ideal as a first course for an elegant luncheon, and could be followed by a fish dish such as wrapped red mullet with mushrooms (page 122) and then Vin Santo Sorbet (page 192).

MAKES ABOUT 30, TO SERVE 6

3 egg whites

180 g / 6 oz / 1½ cups freshly grated Parmesan cheese

a generous pinch of grated nutmeg

olive oil for deep-frying

Whisk the egg whites until stiff, then gently fold in the Parmesan cheese and the nutmeg.

Heat the oil in a deep heavy pan until it reaches 180°C / 350°F.

Using a spoon, shape the mixture into puffs the size of walnuts and immerse them, a few at a time, in the hot oil. Deep-fry them until golden (they will double in size). Remove them with a slotted spoon and drain on paper towels. Serve immediately.

BALSAMIC VINEGAR

Balsamic vinegar is made from the cooked must of unfermented grape-juice. It undergoes an ageing process, at least 10 years, during which time it is transferred to casks of various woods and blended with vinegar of older vintages.

Cappelle di Funghi ai Gamberetti

MUSHROOM CAPS WITH PRAWN (SHRIMP) FILLING

The filling here is also good for hard-boiled egg whites. Ricotta cheese can be substituted for mascarpone to make the mixture less rich. Keep the mushroom stalks for flavouring a soup, sauce or meat stew.

MAKES 18

18 button mushroom caps

90 g / 3 oz shelled raw king prawns (large shrimp)

salt

120 g / 4 oz / ½ cup mascarpone

1 tbsp balsamic vinegar

1 tbsp finely chopped fresh flat-leaf (Italian) parsley

Clean the mushrooms with a damp cloth, but do not wash them. Cook the prawns (shrimp) in boiling salted water for a couple of minutes, then drain them and set aside to cool.

In a food processor fitted with a metal blade, process the mascarpone and prawns (shrimp) until creamy. Add the balsamic vinegar and parsley and process for a few more seconds.

The result is a dark brown, dense liquid with a complex aroma. It is produced in the regions of Modena and Reggio Emilia where, in olden times, it was considered a balsam for curing stomach ailments and colds. I use it as a sauce. Perhaps the best way to enjoy it is to sprinkle a few drops over thin slices of Parmesan cheese.

Put the mixture in a piping bag and fill the mushroom cups. Arrange them on a platter and serve, at room temperature.

Carciofi con Maionese all'Arancia

STUFFED ARTICHOKES WITH ORANGE MAYONNAISE

The Italian artichokes I use are small so I calculate two per person. If you can only find large globe artichokes, one each will suffice. I always save the tender leaves and the stalks to flavour the cooking juices of roast lamb. The leaves can also be cut up and added to vegetable soup.

SERVES 6

juice of 1 lemon

12 small globe artichokes

1 egg and 1 egg yolk

salt

120 ml / 4 fl oz / ½ cup extra virgin olive oil

1 tbsp grated orange zest

1 hard-boiled egg

Fill a bowl with cold water and add the lemon juice. Trim the tops of the artichokes, cut off the tough outer leaves and dig out the chokes. Drop them immediately into the lemon water to prevent them turning black. When all the artichokes have been prepared, cook them in boiling salted water for 15–20 minutes or until tender.

Meanwhile, make the mayonnaise. Work the egg and yolk with salt to taste in a blender. Add the oil in a slow steady stream, with the machine running. Mix in the grated orange zest.

Drain the artichokes upside down and dry them thoroughly. Fill them with the mayonnaise and arrange on a platter. Chop the yolk and white of the hard-boiled egg separately and sprinkle them over the artichokes.

HONEY

*T*he colour, aroma, density and flavour of honey differ according to floral variety. These characteristics have to be considered when you use it as a sweetener in cooking. Chestnut blossom honey is one of the most flavourful and has a slightly bitter but pleasing aftertaste. Acacia and heather honeys are milder and more delicate. Rosemary, lavender and linden are highly aromatic. Natural honey without any preservatives will crystallize at a cold temperature. This does not affect the quality. It will return to liquid form if left in a warm room.

Cipolline al Miele

LITTLE ONIONS IN HONEY

*F*or this dish I generally use our chestnut blossom honey which has a very marked flavour, but a milder honey such as acacia or heather also works well. Place a coloured cocktail stick in each onion and arrange them on a plate covered with grape vine leaves. These onions are also very good served hot with their cooking juices as an accompaniment to boiled or stewed meat. I use small, slightly flat Italian onions, but pickling or pearl onions, although less tender, will do nicely.

SERVES 6

600 g / 1¼ lb small onions

2 tbsp extra virgin olive oil

6 bay leaves

3 tbsp honey

90 ml / 3 fl oz / ⅓ cup red wine vinegar

Bring a saucepan of salted water to the boil. Add the onions and blanch for 5 minutes. Drain and peel.

Pour the oil into a heavy pan and add the onions and bay leaves. Cover and cook them on a low heat until the onions are soft, about 20 minutes.

Stir in the honey and vinegar and cook for a few more minutes, and covered, until almost all the liquid has evaporated.

Leave the onions to cool completely at room temperature, then drain them and arrange on a platter to serve.

DEEP-FRYING

I deep-fry in best quality extra virgin olive oil. The results are light, crisp and healthy because this monounsaturated oil can be heated to a high temperature without releasing toxins. Pour an abundant amount of oil into a deep, heavy pan and heat to 180°C/350°F. Before the oil reaches this temperature, which is just before the smoking point, the colour will change slightly. The temperature of the oil can be measured without a thermometer by dropping in a tiny piece of bread; if it rises almost immediately to the surface and takes on colour in less than a minute, the oil is hot enough. The food must be able to float freely in the oil so fry only a little at a time, removing it with a slotted spoon, and drain on paper towels. If I am unable to serve fried food immediately, I keep it warm in a 100°C/220°F oven with the door slightly ajar, but not for more than 10 minutes.

Crocchette di Riso

RICE AND CHEESE BALLS

*W*hen I have made more risotto than I need, I spread it out to cool and use it for these crisp rice and cheese balls. After frying, they can be kept for about 10 minutes in a warm oven with the door slightly ajar.

SERVES 6

1.2 litres / 2 pints / 5 cups light meat stock (page 216)

450 g / 1 lb / 2 cups arborio rice

120 g / 4 oz uncooked sweet Italian sausage, casing removed

150 g / 5 oz / 1¼ cups freshly grated Parmesan cheese

3 eggs

salt

90 g / 3 oz fontina or Gruyère cheese, diced

180 g / 6 oz / 2 cups fine dry breadcrumbs (page 132)

olive oil for deep-frying

Bring the stock to the boil in a deep saucepan. Add the rice and cook on high heat, stirring frequently, for about 14 minutes or until the rice has absorbed all the stock. Off the heat, add the sausage meat and Parmesan. Allow to cool slightly, then stir in 1 egg. Pour the rice mixture on to a plate and leave to cool completely.

Beat the remaining eggs with a pinch of salt.

With the help of a spoon, form the rice mixture into walnut-size balls. Press a dice of cheese into the centre, closing the ball well to seal in the cheese. Roll

● Little Onions in Honey, Mushroom Caps ●
with Prawn (Shrimp) Filling (p. 13)

each ball in beaten egg and then coat with breadcrumbs.

Heat the oil in a heavy deep pan to 180°C/350°F. Deep-fry the rice balls, a few at a time, until barely golden. Drain them on paper towels and serve.

Crostini all'Arancia e Olive

TOASTS WITH ORANGE SLICES AND OLIVES

These toasts cannot be prepared too far ahead of time because the orange slices tend to dilute the mayonnaise. However, once the mayonnaise is made and put in the refrigerator, the oranges sliced and the bread toasted, all of it can then be assembled in a few seconds. Remember that the eggs for the mayonnaise must be at room temperature.

MAKES 18

1 egg and 1 egg yolk

salt and pepper

120 ml / 4 fl oz / ¹⁄₂ cup extra virgin olive oil

18 slices of French bread (baguette), each 5 mm / ¹⁄₄ inch thick

18 paper-thin orange slices, with skin

18 small black olives

Work the egg and yolk with salt to taste in a blender. Add the oil in a slow steady stream, with the machine running. Season to taste with pepper.

Spread out the bread slices on a large baking sheet and toast in a preheated 180°C/350°F/gas 4 oven until barely golden, about 5 minutes. Allow to cool.

● **Toasts with Orange Slices and Olives** ●
Toasts with Parmesan Cheese and Rocket

Spread the toasts thinly with a little mayonnaise and top each one with a slice of orange. Put the rest of the mayonnaise in a piping bag with a star nozzle and pipe a rosette in the middle of each orange slice. Top with a black olive. Arrange on a platter and serve.

CROSTINI

I use French-style bread for making crostini. Its cylinder shape is ideal and reduces waste. Cut into slices 5-mm/¹⁄₄-inch thick with a saw-edged knife so that the crust does not crumble. Toast the slices in the oven to a golden yellow, the colour of beer. Over-heating will cause a bitter taste.

Crostini al Balsamico

TOASTS WITH BALSAMIC VINEGAR AND
BEEF

Here a delicate *carpaccio* – very thin slices of raw beef, seasoned with balsamic vinegar – tops the toasts. To slice the meat paper-thin, keep it for 1 hour in the freezer before slicing.

MAKES 18

*18 slices of French bread (baguette), each
5 mm / ¼ inch thick*

3 tbsp extra virgin olive oil

2 tbsp balsamic vinegar

salt and pepper

*120 g / 4 oz lean beef topside (top round),
sliced paper-thin*

*90 g / 3 oz Parmesan cheese, thinly sliced
with a vegetable peeler*

1 tbsp finely grated lemon zest

Spread out the bread slices on a large baking sheet and toast in a preheated 180°C / 350°F / gas 4 oven for about 5 minutes, until crisp and barely golden. Allow to cool.

Brush the toast with 1 tbsp of the oil. Make a marinade with the vinegar, the rest of the oil and salt and pepper to taste.

Dip the beef slices quickly in the marinade and place one on each toast. Garnish with the Parmesan and lemon zest, arrange on a platter and serve.

Crostini al Dragoncello

TOASTS WITH TARRAGON AND EGG

Although it is almost unknown in other parts of Italy, tarragon is the aromatic herb most typical of Siena, where it is often used in place of parsley to season sauces, first courses, vegetables and meats. I also use this sauce with steamed fish and on boiled potatoes as well as spaghetti and rice. The sauce will keep in the refrigerator for at least 3 days.

MAKES 18

90 g / 3 oz coarse-textured bread

120 ml / 4 fl oz / ½ cup red wine vinegar

*3 tbsp finely chopped fresh tarragon or flat-
leaf (Italian) parsley*

● Toasts with Tarragon and Egg ●

1 tbsp capers in vinegar, drained and chopped

1 hard-boiled egg, chopped

3 tbsp extra virgin olive oil

salt

*18 slices of French bread (baguette), each
5 mm / ¼ inch thick*

Soak the coarse-textured bread in the vinegar for about 10 minutes, then drain and squeeze dry.

In a bowl, mix the soaked bread with the tarragon, capers, hard-boiled egg, olive oil and a pinch of salt using a fork.

Spread out the bread slices on a large baking sheet and toast in a preheated 180°C / 350°F / gas 4 oven for 5 minutes or until barely golden. Allow to cool.

Spread each slice of toast with some sauce, arrange on a platter and serve.

Crostini al Formaggio di Capra

TOASTS WITH GOAT'S CHEESE

This pairing is so perfect that for once I set aside the rule and use bacon instead of pancetta. Diluted with thick cream or milk, the topping also makes a tasty seasoning for spaghetti.

MAKES 18

18 slices of French bread (baguette), each 5 mm / ¼ inch thick

2 tbsp extra virgin olive oil

120 g / 4 oz / ½ cup fresh goat's cheese

6 thin slices of bacon

pepper

Spread out the slices of bread on a large baking sheet and toast in a preheated 180°C / 350°F / gas 4 oven until barely golden, about 5 minutes. Allow to cool.

In a bowl, blend the olive oil with the cheese until creamy, using a fork.

Place the bacon slices side by side in a heavy frying pan and fry over low heat for about 3 minutes on each side, or until the fat has melted and the slices are crisp and golden. Drain on a paper towel and crumble.

Garnish the toasts with the cheese mixture and sprinkle with the crumbled bacon and freshly ground pepper. Arrange on a platter and serve.

Crostini al Limone e Acciughe

TOASTS WITH LEMON AND ANCHOVIES

To prevent the lemon from making the bread soggy, each toast is buttered first. The ingredients for these toasts can be prepared ahead of time and assembled at the last minute. The garnished lemon slices are also an attractive complement to a fish dish such as fresh tuna in caper sauce (page 120) or to garnish the veal scaloppine on page 100 in place of the tomato.

MAKES 18

18 slices of French bread (baguette), each 5 mm / ¼ inch thick

30 g / 1 oz / 2 tbsp unsalted butter, softened

18 paper-thin lemon slices, with skin

18 anchovy fillets in olive oil, drained

18 capers in vinegar, drained

18 leaves of fresh flat-leaf (Italian) parsley

Spread out the bread slices on a large baking sheet and toast in a preheated 180°C / 350°F / gas 4 oven until barely golden, about 5 minutes. Allow to cool.

Butter the toasts lightly and place a slice of lemon on each one. Roll up the anchovies and place one on each slice of lemon. Top with a caper and garnish with a leaf of parsley. Arrange on a platter and serve.

Crostini di Mare

TOASTS WITH SEAFOOD

If you double the seafood in this recipe, you will have an extra amount to use as a delicious spaghetti sauce. Or add it to a risotto, mixing it into the hot rice at the last moment just before it has finished cooking.

MAKES 18

1.3 kg / 3 lb mixed mussels and clams

4 tbsp extra virgin olive oil

2 tbsp lemon juice

2 tbsp finely chopped fresh flat-leaf (Italian) parsley

a pinch of chili powder

18 slices of French bread (baguette), each 5 mm / ¼ inch thick

Scrub the mussels and clams under cold running water until clean. Put them in a heavy saucepan, cover and cook on moderate heat for about 5 minutes or until the shells open. Drain them and discard any that did not open.

Take the mussels and clams out of their shells. Chop them and fry them in 3 tbsp of the oil on a moderate heat for about 2 minutes. Add the lemon juice and boil to evaporate the liquid. Remove from the heat, sprinkle with the parsley and chili powder and mix well.

Brush the bread slices with the rest of the oil and spread out on a large baking sheet. Toast them in a preheated 180°C / 350°F / gas 4 oven for about 3 minutes. Cover them with the fish mixture and bake for 5 more minutes. Serve hot.

Crostini di Parmigiano e Rucola

TOASTS WITH PARMESAN CHEESE AND ROCKET (ARUGULA)

These toasts are my favourite in summer, when rocket (arugula) grows like a weed in my kitchen garden. In winter I substitute thinly sliced raw artichokes. With 120 g/4 oz of Parmesan cheese and 300 g/10 oz of rocket (arugula) or thinly sliced raw artichokes, seasoned with olive oil, salt and pepper, you can make a lovely salad that is perfect served with the roast chicken with juniper (page 112) for a light lunch.

MAKES 18

18 slices of French bread (baguette), each 5 mm/¼ inch thick

3 tbsp extra virgin olive oil

120 g/4 oz fresh rocket (arugula), julienned

salt and pepper

90 g/3 oz Parmesan cheese, thinly sliced

Spread out the bread slices on a large baking sheet and toast in a preheated 180°C/350°F/gas 4 oven until barely golden, about 5 minutes. Allow to cool.

Brush the toasts with 1 tbsp of the oil.

Mix the rocket (arugula) with the rest of the oil and salt and pepper to taste. Top each slice of toast with some Parmesan. Cover with the rocket (arugula) and serve.

Crostini di Polenta e Formaggio

POLENTA SLICES WITH CHEESE

I always make more polenta than a recipe requires in order to have some for making crostini for the next day. The scraps left when you cut the polenta into crostini can be used for a polenta pie: mix them with a hearty *ragù* and a soft white sauce, then bake. For a special autumn treat I like to cover the polenta rounds with shavings of aromatic white truffle.

SERVES 6

600 g/1¼ lb freshly made polenta (see page 219)

30 g/1 oz/2 tbsp unsalted butter, softened, + extra for the baking sheet

210 g/7 oz fontina or Gruyère cheese, cut into paper-thin slices

a handful of fresh sage leaves

Wet a table or other work surface with cold water and pour the polenta on the table. With a wet spatula or a rolling pin, spread the polenta 1 cm/½ inch thick. Leave to cool. Use a 5-cm/2-inch pastry cutter to cut out rounds.

Brush the polenta rounds on one side with butter. Generously butter a baking sheet and arrange the polenta rounds on the sheet, buttered side up.

Bake in a preheated 180°C/350°F/gas 4 oven for about 15 minutes or until golden, turning once.

Meanwhile, use the same pastry cutter to cut rounds of cheese. Put a round of cheese on each round of polenta, top with a sage leaf and bake for a further 5 minutes or until the cheese starts melting.

Serve immediately.

Melanzane alla Ricotta

AUBERGINE (EGGPLANT) ROLLS WITH RICOTTA CHEESE

If you cannot find long, thin aubergines (eggplants), use the round variety and cut each slice into two or three strips that are big enough to roll. The ricotta cream is also an excellent filling for ravioli. Covered with a raw tomato sauce, such as that on page 157, and heated for 10 minutes in a preheated 180°C/350°F/gas 4 oven, these rolls make an excellent first course.

SERVES 6

2 long oval aubergines (eggplants)

4 tbsp extra virgin olive oil

120 g/4 oz/½ cup ricotta cheese

120 g/4 oz/½ cup fresh goat's cheese

4 tbsp finely chopped fresh basil leaves

Cut the aubergines (eggplants) across into 5-mm/¼-inch thick slices. Brush lightly with 1 tbsp of the oil and grill (broil) them until barely soft, turning them once.

In a bowl, mix the ricotta, goat's cheese, the rest of the oil and the basil until creamy.

Spoon the ricotta cream on top of the aubergine (eggplant) slices, roll them up and secure each with a wooden cocktail stick. Arrange on a platter and serve.

Palline di Formaggio

CHEESE BALLS

These cheese balls can also make an elegant and unusual cold first course for a summer meal: cut three small melons in half and carefully scrape out the seeds and central pulp. Fill with the cheese balls and serve well chilled on individual plates.

SERVES 6

180 g / 6 oz / ³/₄ cup ricotta cheese

120 g / 4 oz gorgonzola cheese

90 g / 3 oz / ¹/₂ cup finely chopped walnuts

90 g / 3 oz / ³/₄ cup freshly grated Parmesan cheese

Put the ricotta, gorgonzola and walnuts in a food processor fitted with a metal blade and process together until a well-blended cream is formed. Or mix with a fork in a bowl. Chill for a couple of hours.

Take a heaped teaspoonful of the mixture and, using the palms of your hands, roll it into a ball about the size of a walnut. Roll gently in the Parmesan and put on a plate. Continue to form into balls until all the cheese mixture has been used.

Return to the refrigerator until ready to serve.

Palline di Prosciutto Cotto

HAM BALLS

You can use this creamed ham in many ways: pipe it on little toasts; fill cherry tomatoes or little pastry puffs, ravioli or crêpes; or spread it on slices of cold roast meat. Arrange on a serving platter with peas or green beans.

MAKES 24

300 g / 10 oz cooked ham

150 g / 5 oz / ²/₃ cup ricotta cheese

90 g / 3 oz / ³/₄ cup freshly grated Parmesan cheese

3 hard-boiled egg yolks

2 tbsp mild paprika

Combine the ham, ricotta, Parmesan and egg yolks in a blender and process until smooth. Chill the mixture for a couple of hours.

Pick up little mounds of mixture with a sugar spoon and roll between the palms of your hands to form balls the size of walnuts. Chill for at least 2 hours.

Just before serving, sprinkle the paprika on a plate and roll the balls in it to coat them completely. Arrange on a platter and serve.

Parmigiano Fritto

PARMESAN CHEESE FRITTERS

I went once to have dinner in a very wonderful restaurant in Castrocaro Terme, called La Frasca, where they make a speciality, among other very particular dishes, of these tasty Parmesan fritters. They can be served warm or cold.

SERVES 6

120 g / 4 oz / 1 cup freshly grated Parmesan cheese

Heat well a non-stick pan on moderate heat.

Put little mounds of the cheese in the pan and flatten each with a spoon to make thin rounds. Fry on one side only until barely golden, then remove the pan from the heat and leave for 1 minute. Detach the fritters with a spatula, arrange on a platter and serve.

Prosciutto e Fichi

PROSCIUTTO AND FIGS

This is a summer classic, simple to prepare and always pleasing. If there are no figs to be found, use melon balls as a substitute. The leftover melon can go into a fruit salad.

MAKES 18

18 ripe but firm figs

1 / 4 bottle of Vin Santo or another sweet dessert wine

9 slices of prosciutto

Peel the figs, then soak them in the Vin Santo for at least 2 hours, turning them from time to time. Drain.

HAM

Italian ham can be bought raw, prosciutto crudo, or cooked, prosciutto cotto, and it comes in various qualities. Perhaps the most esteemed is from San Daniele in Friuli, while the best known is the sweet and aromatic ham from Parma. Tuscany and Umbria also produce excellent prosciutto, saltier and stronger in flavour than the Parma variety. Both prosciutto crudo and prosciutto cotto are made from the thigh of the pig. Cooked ham is boned and sometimes smoked. In the Maremma area of Tuscany, near the sea, prosciutto is also made from the thigh of wild boar and deer. In the recipes, cooked ham means prosciutto cotto and prosciutto means prosciutto crudo (raw ham).

Spread out the slices of prosciutto on a board and cut each lengthwise into two strips. Carefully wrap a strip of ham completely around a fig and secure with a cocktail stick.

Rotolini di Olive

OLIVE ROLLS

You can prepare this antipasto ahead of time and heat it as your guests arrive. I often vary the filling by substituting sweet Italian sausage for the anchovies, or finely chopped salami, or gorgonzola mixed with a few chopped walnuts. Bacon can be used instead of pancetta.

MAKES 18

1 garlic clove, chopped

3 anchovy fillets in oil, drained

1 tbsp extra virgin olive oil

3 tbsp freshly grated Parmesan cheese

2 tbsp fine dry breadcrumbs (page 132)

1 tsp dried oregano

18 big green olives

9 paper-thin slices of pancetta

Mash the garlic and anchovies with a fork. Mix in the olive oil, Parmesan cheese, breadcrumbs and oregano to form a thick cream. Remove the stones from the olives with the special tool and fill them with the anchovy cream. Cut the pancetta slices in half crosswise and roll each piece around an olive. Place the olive rolls on a baking sheet.

Bake in a preheated 200°C/400°F/gas 6 oven for about 6 minutes or until the pancetta becomes translucent and crisp, turning them once. Arrange them on a platter, with cocktail sticks, and serve.

Sedano al Gorgonzola

CELERY STICKS WITH GORGONZOLA CHEESE

You can cut the celery sticks well in advance. To keep them crisp, put them in a bowl of iced water and refrigerate. The gorgonzola cream will keep for several hours, covered, in the refrigerator. The celery trimmings can go into a soup or be used to season a sauce. For a quicker preparation, serve the cream in a bowl as a dip for the celery.

● Parmesan Cheese Fritters, Olive Rolls ●

MAKES ABOUT 18

180 g / 6 oz gorgonzola cheese

1 tbsp fresh lemon juice

1 tbsp extra virgin olive oil

pepper

1.3 kg / 3 lb white celery

Put the gorgonzola, lemon juice, olive oil and pepper to taste into a bowl and mash until soft and creamy.

Remove and discard the hard outer stalks of the celery as well as the thin stalks. Keep the leaves for garnish. Clean the celery stalks and remove the strings by scraping with a vegetable peeler. Wash well and cut across into pieces about 4 cm/1½ inches long.

Fill the hollows in the celery pieces with the gorgonzola cream. Put them on a platter, garnish with the celery leaves and serve.

I Primi

First Courses

*A*lthough I have a particular passion for pasta, the entire class of first courses constitutes my favourite food. From my Milanese upbringing I inherited respect for rice, and relatively recently I have rediscovered the rich heritage of Italian soups. Then, for those occasions when I am feeling more ambitious, there are polenta and gnocchi.

Pasta followed by a green salad and fruit is my idea of a perfect meal, both to prepare and to eat. In Milan I frequently go to the cinema (another passion) with a few friends and afterwards, instead of hassling with restaurant crowds, we go back home and I fix a bowl of spaghetti. What is so immediately appealing about pasta is its simplicity and versatility. There exist, of course, some basic, classic sauces, but the range of recipes is not restricted to these. There are really as many congenial condiments for pasta as there are cooks, and it has always been a part of the Italian culinary tradition to be creative in its preparation.

*I*f I had to choose, I suppose my preference is for the short type of dried pasta partnered with fresh greens. I prepare this dish in the simplest way imaginable by bringing a large pot of water to the boil, cooking the pasta and greens together, draining, and seasoning with extra virgin olive oil, salt, pepper and maybe some freshly grated Parmesan cheese. Here I can be as inventive as my garden is green. As an avid gardener, I am proud to say I seldom have to repeat myself, which also pleases my family inasmuch as this is our standard lunch. I feel, and I think most other Italians do too, that there is something familiar about pasta. It is a dish to be served to family and to friends who are part of the family. And apart from these improvised late-night suppers, it is mid-day fare.

However, even for informal family meals there are certain innate gastronomic imperatives that govern how pasta should be served. During my cooking courses I insist on these so much that one group of students codified them in the form of a 'Decalogue of Culinary Commandments'. The most important (and in my experience the one most transgressed outside of Italy) reads: 'Thou shalt not serve pasta on the same plate or at the

● Linguine with Walnuts and Breadcrumbs (p. 38) ●

same time, even on a side plate, with other foods.' Pasta is a PIATTO, literally a separate plate and course. It merits being enjoyed on its own.

I do not have to renounce pasta at formal meals with guests, but instead I transform it into an elegant TIMBALLO or SFORMATO or CROSTATA — all delicious forms of the ancient baked pasta pie.

I also think of rice, the other staple of Italian first courses, primarily as a good excuse for enjoying an almost infinite variety of such delicious seasonings as saffron with freshly grated Parmesan cheese, flavourful porcini mushrooms, delicate bits of shellfish and, once again, seasonal vegetables, especially tiny peas and asparagus tips. There are also tasty combinations with meat — chicken livers and sausages are two classics. My preference is always for the vegetarian.

As with pasta I would normally serve rice as the first course only for a mid-day meal. But unlike a bowl of pasta, risotto is eminently suitable for more formal occasions. This is not merely a matter of aesthetics. I think the constant care in cooking that risotto requires is somehow communicated to its recipients, especially appropriate for guests.

A very pleasing variation of this classic dish, and one particularly good for a buffet, is risotto prepared in a mould. If you use a ring mould you can put a little bunch of herbs in the centre as a decoration and surround it with a sauce. This brings to mind another difference between rice and pasta. Rice is often served as a CONTORNO, an accompaniment to the main course, and the two can be put together on the same plate. Rice has the agreeable quality of combining well with every flavour.

This is an attribute it has in common with another popular first course, polenta, which I often substitute for rice on winter menus. In Italy we consider polenta mostly a cold weather dish. Not only does it warm the stomach, it also warms the cook, who must patiently stir it to readiness over a hot stove for about 40 minutes! It is also richer fare than either pasta or rice, especially if you cook it in stock instead of water.

Polenta is usually made from coarsely ground yellow cornmeal. In the region of the Veneto, however, they sometimes use a very fine white cornmeal which gives this dish a more refined appearance as well as taste. Polenta is tasty on its own and, notwithstanding its humble origins as a poor man's substitute for bread, it also lends itself to more sophisticated preparations. You can slice and layer it with cheese, or mould and marble it with diced cooked vegetables.

*A*nother first course of undoubtedly humble origins, but which has also assumed a certain elegance over the centuries thanks to a bit of imaginative preparation, is gnocchi. In their most basic form, these small dumplings are made from potatoes, but there are many variations. Because gnocchi satisfy one of my primary cooking requirements, I often choose them for party menus. They can be prepared ahead of time, then covered with a veil of white sauce, cream or butter and put into the oven to bake while I am greeting and visiting with my guests.

A first course that vies with pasta for variety and down-to-earth goodness is soup. While researching recipes over the years, I have come to think of Italy as the country of soups even more than of pasta. Often we combine these two in a simple and light pasta IN BRODO, pasta in broth. Whereas the other first courses I have mentioned are more suitable for the mid-day meal, soups are the usual first course for an Italian supper in the evening. I think of hearty vegetable soups as family fare, but the same minestrone puréed can become an inviting dish for guests.

*Y*ears ago I had a rather formidable menu problem to resolve. What could I serve at a summer garden buffet supper to 300 guests whose ranks could easily swell to over 400 at the last minute? The event in question is our annual August concert of chamber music, which we hold in the grand courtyard of Coltibuono. We invite our friends and neighbours and afterwards there is feasting and dancing. Over the years I had tried everything from roasted whole pigs to huge quantities of pasta until I struck upon the satisfying solution of serving a series of first courses. We prepare five classics: a pasta salad with fresh tomatoes and basil; a rice salad with fresh pesto sauce; a soup of chickpeas and fresh tagliatelle with extra virgin olive oil and ground pepper; bucatini timbales with porcini mushrooms; and rice moulds with herbed mayonnaise. So every August, with these first courses, together with a variety of SCHIACCIATA, Tuscan flat bread seasoned with herbs, and lots of wine, I am able to work my version of the miracle of the loaves and fishes.

Anello di Riso al Dragoncello

RICE RING WITH TARRAGON MAYONNAISE

If you serve this rice ring at a summer lunch, you could accompany it with plates of cold cooked green beans, courgettes (zucchini) and potatoes, all diced. Make double the quantity of mayonnaise to dress the cold vegetables. A main course to follow could be monkfish in mustard sauce (page 96).

● **Rice Ring with Tarragon Mayonnaise** ●

SERVES 6
600 g / 1¼ lb / 2⅔ cups arborio rice
210 ml / 7 fl oz / ⅞ cup extra virgin olive oil
1 egg and 2 egg yolks
3 tbsp chopped fresh tarragon, or 1 tbsp dried tarragon
salt and pepper
juice of ½ lemon
4 tbsp milk

Bring a large saucepan of salted water to the boil. Add the rice and boil over moderate heat, without stirring, for 15 minutes. Drain the rice and, leaving it in the colander, rinse it quickly under cold running water to prevent any further cooking.

Using 1 tbsp of the oil, grease a 20-cm/8-inch ring mould. Spoon all the rice into the mould and press it down firmly and evenly. (The rice can now be refrigerated for several hours.)

Put the egg and yolks into the bowl of a food processor fitted with the metal blade. Add the tarragon and a pinch of salt. Process for a few seconds. With the motor running, pour in the remaining oil in a slow steady stream. When the mayonnaise is made, add the lemon juice and milk and process briefly. Taste and correct the seasoning. Spoon into a bowl, cover tightly and refrigerate.

Before serving, return the rice and mayonnaise to room temperature. Turn out the rice ring on to a platter and fill the centre with the mayonnaise.

Brodo con Frittatine

OMELETTE STRIPS IN BROTH

For a quick evening supper I make a bigger quantity of these omelette strips and I serve them with a Milanese tomato sauce like the one on page 157.

SERVES 6
3 eggs
1 tbsp chopped fresh thyme
2 tbsp chopped fresh flat-leaf (Italian) parsley
salt and pepper
15 g / ½ oz / 1 tbsp unsalted butter
1.5 litres / 2½ pints / 1½ quarts light meat or chicken stock (page 216)

In a bowl whisk the eggs with the herbs and seasoning to taste. Butter a 15-cm/6-inch non-stick frying pan and pour a little of the egg mixture into the pan, shaking to spread it out, to make a layer about 3 mm/⅛ inch thick. Cook over very low heat for a few minutes, so that the egg sets without changing colour. Turn the omelette on to a plate. Continue making omelettes until the egg mixture is finished.

Roll up the omelettes and cut them across into narrow strips. At this point you can keep the omelette strips in the refrigerator for a few hours.

Heat the stock and add the omelette strips. Serve immediately in a warm tureen.

Consommé in Gelatina

JELLIED CONSOMME

I enjoy jellied consommé throughout the year, not just during the summer. It makes a delicate first course that can be prepared well in advance, and the flavour can be varied by the wine you use as well as the herbs. Try chopped fresh flat-leaf (Italian) parsley, basil or chives and any semi-sweet white dessert wine.

SERVES 6

---

600 g / 1¼ lb oxtail, in pieces

---

600 g / 1¼ lb beef shin (shank)

---

1 pig's trotter

---

1 medium-size carrot, quartered

---

1 celery stalk, chopped

---

a small bunch of fresh flat-leaf (Italian) parsley

---

1 bay leaf

---

salt

---

1 egg white

---

120 g / 4 oz lean boneless beef, chopped

---

6 tbsp Vin Santo

---

6 sprigs of fresh thyme

In a large pot combine the oxtail, beef shin (shank), pig's trotter, carrot, celery, parsley and bay leaf. Add 5 litres/8 pints/5 quarts of water and slowly bring it to the boil. Lower the heat, cover and simmer for about 3 hours, when you should have about 1.5 litres/2½ pints/1½ quarts of stock. Remove the meat and strain the stock through a very fine sieve into a bowl. Season with salt to taste and leave to cool.

In a saucepan whisk the egg white lightly. Add the chopped beef and stir well. Pour in the stock and bring to the boil. To clarify the stock, allow it to boil for a further 5 minutes. Strain through a fine sieve and stir in the Vin Santo.

Chill the consommé for about 3 hours or until it solidifies. Break the jelly with a fork and spoon it into 6 cups. Garnish with the thyme and serve.

● Onion and Almond Soup (p. 28), Jellied ●
Consommé

Crema di Ceci

CREAM OF CHICKPEA SOUP

Unfortunately chickpeas must be carefully washed and sorted before cooking because there are sometimes little stones among them, and they also take a long time to cook. However, they are popular all over Italy. I sometimes serve them on small slices of toast. The fillets of sole in cream sauce (page 102) would go well after this soup.

SERVES 6

300 g / 10 oz / 1½ cups dried chickpeas

2 litres / 3½ pints / 2 quarts light meat stock (page 216)

6 tbsp extra virgin olive oil

2 garlic cloves, chopped

1 tbsp chopped fresh rosemary

300 g / 10 oz Italian plum tomatoes, peeled and chopped (or use canned)

salt and pepper

Rinse and pick over the chickpeas, then soak in water to cover for about 12 hours.

Drain the chickpeas and transfer them to a deep pot. Add the stock and bring slowly to the boil. Simmer gently over low heat for about 3 hours.

Drain the chickpeas, reserving the stock, and purée them in a food processor or put them through a food mill. Return the purée to the stock and stir well.

In a frying pan, heat the olive oil, garlic and rosemary and fry over low heat until the garlic is translucent. Add the tomatoes and cook for 10 minutes to blend the flavours, stirring occasionally.

Add the tomato sauce to the chickpea soup and, stirring well, return it to the boil. Season to taste. Transfer the soup to a tureen and serve at once.

Crema di Cipolle alle Spezie

ONION AND ALMOND SOUP

This is a modern version of a very famous Renaissance soup, when instead of herbs food was seasoned with spices. I like to serve this soup in wintertime, followed by roast pork in fennel sauce (page 90).

SERVES 6

4 tbsp extra virgin olive oil

6 medium-size onions, preferably red, thinly sliced

1.5 litres / 2½ pints / 1½ quarts light chicken stock (page 216)

180 g / 6 oz / 1¼ cups blanched almonds, powdered in a blender

1 tsp ground cinnamon

1 tsp grated nutmeg

2 tbsp crushed amaretti biscuits (cookies)

salt and pepper

In a large saucepan heat the olive oil, add the onions and sauté over low heat until translucent, about 10 minutes. Add the stock and the almonds and allow to simmer for about 30 minutes.

Transfer the soup, in batches, to a blender or food processor and purée. Add the cinnamon, nutmeg, amaretti crumbs, and salt and pepper to taste. Process until creamy. Return the soup to the saucepan and bring to the boil.

Pour the soup into a tureen and serve at once.

Crema di Patate e Porri

CREAM OF POTATO AND LEEK SOUP

Onions can be used instead of leeks, and although they are more strongly flavoured they make an excellent cream. For a dinner party I occasionally put three or four large prawns or shrimp tails in the middle of each bowl. The prawns or shrimp should be tossed in a little hot oil for a couple of minutes, just until cooked and hot. After the soup serve roast pork with prunes (page 92).

SERVES 6

600 g / 1¼ lb leeks

30 g / 1 oz / 2 tbsp unsalted butter

1 tbsp extra virgin olive oil

4 tbsp dry white wine

6 medium-size boiling potatoes

120 g / 4 oz / 1 cup grated Gruyère or emmenthal cheese

600 ml / 1 pint / 2½ cups milk

600 ml / 1 pint / 2½ cups light meat stock (page 216)

salt and pepper

1 tsp grated nutmeg

Remove the tough green leaves and the roots from the leeks. Wash carefully and slice thinly. Heat the butter and olive oil in a saucepan, add the sliced leeks and cook gently for about 10 minutes until translucent. Add the wine and 120 ml / 4 fl oz / ½ cup water and leave to simmer over low heat for another 10 minutes.

Scrub the potatoes and cook them, in their skins, in boiling water until tender. Drain, then peel and slice the potatoes.

Purée the leeks with their liquid, the sliced potatoes and grated cheese in a blender or food processor. Transfer the purée to a clean saucepan and stir in the milk and stock. Slowly return to the boil. Season with salt, pepper and nutmeg and serve in individual bowls.

Crostata di Spaghetti

SPAGHETTI TART

I once prepared a linguine tart, similar to this version with spaghetti, for over 90 people. It was very easy because all the pastry cases could be baked well in advance. So our time could be dedicated to the turkey breast rolls on page 114, which were the second course.

MAKES 1 TART TO SERVE 6

For the pastry

10 oz / 2½ cups flour

150 g / 5 oz / 10 tbsp unsalted butter, softened, + extra for the pan

1 egg yolk

For the filling

200 g / 7 oz spaghetti

45 g / 1½ oz / 3 tbsp unsalted butter

120 ml / 4 fl oz / ½ cup whipping cream

90 g / 3 oz / ¾ cup freshly grated Parmesan cheese

a pinch of grated nutmeg

90 g / 3 oz / ⅔ cup chopped cooked ham

90 g / 3 oz / ½ cup shelled fresh peas, lightly cooked

salt and pepper

To make the pastry dough, combine the flour, softened butter and egg yolk in a food processor. Process just until a ball of dough forms around the metal blade. Wrap and refrigerate for about 1 hour.

Butter a 23-cm / 9-inch flan or tart pan with a removable bottom. Roll out the dough between two sheets of plastic film to a round 5 mm / ¼ inch thick. Line the prepared pan with the dough. Cover with foil and weigh down with dried beans. Bake in a preheated 180°C / 350°F / gas 4 oven for about 40 minutes. Remove the foil and beans and set the pastry case aside.

● Spaghetti Tart ●

In a large saucepan bring 5 litres / 8 pints / 5 quarts of salted water to the boil. Add the spaghetti and cook until *al dente*. Drain and transfer to a bowl. Add the butter, cream, cheese, nutmeg, ham and peas; toss well. Season to taste.

Pour the filling into the pastry case while it is still in the pan. At this point the tart can be refrigerated for several hours and later reheated in a 180°C / 350°F / gas 4 oven for about 10 minutes. Remove the rim from the pan, transfer the tart to a platter and serve.

Farinata con le Verze

CABBAGE AND POLENTA SOUP

When I am in Tuscany during the winter I make this soup with the local long-leaved black cabbage. However, as it is only available there, when I am in Milan I make the soup very successfully with Savoy cabbage. If you are fond of broccoli, it is a wonderful substitute. Braised lamb with artichokes (page 90) could follow this soup.

SERVES 6

300 g / 10 oz Savoy cabbage leaves

2 litres / 3½ pints / 2 quarts light meat or chicken stock (page 216)

120 g / 4 oz / 1 cup coarse yellow cornmeal

salt

Remove any tough stalks from the cabbage and shred it finely.

In a deep pot bring the stock to the boil. Add the cornmeal in a steady stream, whisking constantly to avoid the formation of lumps. Add the cabbage. Lower the heat and simmer for about 1 hour, stirring occasionally with a wooden spoon.

Check for salt and serve immediately.

SUCCESS WITH POLENTA

Polenta is generally made with coarse yellow cornmeal, except in the Veneto where fine white cornmeal is used; fairly coarse cornmeal makes the more tasty polenta. For polenta, the cornmeal should normally boil for about 40 minutes (for gnocchi it need only be boiled for 10 minutes because the cornmeal continues to cook in the oven). After boiling, do not be too concerned if some of the polenta sticks to the bottom of the pot. Just leave the pot to soak in cold water for a couple of hours and the polenta will come away without any trouble.

Gnocchetti di Semolino in Brodo

BABY DUMPLINGS IN BROTH

If you need a quick, easy and unusual soup, this is the answer. The fresh marjoram can be replaced by thyme or oregano. The soup could be followed by marinated rabbit (page 96).

SERVES 6

240 g / 8 oz / 1⅓ cups coarse semolina or farina

30 g / 1 oz / 2 tbsp unsalted butter, softened

2 eggs

45 g / 1½ oz / 6 tbsp freshly grated Parmesan cheese

salt and pepper

1.5 litres / 2½ pints / 1½ quarts light meat or chicken stock (page 216)

fresh marjoram sprigs, to garnish

In a bowl, combine all but 2–3 tbsp of the semolina with the butter, eggs, Parmesan, and salt and pepper to taste. Stir until a well-blended dough is formed.

Sprinkle a little of the reserved semolina on your hands and roll the dough into balls about the size of walnuts. Spread the balls on a plate dredged with semolina. They can be kept for several hours in the refrigerator.

In a large saucepan bring the stock to the boil. Carefully submerge the dumplings in the stock with the aid of a slotted spoon. Cook over very low heat for about 10 minutes.

Serve immediately, sprinkled with tiny sprigs of fresh marjoram.

Gnocchi agli Asparagi

CHEESE PUFFS WITH ASPARAGUS SAUCE

I generally serve this dish at a fairly formal luncheon or a buffet supper. The asparagus can be replaced by peas or, in winter, with fresh-flavoured fennel or broccoli. The cheese puffs could be followed by leg of lamb with mint and thyme (page 98), with chocolate custards (page 189) for dessert.

SERVES 6

For the dough

120 g / 4 oz / 1 stick unsalted butter + extra for the dish

½ tsp grated nutmeg

salt and pepper

240 g / 8 oz / 2 cups flour

150 g / 5 oz / 1¼ cups finely grated Gruyère or emmenthal cheese

4 eggs

For the sauce

300 g / 10 oz asparagus tips

1 tbsp extra virgin olive oil

30 g / 1 oz / 2 tbsp unsalted butter

30 g / 1 oz / ¼ cup flour

● **Baby Dumplings in Broth** ●

600 ml / 1 pint / 2½ cups milk

120 ml / 4 fl oz / ½ cup whipping cream

90 g / 3 oz / ¾ cup freshly grated Parmesan cheese

To make the dough, in a large saucepan combine the butter, nutmeg and a pinch of salt with 480 ml / 16 fl oz / 2 cups of water. Bring to the boil. Remove the saucepan from the heat and add the flour all at once, stirring vigorously with a wooden spoon. Return to moderate heat and stir constantly until the dough leaves the sides of the pan and forms a ball. Remove the pan from the heat and leave to cool for several minutes.

Add the Gruyère cheese and then the eggs, one by one, adding the next one only after the previous egg is well incorporated. Beat until the dough is smooth.

Bring 5 litres / 8 pints / 5 quarts of salted water to the boil. Fill a piping bag fitted with a large plain nozzle with the dough. Squeeze 2-cm / ¾-inch lengths of dough into the boiling water, cutting the dough with a knife as it comes out of the bag. As soon as the puffs rise to the surface, remove them with a slotted spoon and drop them into a bowl of cold water.

Prepare the sauce: blanch the asparagus tips in boiling salted water for 5 minutes, then drain. In a frying pan heat the oil and sauté the asparagus tips for a few minutes. Purée the asparagus in a blender.

In a medium saucepan melt the butter over low heat. Add the flour and stir well. Raise the heat and gradually add the milk, stirring constantly. Allow to boil for a few minutes. Remove from the heat and stir in the cream, puréed asparagus and Parmesan cheese. Mix well. Season with salt and pepper to taste.

Butter an ovenproof dish well. Drain the puffs and arrange them in the dish in a single layer. Cover with the sauce. Bake in a preheated 180°C / 350°F / gas 4 oven until bubbling, about 20 minutes. Serve piping hot.

Gnocchi di Patate in Salsa di Melanzane

POTATO DUMPLINGS IN AUBERGINE (EGGPLANT) SAUCE

This sauce is one of my favourites and I often serve it with spaghetti, tagliatelle or simply boiled rice. To make the rice more elegant I drain it, toss it with a little olive oil and press it into a ring mould. While it is still hot, I unmould the rice ring and pour the sauce into the middle.

SERVES 6

2 medium-size aubergines (eggplants)

2 ripe tomatoes, peeled and seeded

4 tbsp extra virgin olive oil

½ medium-size onion, finely chopped

salt and pepper

1 tbsp dried oregano

1 kg / 2¼ lb boiling potatoes

210 g / 7 oz / 1¾ cups flour

2 egg yolks

Slice the aubergines (eggplants) in half lengthwise and bake them, cut sides up, in a preheated 180°C / 350°F / gas 4 oven for about 20 minutes. Remove the skins and purée the flesh in a blender with the tomatoes.

Heat the oil in a saucepan, add the onion and cook over low heat until trans-lucent. Add the purée, season with salt and pepper and simmer for a further 15 minutes. Stir in the oregano and set aside.

In a large saucepan cook the potatoes, in their skins in boiling water until tender. Drain, peel and mash them well.

In a bowl combine the mashed potatoes with half the flour and the egg yolks. Season with salt and pepper and knead the mixture until a firm, smooth dough is formed. Divide the dough into pieces. Using the palms of your hands, well floured, roll each piece into a long, narrow sausage shape on a surface sprinkled with most of the remaining flour. Cut these into sections about 3 cm / 1¼ inches long. Roll each section on the prongs of a fork while pressing lightly with your thumb. Drop the shaped dumplings onto a well-floured board. At this point they can be kept for a couple of hours, at room temperature.

Bring a large pot of lightly salted water to the boil. Add the dumplings a few at a time and remove them with a slotted spoon as soon as they rise to the surface. Arrange on a warm serving plate.

Meanwhile reheat the sauce. If it seems too thick, add a little water.

As soon as all the gnocchi are cooked, pour the sauce over them and serve at once.

SUCCESS WITH POTATO GNOCCHI

The only really good potato gnocchi are home-made. Bought gnocchi are always heavy because to be kept for any length of time a lot of flour has to be added to bind the mashed potato. So that just the minimum amount of flour need be used, gnocchi should not be prepared too far in advance. It is a good idea to boil, peel and mash the potatoes well ahead of time and to leave them standing, covered with a cloth, for a few hours so they can dry out a little. Then add the flour and eggs at the last minute.

Gnocchi di Polenta con Funghi

POLENTA DUMPLINGS WITH MUSHROOM SAUCE

In autumn, when porcini mushrooms are gathered in the woods, this is one of my favourite dishes. If you can't find fresh porcini, use button mushrooms plus a handful – about 30 g/1 oz – dried porcini to improve their flavour. Soak the dried porcini in warm water to cover for about 30 minutes before using. As this is a rather rich first course. I usually follow it with a vegetable dish such as onions stuffed with ham (page 133).

SERVES 6

270 g / 9 oz / 2 cups coarse yellow cornmeal

90 g / 3 oz / 6 tbsp unsalted butter + extra for the dish

300 g / 10 oz fresh porcini mushrooms

120 ml / 4 fl oz / ½ cup whipping cream

salt and pepper

90 g / 3 oz / ¾ cup freshly grated Parmesan cheese

In a large saucepan bring 1.5 litres/ 2½ pints/6 cups of lightly salted water to the boil. Pour in the cornmeal in a steady stream, whisking constantly. Lower the heat and cook for about 10 minutes, stirring occasionally with a wooden spoon.

Dampen a wooden board with a little water. Pour on the polenta and, using a slightly wet spatula, spread it until it is about 1 cm/½ inch thick. Leave it to cool completely.

Using a 5-cm/2-inch pastry cutter, cut the polenta into rounds. Reserve the trimmings. Butter an ovenproof dish. Cover the bottom with the polenta trimmings and arrange the rounds, in slightly overlapping rings, on top. Set aside while preparing the sauce. At this point the dish can be kept in the refrigerator for up to 10 hours.

Clean the mushrooms with a damp cloth and slice them about 3 mm/⅛ inch thick. (If using button mushrooms add to them, squeezed dry and chopped, the soaked porcini.) In a frying pan heat 30 g/1 oz/2 tbsp butter, add the mushrooms and sauté over moderate heat for about 5 minutes, stirring occasionally. Add the cream, stir and season with salt and pepper.

Pour the sauce over the polenta. Sprinkle with the Parmesan and dot with small pieces of the remaining butter. Bake in a preheated 180°C/350°F/gas 4 oven for 20 minutes. Serve piping hot.

Gnocchi di Polenta alla Salvia

POLENTA DUMPLINGS WITH SAGE AND BUTTER

This delicious way of serving polenta is popular also for boiled rice or tagliatelle. And polenta, rice or tagliatelle in this sauce can be followed by beef braised in Chianti (page 94).

SERVES 6

270 g / 9 oz / 2 cups coarse yellow cornmeal

salt

90 g / 3 oz / 6 tbsp unsalted butter + extra for the dish

about 20 fresh sage leaves

90 g / 3 oz / ¾ cup freshly grated Parmesan cheese

In a large saucepan bring 1.5 litres/ 2½ pints/6 cups of salted water to the boil. Pour in the cornmeal in a steady stream, whisking constantly. Lower the heat and cook for about 10 minutes, stirring occasionally with a wooden spoon.

Transfer the polenta to a wet rectangular dish and leave it to cool completely.

Unmould the polenta and cut it into slices about 1 cm/½ inch thick. At this point the polenta can be kept for several hours in the refrigerator.

In a frying pan heat the butter, add the sage leaves and fry until the sage is crisp and the butter fairly brown.

Butter an ovenproof dish. Arrange the polenta slices in it and pour over the sage and butter mixture. Sprinkle with the Parmesan and bake in a preheated 180°C/350°F/gas 4 oven for about 20 minutes. Serve immediately.

Gnocchi al Prosciutto

SEMOLINA DUMPLINGS WITH HAM

A very rich dish, this can be followed by a simple vegetable such as Swiss chard rolls (page 139) for a family luncheon, or roast veal with mushrooms (page 94) for a more formal meal.

SERVES 6

1.2 litres / 2 pints / 5 cups milk

270 g / 9 oz / 2 cups coarse semolina or farina

3 egg yolks

90 g / 3 oz / ¾ cup finely grated Gruyère or emmenthal cheese

120 g / 4 oz cooked ham, finely chopped

salt

90 g / 3 oz / 6 tbsp unsalted butter + extra for the dish

6 tbsp freshly grated Parmesan cheese

Bring the milk to the boil in a heavy saucepan. Slowly drizzle in the semolina, beating with a whisk to avoid the formation of lumps. Continue stirring with a wooden spoon.

Cook for 10 minutes, until the mixture comes away from the sides of the pan, then remove it from the heat. Allow to cool for several minutes, then stir in the egg yolks, one by one, the Gruyère cheese and chopped ham. Season with salt. Pour the mixture on to a wet surface and spread out to 1 cm / ½ inch thick with a wet spatula. Leave to cool, then cut out rounds with a 4-cm / 1½-inch pastry cutter.

Butter an ovenproof dish. Arrange the rounds in it. Dot with the butter and sprinkle with the Parmesan cheese. At this point you can keep the dish in the refrigerator for several hours. Bake in a preheated 180°C/350°F/gas 4 oven for 30 minutes, or until golden. Serve hot.

● **Semolina Dumplings with Ham (p. 33),** ●
Spinach Dumplings with White Sauce

Gnocchi di Spinaci alla Crema

SPINACH DUMPLINGS WITH WHITE SAUCE

I don't know anyone who doesn't love these spinach dumplings. They are useful for serving at a dinner party, as they can be prepared in advance, refrigerated in the baking dish and popped into the oven at the last minute. They could be followed by herbed veal chops (page 120) and potatoes with rosemary (page 141).

SERVES 6

2 kg / 4½ lb fresh spinach

150 g / 5 oz / 1¼ cups freshly grated Parmesan cheese

150 g / 5 oz / 1¼ cups flour

300 g / 10 oz / 1¼ cups ricotta cheese

2 egg yolks

a pinch of grated nutmeg

salt and pepper

30 g / 1 oz / 2 tbsp unsalted butter + extra for the dish

600 ml / 1 pint / 2½ cups milk

10 g / ⅓ oz dried porcini mushrooms, soaked in warm water for 30 minutes, squeezed and chopped

Blanch the spinach in boiling water until it wilts, then drain. When cool enough to handle, squeeze the spinach dry and chop it finely.

In a large mixing bowl combine the spinach, half the Parmesan cheese, 60 g/2 oz/½ cup of flour, the ricotta, egg yolks, nutmeg, and salt and pepper to taste. Mix well to blend the ingredients thoroughly. Set aside.

In a medium saucepan melt the butter over moderate heat. Add 30 g/1 oz/¼ cup flour and stir well. Gradually add the milk and bring it to the boil, stirring constantly. Allow to boil for a couple of minutes. Remove from the heat and add the chopped mushrooms, stirring carefully.

Flour a board well. Divide the spinach mixture into pieces. Using the palms of your hands, well floured, roll each piece into a long, narrow sausage shape on a surface sprinkled with most of the remaining flour. Cut into sections about 3 cm/1¼ inches long and shape them into ovals. Arrange the dumplings on a well-floured board.

Bring a large pot of lightly salted water to the boil. Add the dumplings a few at a time and cook until they rise to the surface. Remove with a slotted spoon and drain.

Butter an ovenproof dish and arrange the dumplings in it. (At this point the dish can be chilled for several hours.) Pour the sauce over the dumplings and bake in a preheated 180°C/350°F/gas 4 oven until the sauce bubbles, about 20 minutes. Serve hot.

Lasagne agli Asparagi

LASAGNE WITH ASPARAGUS SAUCE

At a more formal luncheon I serve this followed by a main course such as roast guinea fowl with peaches (page 101). But for a few close friends, I cut the lasagne in the traditional rectangular shape and follow this with a green salad and fresh fruit.

SERVES 6

For the pasta dough

300 g/10 oz/2½ cups flour

2 eggs

60 g/2 oz/⅓ cup cooked spinach, squeezed well and puréed in a blender

For the sauce

36 asparagus spears

3 tbsp extra virgin olive oil

30 g/1 oz/2 tbsp unsalted butter

30 g/1 oz/¼ cup flour

900 ml/1½ pints/3¾ cups milk

90 g/3 oz/¾ cup freshly grated Parmesan cheese

salt and pepper

180 g/6 oz smoked ham, diced

Heap the flour on a board. Make a well in the centre and break in the eggs. Beat them lightly with a fork. Add the spinach and start working the flour into the eggs with the fork. Knead with the hands until a smooth elastic dough is formed (see page 199).

Using a pasta machine, roll out the dough in large strips 1 mm/¹⁄₃₂ inch thick. With a pastry cutter, cut out 7-cm/3-inch rounds.

Bring a large pot of lightly salted water to the boil. Add the lasagne rounds a few at a time. Cook for 2 minutes. Remove with a slotted spoon and transfer to a bowl of cold water. Drain and spread out on paper towels.

Clean the asparagus spears and break off the tough part of the stalks, saving only the tender green part and the tips. Blanch the asparagus in boiling salted water for 5 minutes. Drain and refresh in a bowl of iced water, then drain them again and spread out on paper towels.

Heat the oil in a frying pan. Add the asparagus and cook, covered, over low heat until tender, about 5 minutes. Set aside 12 asparagus tips for garnish and purée the rest in a blender.

In a saucepan melt the butter over moderate heat. Stir in the flour with a wooden spoon. Gradually add the milk, stirring constantly, and bring to the boil. Allow to boil for a couple of minutes, then remove from the heat and add the Parmesan and puréed asparagus with salt and pepper to taste. Stir well.

Brush an ovenproof dish with a little of the sauce. Arrange a slightly overlapping layer of lasagne rounds in the dish. Cover with a thin layer of sauce and sprinkle with ham. Continue making layers until all the ingredients are used, adding the reserved asparagus tips before the final layer of sauce.

Bake the lasagne in a preheated 180°C/350°F/gas 4 oven for about 20 minutes. Serve at once.

Lasagnette di Pane con Pesto

NARROW BREADCRUMB LASAGNE WITH PESTO SAUCE

I generally make these when I have a lot of stale bread. Fine dry breadcrumbs can be bought in Italian shops, or you can make them yourself (see page 202). The lasagne can be made ahead of time and kept in the refrigerator until just before they are boiled. The dish can be followed by a vegetable mould, for example pea and tomato (page 76).

SERVES 6

For the pasta dough

210 g / 7 oz / 1¾ cups flour

210 g / 7 oz / 2¼ cups fine dry breadcrumbs (page 132)

1 egg

salt

For the pesto sauce

90 g / 3 oz / 1½ cups fresh basil leaves

1 garlic clove

30 g / 1 oz / ¼ cup pine nuts

2 walnuts, shelled

4 tbsp freshly grated Parmesan cheese

120 ml / 4 fl oz / ½ cup extra virgin olive oil

● **Lasagne with Asparagus Sauce (p. 35)** ●

For the garnish

1 ripe tomato, peeled, seeded and diced

12 green beans, blanched and cut into 2.5-cm / 1-inch pieces

fresh basil leaves

Heap the flour and breadcrumbs on a board. Make a well in the centre and break in the egg. Add 120 ml / 4 fl oz / ½ cup water to the egg with salt to taste and beat lightly together with a fork. Gradually start working the flour into the egg mixture with the fork. Knead with your hands until you have a soft elastic dough (see page 199).

On a floured surface, roll out the dough until it is about 2 mm / 1⁄16 inch thick. Using a fluted pasta wheel, cut into strips about 2.5 cm / 1 inch wide and

5 cm / 2 inches long. Transfer to a well-floured board.

To prepare the pesto, in a blender combine the basil, peeled garlic, pine nuts, walnuts, Parmesan, oil and salt to taste. Blend until a smooth sauce is formed. (It can be stored for a few days in the refrigerator.)

Bring a large pot of lightly salted water to the boil. Add the lasagne strips and cook for 2 minutes. Drain well, reserving 120 ml / 4 fl oz / ½ cup of the cooking water, and transfer to a warm serving dish. Mix the reserved cooking water with the pesto sauce and toss with the lasagne strips. Sprinkle with the diced tomatoes and beans as well as a few basil leaves. Serve immediately.

● **Narrow Breadcrumb Lasagne with** ●
Pesto Sauce

Lattughe in Brodo

STUFFED LETTUCE IN BROTH

I like to serve this soup in spring when the first tender lettuce appears. There are a number of recipes for the stuffing, but I prefer to use a simple one so its flavour does not interfere with the soup. Only excellent home-made chicken or beef stock should be used. The soup could be followed by veal medallions with orange (page 106).

SERVES 6

3 slices of plain white bread

240 ml / 8 fl oz / 1 cup milk

18 large leaves of soft lettuce such as round, butterhead or Boston

300 g / 10 oz boned chicken breast, skinned and diced

1 egg

1 tbsp chopped fresh flat-leaf (Italian) parsley

1 tbsp chopped fresh mint leaves

a pinch of grated nutmeg

salt and pepper

1.5 litres / 2½ pints / 1½ quarts light chicken or meat stock (page 216)

Soak the bread in the milk for 10 minutes, then drain and squeeze out excess liquid.

Bring a large saucepan of lightly salted water to the boil and blanch the lettuce

leaves for 30 seconds. Drain and transfer to a bowl of iced water. Drain again and place the leaves flat on paper towels.

In a blender combine the chicken breast meat, egg, bread, parsley, mint, nutmeg and seasoning to taste. Process until creamy.

In the middle of each lettuce leaf place 1 tbsp of the chicken mixture squeezed into the shape of a cocktail sausage. Wrap up carefully, folding in the sides of the lettuce leaf and then rolling up to enclose the filling. These can be kept for a few hours in the refrigerator before cooking.

Arrange the stuffed lettuce leaves carefully in the bottom of a shallow saucepan. Add about one-third of the stock. Cover the saucepan and simmer gently over low heat for about 10 minutes. Meanwhile, heat the rest of the stock in another pan.

Place three stuffed lettuce leaves in each soup bowl, cover with the boiling stock and serve immediately.

Linguine alla Crema di Piselli

LINGUINE WITH CREAMED PEAS

Although this sauce is very quick and easy to prepare, it is bound to be a success. I generally use fresh peas, but if they are not available use frozen. If you don't have fresh tarragon, substitute 3 sprigs of flat-leaf (Italian) parsley or a handful of fresh basil. A plate of cheese and the fruit soufflé omelette on page 186 make a lunch for unexpected guests.

SERVES 6

240 g / 8 oz / 1²⁄₃ cups freshly shelled peas

1 tbsp sugar

3 sprigs of fresh tarragon

6 tbsp extra virgin olive oil

salt and pepper

600 g / 1¹⁄₄ lb linguine

Blanch the peas in boiling water for 1 minute. Drain and refresh in a bowl of iced water. Drain the peas once more.

In a saucepan bring 240 ml / 8 fl oz / 1 cup of water to the boil. Add the peas, sugar and tarragon and cook, covered, over moderate heat for about 10 minutes.

Remove the saucepan from the heat and discard the tarragon or other herbs. Pour the contents of the pan into a blender and add the oil. Process until you have a sauce that is not too thick. Season with salt and pepper to taste.

Bring a large pot of salted water to the boil. When the water is boiling briskly, put in the linguine, stir once and cook until the pasta is just *al dente*.

Drain the linguine quickly and transfer to a warm serving bowl. Pour on the sauce, toss well and serve immediately.

Linguine al Pangrattato

LINGUINE WITH WALNUTS AND BREADCRUMBS

The walnut and breadcrumb mixture can be prepared in bigger quantity and kept in the refrigerator for a few days. It is excellent used instead of Parmesan cheese on spaghetti or linguine, or sprinkled over sautéed Swiss chard or boiled asparagus.

SERVES 6

120 ml / 4 fl oz / ¹⁄₂ cup extra virgin olive oil

90 g / 3 oz shelled walnuts, chopped

3 garlic cloves, finely chopped

120 g / 4 oz / 1¹⁄₃ cups fine dry breadcrumbs (page 132)

salt

600 g / 1¹⁄₄ lb linguine

In a frying pan, heat half the oil. Add the nuts, garlic and breadcrumbs and fry until the garlic is just golden, about 5 minutes. This mixture can be stored for a few days in the refrigerator.

Meanwhile, bring a large pot of salted water to the boil. Add the pasta and cook until *al dente*.

Drain the pasta and transfer it to a warm serving bowl. Toss with the rest of the oil and the nut mixture and serve immediately.

Linguine al Tonno

LINGUINE WITH TUNA SAUCE

When buying dried pasta always choose that which has been imported from Italy, to be sure it is made with hard or durum wheat. Such pasta is easy to cook *al dente*, whereas pasta made of soft wheat is practically impossible to cook to the right texture. This is a very useful emergency recipe because all the ingredients are generally in the kitchen store cupboard.

SERVES 6

120 ml / 4 fl oz / $\frac{1}{2}$ cup extra virgin olive oil

2 whole garlic cloves

a small piece of hot chili pepper

900 g / 2 lb plum tomatoes, peeled (or use canned)

salt

300 g / 10 oz canned tuna fish, drained and flaked

2 tbsp small capers in vinegar, drained

600 g / 1 $\frac{1}{4}$ lb linguine

2 tbsp chopped fresh parsley

Heat the oil in a saucepan with the peeled garlic and chili and sauté over low heat until the garlic is just golden. Add the tomatoes and season with salt to taste. Bring to the boil and cook over moderate heat, stirring occasionally, until all the excess liquid has evaporated.

Remove the garlic from the tomato sauce. Add the tuna fish and capers. Stir well and keep warm over low heat.

Bring a large pot of salted water to the boil. Add the linguine and cook until *al dente*. Drain the pasta and transfer it to a warm serving bowl. Pour over the sauce, then sprinkle with the parsley, toss well and serve immediately.

Minestra di Funghi e Piselli

MUSHROOM AND PEA SOUP

This very quick soup is elegant enough to serve at a dinner party. Although cured boiled tongue adds good texture to the soup, if you are not fond of it, substitute cooked ham. As the soup is very light, it should be followed by a fish dish such as fish fillets with artichokes (page 102).

SERVES 6

90 g / 3 oz fresh porcini or button mushrooms

90 g / 3 oz cured tongue or ham

1.5 litres / 2 $\frac{1}{2}$ pints / 1 $\frac{1}{2}$ quarts light meat stock (page 216)

90 g / 3 oz / $\frac{2}{3}$ cup freshly shelled peas, blanched

90 g / 3 oz taglierini

salt

Wipe the mushrooms with a damp cloth but do not immerse them in water. Cut them into julienne stips. Cut the tongue or ham into julienne strips.

In a large pot bring the stock to the boil over moderate heat. Add the peas, mushrooms and tongue or ham. As soon as the stock returns to the boil, add the taglierini. Stir once and boil until *al dente*. Season with salt to taste.

Pour the soup into a soup tureen and serve at once.

Minestra di Ricotta

RICOTTA DUMPLINGS IN BROTH

The ricotta dumplings have a very subtle flavour, and also have the advantage of being prepared well ahead and added to the stock at the last moment. I suggest you follow this with chicken breasts with grapes (page 109) and the lemon tart on page 192.

SERVES 6

240 g / 8 oz / 1 cup ricotta cheese

30 g / 1 oz / $\frac{1}{4}$ cup flour

2 eggs

60 g / 2 oz / $\frac{1}{2}$ cup freshly grated Parmesan cheese

grated zest of $\frac{1}{2}$ lemon

a pinch of grated nutmeg

1.5 litres / 2 $\frac{1}{2}$ pints / 1 $\frac{1}{2}$ quarts light meat stock (page 216)

Push the ricotta through a sieve and whisk it well to get rid of any lumps. Whisk in the flour, then the eggs one at a time, and then the Parmesan, lemon zest and nutmeg.

Spoon the mixture into a rectangular pan and spread it out into a layer about 1 cm / $\frac{1}{2}$ inch thick. Cover the pan with foil and place it in a larger pan containing 2.5 cm / 1 inch of water. Cook over low heat on top of the stove until the mixture is firm, about 40 minutes. Leave to cool completely.

Turn the cold ricotta mixture out of the pan and cut it into 1-cm / $\frac{1}{2}$-inch squares. (At this point the dumplings can be refrigerated for several hours.)

Bring the stock to the boil. Add the ricotta dumplings and cook until they rise to the surface. Remove them with a slotted spoon and arrange them in the bottom of a soup tureen. Pour in the boiling stock and serve.

Minestra di Riso e Prezzemolo

RICE AND PARSLEY SOUP

I very often prepare this light and tasty soup, not just for the family but even on quite elegant occasions. Its success depends entirely on the quality of the stock. Afterwards I often serve the cheese pie on page 79.

SERVES 6

1.4 litres / scant 2½ pints / scant 6 cups light meat stock (page 216)

300 g / 10 oz / 1⅓ cups arborio rice

salt

3 tbsp chopped fresh flat-leaf (Italian) parsley

In a large pot bring the stock to the boil on moderate heat. Pour in the rice, stir and check the salt. Cook for exactly 15 minutes.

Sprinkle with the parsley, pour into a tureen and serve immediately.

Minestrone al Pesto

MINESTRONE WITH PESTO

Minestrone is never served boiling hot because when you add the pesto it would soften the flavour. Served at room temperature, this is an ideal summer soup.

SERVES 6

120 g / 4 oz / ⅔ cup dried cannellini, haricot or great northern beans

30 g / 1 oz dried porcini mushrooms

2 globe artichokes

lemon juice

120 ml / 4 fl oz / ½ cup extra virgin olive oil

1 onion, chopped

1 tbsp chopped fresh flat-leaf (Italian) parsley

1 leek, white part only, thinly sliced

1 celery stalk, diced

1 medium-size carrot, diced

1 medium-size courgette (zucchini), diced

1 medium-size potato, peeled and diced

210 g / 7 oz / 1⅔ cups freshly shelled peas

salt and pepper

300 g / 10 oz / 1⅓ cups arborio rice

30 small fresh basil leaves

2 tbsp freshly grated pecorino cheese

4 tbsp freshly grated Parmesan cheese

2 garlic cloves

50 g / 1⅔ oz / 9 tbsp pine nuts

Soak the beans in water to cover for 12 hours; drain. Soak the mushrooms in warm water to cover for 30 minutes; drain and chop.

Cut off all the artichoke leaves and the chokes, leaving just the fleshy bottoms. Sprinkle with lemon juice to prevent discolouring, then dice the bottoms.

In a large soup pot heat 2 tbsp oil. Add the onion, parsley and leek and fry over low heat, stirring, until translucent, about 5 minutes. Add the diced vegetables, beans, mushrooms and peas and stir well. Pour in 1.4 litres / scant 2½ pints / scant 6 cups water and bring to the boil over high heat. Lower the heat and simmer for about 3 hours.

Season with salt and pepper. Add the rice and cook for a further 15 minutes.

Meanwhile, in a blender combine the basil, pecorino, Parmesan, peeled garlic and pine nuts with the rest of the oil. Process until a thick cream is formed.

Pour the minestrone into a soup tureen and leave to cool slightly, then add the pesto. Stir well and serve.

Pappa ai Funghi

BREAD AND MUSHROOM SOUP

This is a variation of a well-known Tuscan soup called *Pappa al pomodoro* that is always a great success when I serve it. It is also a wonderful way to use up stale bread. If you only have fresh bread, dry it a bit in the oven first.

SERVES 6

30 g / 1 oz dried porcini mushrooms

180 ml / 6 fl oz / ¾ cup extra virgin olive oil

2 garlic cloves, crushed

180 g / 6 oz stale wholewheat bread, sliced

600 g / 1¼ lb plum tomatoes, peeled and chopped (or use canned)

1.5 litres / 2½ pints / 1½ quarts light meat stock (page 216)

3 tbsp fresh thyme leaves

salt and pepper

Soak the mushrooms in water to cover for 30 minutes. Drain and chop.

In a large pot heat 120 ml / 4 fl oz / ½ cup oil. Add the garlic and bread. Sauté over moderate heat, stirring frequently, until the garlic is translucent, about 2 minutes. Add the mushrooms, tomatoes, stock and thyme. Simmer over

● **Egg, Bread and Parmesan in Broth (p. 42)** ●

low heat for about 30 minutes, stirring occasionally to break up the bread.

Season to taste with salt and pepper. Ladle into individual bowls and top each serving with some of the remaining oil.

Passatelli in Brodo

EGG, BREAD AND PARMESAN IN BROTH

Traditionally this soup comes from Emilia Romagna. If you cannot find bone marrow, substitute 30 g/1 oz/ 2 tbsp butter.

SERVES 6

240 g/8 oz/2 cups freshly grated Parmesan cheese

240 g/8 oz/5 cups fresh breadcrumbs made from coarse-textured bread

3 eggs

1 tbsp grated nutmeg

1 tbsp grated lemon zest

30 g/1 oz bone marrow, softened

salt and pepper

1.5 litres/2½ pints/1½ quarts light meat stock (page 216)

In the bowl of a food processor fitted with the plastic blade, combine the Parmesan, breadcrumbs, eggs, nutmeg, lemon zest and bone marrow. Season with salt and pepper. Process until the mixture is well blended but not too creamy. (The mixture can be kept in the refrigerator for a few hours.)

In a large pot bring the stock to the boil. Push the marrow mixture through a food mill fitted with a large-holed disc, straight into the stock. Cook until the pieces rise to the surface, about 1 minute. Pour into a tureen and serve.

Passato di Spinaci alle Nocciole

CREAM OF SPINACH SOUP WITH HAZELNUTS

Although, strictly speaking, this is a cream soup, I don't like the spinach to be too smooth, so instead of processing it in a machine I put it through a food mill. I always use fresh spinach, but in an emergency frozen spinach will do. Afterwards I suggest you serve roast chicken in Vin Santo (page 112).

SERVES 6

90 g/3 oz/1½ cups shelled hazelnuts

1.2 kg/2½ lb fresh spinach with stalks

30 g/1 oz/2 tbsp unsalted butter, at room temperature

30 g/1 oz/¼ cup flour

240 ml/8 fl oz/1 cup milk

1 tsp grated nutmeg

1.2 litres/2 pints/5 cups light chicken stock (page 216)

salt

Toast the hazelnuts in a preheated 180°C/350°F/gas 4 oven for just a few minutes. Remove and rub off the skins in a coarse towel. Chop the nuts coarsely. Set aside.

Bring a large pot of salted water to the boil. Add the spinach, cover and cook until tender, about 3 minutes. Drain the spinach and refresh it in a bowl of iced water to prevent it losing colour. Drain and squeeze out excess liquid. Put the spinach through a food mill.

In a saucepan large enough to contain all the ingredients, melt the butter over moderate heat. Add the flour and stir with a wooden spoon until well blended.

In Italy pasta, rice, polenta and gnocchi, called *minestre asciutte*, are traditionally served at lunch, while soups of all kinds are served as the first course at dinner. In recent years pasta and rice have started appearing on the dinner table, but in this case they should be presented in the shape of a timbale, pie or mould. These baked dishes are also very useful for large buffets and can be prepared ahead of time and put in the oven just before the guests arrive.

Gradually stir in the milk and continue stirring until you have a smooth, thick sauce. Add the spinach and nutmeg and stir well. Pour in the stock and blend well.

Allow the soup to simmer for about 5 minutes. Check for salt, then pour into a soup tureen, sprinkle with the chopped hazelnuts and serve at once.

Pasta e Carciofi Gratinati

BAKED PASTA WITH ARTICHOKES

Baked pasta is a great solution for dinner parties because it can be prepared well in advance. I think your guests will enjoy this rather unusual combination that can be followed by veal olives in tomato sauce (page 104) and turnip leaves sautéed with garlic and breadcrumbs (page 132).

SERVES 6

juice of 1 lemon

6 small globe artichokes

60 g/2 oz/4 tbsp unsalted butter + extra for the dish

450 g / 1 lb rigatoni

2 eggs

480 ml / 16 fl oz / 2 cups whipping cream

salt and pepper

a pinch of grated nutmeg

180 g / 6 oz cooked ham, cut into narrow strips

120 g / 4 oz / 1 cup freshly grated Parmesan cheese

Fill a bowl with cold water and add the lemon juice. Trim the tops, hard outer leaves and spikes from the antichokes. Scoop out the chokes and drop immediately into the lemon water to prevent them turning black.

When all the artichokes have been prepared, blanch them in a saucepan of boiling salted water for 2 minutes. Drain well, then cut the artichokes lengthwise into slices.

In a frying pan melt 15 g / ½ oz / 1 tbsp butter over low heat. Add the artichoke slices and cook, covered, for 5 minutes, stirring frequently.

Bring a large pot of salted water to the boil. Add the rigatoni and cook until still very firm – about 6 minutes less than the usual cooking time. Drain and transfer to a bowl. Stir in the remaining butter and set aside. (All the prepared ingredients can be refrigerated for several hours, if desired.)

In a bowl, beat the eggs together. Add the cream and season with salt, pepper and nutmeg.

Butter an overproof dish. Pour in a thin layer of the egg and cream mixture and cover with a layer of pasta. Top it with a little ham and a layer of artichoke slices. Sprinkle with a little Parmesan. Repeat until you have used all the ingredients, finishing with the egg and cream and sprinkling with the rest of the Parmesan.

Bake in a preheated 180°C/350°F/gas 4 oven until bubbling, about 20 minutes. Serve hot.

Pasta con Melanzane e Basilico

BAKED PASTA WITH AUBERGINE (EGGPLANT) AND BASIL

This dish can be assembled and then frozen, but as basil will turn black when frozen, add the last layer of basil just before putting the dish in the oven. Defrost completely before cooking.

SERVES 6

½ medium-size onion, chopped

2 garlic cloves, finely chopped

6 tbsp extra virgin olive oil

900 g / 2 lb fresh plum tomatoes, peeled and chopped (or use canned)

extra virgin olive oil for deep-frying

2 oval, Asian-type aubergines (eggplants), about 300 g / 10 oz in total, sliced crosswise

30 g / 1 oz / 2 tbsp unsalted butter

30 g / 1 oz / ¼ cup flour

480 ml / 16 fl oz / 2 cups milk

120 g / 4 oz / 1 cup freshly grated Parmesan cheese

salt and pepper

450 g / 1 lb penne or other short pasta

a generous handful of fresh basil leaves

In a saucepan, sauté the onion and garlic in 4 tbsp oil over low heat until translucent, about 10 minutes. Add the tomatoes and bring to the boil. Cook over moderate heat, stirring occasionally, until all excess liquid has evaporated, about 50 minutes. Meanwhile, in a deep pan heat the oil for deep-frying to 180°C/350°F. Add the aubergine (eggplant) slices, a few at time, and fry until golden. Drain on paper towels.

In a heavy saucepan melt the butter on moderate heat. Add the flour and stir well. Gradually add the milk, stirring constantly, and bring to the boil. Boil for a couple of minutes until a creamy white sauce is formed. Add two-thirds of the grated Parmesan and salt and pepper to taste. Stir well and set aside.

Bring a large pot of salted water to the boil. Add the pasta and cook for 6 minutes (less than the usual cooking time). Drain and transfer to a bowl. Toss with the remaining 2 tbsp oil and set aside.

Cover the bottom of an ovenproof dish with one-third of the tomato sauce. Arrange a layer of pasta over the tomato sauce and cover it with half the white sauce. Place a layer of aubergine (eggplant) slices over the pasta and top with more tomato sauce and half the basil leaves. Repeat the layers once more. Sprinkle with the rest of the cheese. (The dish can now be kept for a few hours in the refrigerator or even frozen, omitting the top layer of basil.)

Bake in a preheated 180°C/350°F/gas 4 oven for 20 minutes, until bubbling. Serve immediately.

PASTA SHAPES

Dried pasta comes in so many different shapes and sizes that it would be almost impossible to list them all here. The most popular types of pasta served with sauce are spaghetti, penne, rigatoni, linguine, fusilli, bucatini, capelli d'angelo, zite and orecchiette. The small shapes are used in soups: ditalini, the biggest of these, in minestrone, and stelline, anellini and tempestina in broth. An excellent soup may be prepared by boiling 2 tbsp of small pasta shapes per person in good home-made stock. With a sprinkling of Parmesan cheese, you have a delicious first course in no time at all.

Pasta alle Zucchine

BAKED PASTA WITH COURGETTES (ZUCCHINI)

This delicious baked pasta is very useful because it can be prepared ahead of time and even frozen, then popped into the oven at the last minute. It can be followed by the tomato omelette on page 70.

SERVES 6

450 g / 1 lb penne or other short pasta

6 tbsp extra virgin olive oil

6 medium-size courgettes (zucchini), about 480 g / 1 lb or so total weight, thinly sliced

30 large fresh basil leaves

salt and pepper

30 g / 1 oz / 2 tbsp unsalted butter + extra for the dish

30 g / 1 oz / 1/4 cup flour

600 ml / 1 pint / 2 1/2 cups milk

120 g / 4 oz / 1 1/4 cups freshly grated Parmesan cheese

Bring a large pot of salted water to the boil. Add the pasta and half cook it, about 6 minutes (less than the usual cooking time). Drain the half-cooked pasta and transfer to a bowl. Stir in 2 tbsp oil.

Heat the rest of the oil in a frying pan. Add the courgettes (zucchini) and cook over moderate heat for about 10 minutes, or until tender and the excess liquid has evaporated. Add the basil, stir and season with salt and pepper. Set aside.

In a saucepan melt the butter over moderate heat. Stir in the flour, then gradually add the milk, stirring constantly, until a smooth white sauce is formed. Season with salt and pepper and set aside.

Butter an ovenproof dish. Make a layer of pasta on the bottom of the dish, then cover with a layer of courgettes (zucchini). Sprinkle with Parmesan and cover with a layer of white sauce. Continue making layers until all the ingredients are used, finishing with a layer of white sauce. (At this point the dish can be kept for a few hours in the refrigerator or frozen. Defrost before cooking.)

Bake in a preheated 180°C/350°F/gas 4 oven for 20 minutes until bubbling. Serve piping hot.

Penne con le Bietole

PENNE WITH SWISS CHARD

Here breadcrumbs, sautéed in oil, make a wonderful substitute for the more usual Parmesan cheese topping. It is worthwhile preparing a bigger quantity of them, to have them handy. They can be kept in the refrigerator for a few days. This delicious pasta can be followed by a nice dish of rocket and pear salad (page 145).

SERVES 6

120 ml / 4 fl oz / 1/2 cup extra virgin olive oil

150 g / 5 oz / 1 1/2 cups dry breadcrumbs (page 132)

450 g / 1 lb Swiss chard

salt

450 g / 1 lb penne or other short pasta

6 garlic cloves

1 dried hot red chili pepper, very finely chopped

6 flat anchovy fillets in oil, drained

In a frying pan heat half the oil over moderate heat. Add the breadcrumbs and stir gently with a wooden spoon until golden. Set aside.

Clean the Swiss chard and cut it into 2.5-cm/1-inch pieces, including the stalks. Bring a large pot of salted water to the boil. Add the pasta and Swiss chard and cook until the pasta is *al dente*.

While the pasta is cooking, heat the rest of the oil in a frying pan and sauté the garlic, chili pepper and anchovy fillets over moderate heat until the garlic is lightly coloured, about 3 minutes.

Drain the pasta and Swiss chard. Transfer to a bowl, add the garlic mixture and toss well to mix. Sprinkle with the breadcrumbs and serve.

Penne al Gorgonzola

PENNE WITH GORGONZOLA CREAM

This dish is quick, easy and impressive. Gorgonzola is the only suitable blue cheese to use – others will taste harsh. If you don't want to use Gorgonzola, substitute Gruyère or emmenthal. To follow, you can serve the tomato omelette (page 70).

SERVES 6

240 ml / 8 fl oz / 1 cup milk

1 tbsp grated lemon zest

150 g / 5 oz gorgonzola cheese, cut into small pieces

salt and pepper

600 g / 1 1/4 lb penne or other short pasta

60 g / 2 oz / 1/2 cup freshly grated Parmesan cheese

Put the milk, lemon zest and gorgonzola into a small saucepan over low heat. Stir with a wooden spoon until the cheese has melted and a smooth cream has formed, just a few minutes.

Meanwhile, bring a large pot of salted water to the boil. Add the penne and cook until *al dente*.

Drain the pasta and transfer it to a warm serving bowl. Mix immediately with the gorgonzola cream, then sprinkle with the Parmesan cheese and add pepper to taste. Serve at once.

Penne all'Uvetta

Penne with Raisins and Almonds

This rather unusual combination of flavours in a savoury dish comes from the Austrian influence on Northern Italian cooking. Occasionally I substitute poppy seed or a little cinnamon for the paprika. I like to follow this slightly sweet flavour with roast leg of lamb with anchovies (page 97) or the potato and onion mould on page 76, both of which complete the menu very well.

SERVES 6

90 g / 3 oz / ²⁄₃ cup sultanas (golden raisins)

90 g / 3 oz / ²⁄₃ cup blanched almonds

240 ml / 8 fl oz / 1 cup whipping cream

salt

600 g / 1¼ lb penne or other short pasta

60 g / 2 oz / 4 tbsp unsalted butter

1 tsp sweet paprika

Soak the raisins in water to cover for about 30 minutes; drain. In a blender grind the almonds. Transfer the ground almonds to a large saucepan. Gradually stir in the cream and then the raisins. Set aside.

Bring a large pot of salted water to the boil. Add the pasta and cook until *al dente*.

Meanwhile, warm the almond and

● **Penne with Raisins and Almonds** ●

raisin cream with the butter over low heat.

Drain the pasta and add it to the raisin and almond cream. Stirring frequently, cook on moderate heat for 2 minutes.

Pile the pasta on a warm platter, sprinkle with the paprika and serve at once.

Polenta Pasticciata con il Gorgonzola

POLENTA STUFFED WITH GORGONZOLA CHEESE

This is one of my favourite ways of eating polenta, provided that the cheese is very fresh. I can even prepare the dish ahead of time, and put it in the oven to reheat for about 10 minutes when needed. In that case I cover the top with foil so that it will not form a crust on the surface. In season I put a layer of thinly shaved white truffles on top of the gorgonzola. Polenta could be followed by baked stuffed sardines (page 116).

SERVES 6

270 g / 9 oz / 2 cups coarse yellow cornmeal

extra virgin olive oil for the dish

300 g / 10 oz gorgonzola cheese, sliced

Bring 1.5 litres / 2½ pints / 6 cups salted water to the boil in a large saucepan. Sprinkle in the cornmeal, stirring constantly with a whisk to prevent lumps. Lower the heat and, stirring frequently with a wooden spoon, cook for about 40 minutes.

Pour half of the polenta into an oiled round shallow dish and smooth the surface with a wet spatula. Spread over the gorgonzola to cover completely, then cover with the rest of the polenta. Smooth the surface again and turn out the polenta on to a platter. Serve immediately, cut into slices.

Ravioli di Patate

POTATO RAVIOLI

These ravioli are a speciality of Friuli, in north-eastern Italy. They are often flavoured with cinnamon or poppy seeds, but I have given them a touch of Tuscany by flavouring the sauce with rosemary. Uncooked ravioli can be frozen successfully. To cook from frozen, put into boiling water for about 6 minutes. During the cooking courses, we usually have pigeons stuffed with pear (page 110) to follow.

SERVES 6

For the pasta dough

300 g / 10 oz / 2½ cups flour

3 eggs

For the filling and sauce

450 g / 1 lb boiling potatoes, peeled and thinly sliced

1 large onion, thinly sliced

120 ml / 4 fl oz / ½ cup extra virgin olive oil

2 tbsp finely chopped fresh rosemary

salt and pepper

60 g / 2 oz bacon, chopped

240 g / 8 oz / 1 cup ricotta cheese

60 g / 2 oz / ½ cup freshly grated Parmesan cheese

2 egg yolks

¼ tbsp grated nutmeg

Heap the flour on a board. Make a well in the centre and break in the eggs. Using a fork, gently break them up. With a circular motion, gradually work the flour into the eggs until it is all well incorporated and a dough has formed. Knead the dough until it is smooth and elastic (see page 199). Roll the dough into a ball, wrap it and set aside in a cool place. (It can be refrigerated for a few days or frozen.)

In a saucepan combine half the potatoes and half the onion with 480 ml / 16 fl oz / 2 cups water. Cover and simmer over low heat for about 30 minutes. Transfer the contents of the saucepan to a blender and purée with 6 tbsp of the oil. Add the rosemary, season to taste and set aside. (This sauce can be refrigerated for a few hours.)

In a large non-stick frying pan heat the remaining 2 tbsp oil over moderate heat. Add the bacon and the rest of the potatoes and onion. Cover and cook, stirring frequently, for about 20 minutes. Allow to cool, then stir in the ricotta, Parmesan, egg yolks and nutmeg. Season with salt and pepper. Blend well and set aside. (This filling can be kept chilled for a few hours.)

Divide the pasta into pieces and, using a pasta machine, roll out into very thin strips (about 0.5 mm thick).

Arrange small mounds of the filling at 5-cm / 2-inch intervals down one half of each strip of pasta. Brush the edges with a little water, then fold over the strip lengthwise to cover the filling. Press the edges to seal. Cut around the mounds of filling with a round pastry cutter about 5-cm / 2-inches in diameter. (The ravioli can be kept in the refrigerator for a few hours before cooking.)

Bring a large pot of salted water to the boil. Return the sauce to its saucepan and reheat it. Add the ravioli to the boiling water and cook over high heat for about 2 minutes.

Drain the ravioli well and arrange on a warm platter. Spoon over the sauce and serve at once.

● **Potato Ravioli** ●

Rigatoni ai Peperoni

BAKED RIGATONI WITH PEPPERS

As this dish is so rich and tasty, I usually serve it in the summer, followed only by hot or cold courgettes (zucchini) stuffed with ham (page 84).

SERVES 6

6 large sweet peppers, 3 red and 3 yellow

7 tbsp extra virgin olive oil

2 garlic cloves, chopped

600 g / 1¼ lb ripe plum tomatoes, peeled and chopped (or use canned)

90 g / 3 oz / ½ cup capers in vinegar or salt, drained or rinsed

90 g / 3 oz / ½ cup black olives, stored

6 tbsp fine dry breadcrumbs (page 132)

1 tbsp dried oregano

salt and pepper

450 g / 1 lb rigatoni

unsalted butter for the dish

Wash the peppers and place them on the shelf in a preheated 200°C/400°F/gas 6 oven. Bake, turning once, until the skins blister, about 20 minutes. Wrap the peppers in foil and leave them to cool for about 2 minutes, then peel them. Cut the peppers in half and remove the seeds and core. Cut them into strips about 1 cm/½ inch wide.

In a large frying pan heat 6 tbsp of oil with the garlic and cook until the garlic is translucent. Add the pepper strips, tomatoes, capers, olives, breadcrumbs and oregano. Season with salt and pepper. Cook over moderate heat for about 10 minutes, stirring occasionally.

Meanwhile, bring a large pot of salted water to the boil. Add the rigatoni and cook for 6 minutes (less than the usual cooking time). Drain the pasta and quickly coat it with the remaining oil.

Butter an ovenproof dish and cover the bottom with a layer of pasta. Spread a layer of the pepper mixture over it. Continue making alternate layers until all the ingredients are used, finishing with the pepper mixture. (At this point the dish can be refrigerated for a few hours.)

Bake in a preheated 180°C/350°F/gas 4 oven for about 20 minutes. Serve immediately.

Rigatoni al Pomodoro e Ricotta

RIGATONI WITH TOMATO AND RICOTTA SAUCE

When buying canned tomatoes, I suggest you always choose an Italian brand, because in Italy the tomatoes are picked when perfectly ripe and they are canned in their natural juices. This dish can be followed by the soufflé omelette with herbs on page 83.

SERVES 6

3 tbsp extra virgin olive oil

3 garlic cloves, chopped

900 g / 2 lb canned Italian plum tomatoes with their juice, chopped

salt and pepper

450 g / 1 lb rigatoni

240 g / 8 oz / 1 cup ricotta cheese

2 tbsp chopped fresh basil leaves

3 tbsp freshly grated Parmesan cheese

Pour the oil into a medium-size saucepan. Add the garlic and cook over low heat until it is just translucent, about 3 minutes. Add the tomatoes and simmer over low heat until the liquid has evaporated, about 50 minutes.

Bring a large pot of salted water to the boil. Cook the rigatoni until *al dente*.

Meanwhile, put the ricotta in a bowl and crumble it with a fork. Set the bowl in a pan of hot water and leave to heat the cheese.

Add the basil to the tomato sauce and season with salt and pepper. Stir well.

Drain the pasta and transfer it to a warm serving bowl. Add the tomato sauce and half of the ricotta and toss gently. Cover with the rest of the ricotta, sprinkle with Parmesan and serve at once.

Riso al Burro e Salvia

RICE WITH SAGE AND BUTTER

At an elegant luncheon I sometimes serve this dish moulded: as soon as the rice is cooked, pack it into a ring mould and turn it out on to a serving plate almost immediately. Pour the sage and butter into the hollow and garnish the plate with fresh sage leaves. For a simple luncheon, follow it with a tomato omelette (page 70). On a more elegant occasion it could be followed by sole fillets with courgettes (zucchini) and tomato (page 102).

SERVES 6

600 g / 1¼ lb / 2⅔ cups arborio rice

salt

about 30 fresh sage leaves

150 g / 5 oz / 10 tbsp unsalted butter

90 g / 3 oz / ¾ cup freshly grated Parmesan cheese

● **Rigatoni with Tomato and Ricotta Sauce** ●

Bring about 3 litres/5 pints/3 quarts of salted water to the boil in a large pot. Pour in the rice and leave to cook over moderate heat, without stirring, for about 15 minutes.

Meanwhile, in a saucepan over moderate heat fry the sage in the butter until the butter is fairly dark and the sage leaves are crisp, about 10 minutes.

Drain the rice. Pile it on a serving dish (or mould it). Sprinkle with the Parmesan, pour over the sage and butter, and serve immediately.

Risotto al Finocchio

FENNEL RISOTTO

Y ou can substitute artichoke bottoms, shredded cabbage leaves or sliced broccoli for the fennel. As risotto should be made at the last minute. I like to follow this with roast pork in almond sauce (page 106) because it can be prepared a day ahead.

SERVES 6

3 medium-size fennel bulbs

1.2 litres/2 pints/5 cups light meat stock (page 216)

6 tbsp extra virgin olive oil

450 g/1 lb/2 cups arborio rice

120 ml/4 fl oz/$\frac{1}{2}$ cup dry white wine

1 tbsp fennel seeds

6 tbsp freshly grated Parmesan cheese

salt and pepper

Remove the tough outer leaves of the fennel. Wash the bulbs thoroughly, drain and dry. Slice very finely.

Heat the stock and keep it simmering over low heat.

In a saucepan heat the oil. Add the fennel and cook, covered, over low heat for about 10 minutes. Add the rice, raise the heat to moderate and allow it to heat for a couple of minutes, stirring frequently. Pour in the wine and enough boiling stock to cover the rice. Add the fennel seeds. Simmer, stirring, adding the rest of the stock in batches in order to keep the rice always covered with a veil of liquid.

Remove the saucepan from the heat exactly 14 minutes after adding the first stock. Stir in the Parmesan and season to taste. Cover and allow the risotto to rest for a couple of minutes. Transfer to a serving plate and serve immediately.

Risotto in Forma al Prosciutto

RISOTTO MOULD WRAPPED IN PROSCIUTTO

As delicious as it is beautiful, this dish is ideal for a buffet party. I prepare it ahead of time, so it can be popped into the oven as soon as the guests have arrived. It can be served with the veal rolls in tomato sauce (page 104) or with the sauté of veal with peas on page 117.

SERVES 6

100 g / 3½ oz / 7 tbsp unsalted butter + extra for the mould

6 thin slices of Parma prosciutto

1.2 litres / 2 pints / 5 cups light chicken stock (page 216)

1 tbsp chopped onion

600 g / 1¼ lb / 2⅔ cups arborio rice

90 g / 3 oz / ¾ cup freshly grated Parmesan cheese

salt and pepper

Butter a 1.5-litre/2½-pint/1½-quart mould. Line it with slightly overlapping layers of prosciutto and keep in a cool place.

In saucepan, heat the stock and keep it at a simmer.

In a heavy saucepan heat 60 g/ 2 oz/4 tbsp butter. Add the chopped onion and, stirring frequently, cook over low heat until translucent, about 5 minutes. Add the rice, raise the heat to moderate and stir until the rice is hot, about 2 minutes.

Add 3 ladles of stock. Simmer, stirring constantly, gradually adding the rest of the stock, about a ladle at a time, so that the rice is always covered with a veil of liquid.

After exactly 12 minutes remove the saucepan from the heat. Stir in the Parmesan and the rest of the butter. Season with salt and pepper. Pour the risotto on to a large plate to stop the rice cooking. Leave to cool for a couple of minutes.

Spoon the rice into the prepared mould. Transfer to the lowest shelf of a preheated 200°C/400°F/gas 6 oven and bake for 10 minutes. Cover with foil and bake for a further 10 minutes.

Unmould on to a platter and serve at once.

RICE

Several different kinds of rice are grown in the Padana plains around Vercelli and in the Veneto. Although the width varies, they are all short-grain rices. They are divided into categories – semifine, fine and superfine. Superfine is used for risotto, the best being carnaroli, followed by arborio and vialone nano. Semifine, such as maratelli, is used in soups. When making risotto, the finished dish should have a creamy consistency but the rice itself should be firm to the bite and you should be able to distinguish individual grains.

● **Risotto Mould Wrapped in Prosciutto** ●

Risotto al Funghi

MUSHROOM RISOTTO

I sometimes dissolve a large pinch of saffron in the first ladle of stock because it enhances the flavour of the mushrooms and gives the rice a cheerful colour. I always have dried porcini and saffron in my larder so I can make this risotto for unexpected guests, followed by a salad, such as the rocket (arugula) and pear salad on page 145.

SERVES 6

10 g / 1/3 oz dried porcini mushrooms, crumbled

1.5 litres / 2 1/2 pints / 1 1/2 quarts light meat stock (page 216)

120 g / 4 oz / 1 stick unsalted butter

2 tbsp chopped onion

600 g / 1 1/4 lb / 2 2/3 cups arborio rice

a pinch of saffron threads (optional)

90 g / 3 oz / 3/4 cup freshly grated Parmesan cheese

salt and pepper

Soak the porcini in lukewarm water to cover for 30 minutes. Remove the mushrooms and squeeze out excess liquid. Strain the mushroom water through a fine sieve into the stock and heat it, then keep it at a simmer.

In a heavy saucepan melt half the butter over low heat. Add the onion and, stirring constantly, sauté until translucent, about 3 minutes. Raise the heat to moderate, add the rice and heat, stirring, for about 2 minutes. Add 3 ladles of stock with the saffron, if used, and the mushrooms. Simmer, stirring constantly, adding the rest of the stock gradually so that the rice is always covered with a veil of liquid.

Exactly 14 minutes after the first

● **Lemon Risotto** ●

stock was added, remove the saucepan from the heat. Stir in the Parmesan cheese and the rest of the butter and season with salt and pepper to taste. Cover the saucepan with a lid and leave for 2 minutes before serving on a warm platter.

Risotto al Limone

LEMON RISOTTO

This is the risotto I prepare most often during the cookery courses, because it is easy to make with readily available ingredients and it has a lovely fresh flavour. Generally I follow it with the grilled wrapped trout on page 122, and have raspberries in wine jelly (page 186) for dessert.

SERVES 6

5 litres / 2 1/2 pints / 1 1/2 quarts light meat or chicken stock (page 216)

120 g / 4 oz / 1 stick unsalted butter

1 small onion, finely chopped

600 g / 1 1/4 lb / 2 2/3 cups arborio rice

300 ml / 1/2 pint / 1 1/4 cups dry white wine

90 g / 3 oz / 3/4 cup freshly grated Parmesan cheese

3 tbsp chopped fresh flat-leaf (Italian) parsley

grated zest and juice of 1 lemon

salt and pepper

Heat the stock and keep it simmering over low heat.

In a saucepan melt half the butter over low heat. Add the onion and, stirring frequently, cook until translucent, about 5 minutes. Add the rice and raise the heat to moderate. Stir for 2 minutes to warm the rice. Add 3 ladles of the stock. Simmer stirring constantly, adding the rest of the stock gradually, alternating it with a little wine, so that the rice is always covered with a veil of liquid.

Exactly 14 minutes after adding the first stock, remove the pan from the heat. Add the Parmesan, the rest of the butter, the parsley, and lemon zest and juice. Stir well and season with salt and pepper. Cover and allow to rest for 2 minutes.

Transfer to a warm platter and serve immediately.

Risotto al Pomodoro e Basilico

TOMATO AND BASIL RISOTTO

Although it is a well-known fact that Neapolitans much prefer pasta to rice, the traditional Neapolitan cuisine has several famous rice recipes. Inevitably they involve a lot of tomato. This could be followed by squid stuffed with prawns (page 117).

SERVES 6

900 g / 2 lb Italian plum tomatoes, peeled (or canned) and puréed in a blender

salt and pepper

6 tbsp extra virgin olive oil

1 medium-size onion, chopped

1 medium-size carrot, chopped

1 celery stalk, chopped

600 g / 1¼ lb / 2⅔ cups arborio rice

2 tbsp chopped fresh basil leaves

90 g / 3 oz / ¾ cup freshly grated Parmesan cheese

Put the tomatoes in a medium-size saucepan, add 600 ml / 1 pint / 2½ cups of water and simmer over low heat for about 10 minutes. Season with salt and pepper. The tomato sauce should be very runny. Keep on a low boil.

Pour the oil into a heavy saucepan. Add the onion, carrot and celery and sauté over moderate heat for about 5 minutes. Add the rice and, stirring constantly, allow the flavours to amalgamate for about 2 minutes. Add just enough tomato sauce to cover the rice. Simmer, stirring, adding the rest of the sauce gradually so that the rice is always covered with a veil of liquid.

Exactly 14 minutes after adding the first sauce, remove the saucepan from the heat. Stir in the basil and Parmesan cheese. Cover and allow to rest for 2 minutes.

Pour on to a serving dish and serve at once.

Risotto al Radicchio Rosso

RED RADICCHIO RISOTTO

This recipe comes from Veneto where the best varieties of radicchio are grown. The Austrian influence in the regional cooking can be seen in the smoky bacon used instead of pancetta.

SERVES 6

1.2 litres / 2 pints / 5 cups light meat stock (page 216)

90 g / 3 oz smoked bacon, chopped

600 g / 1¼ lb red radicchio, shredded

450 g / 1 lb / 2 cups arborio rice

salt and pepper

Bring the stock to the boil, then keep it simmering gently.

In a large saucepan fry the bacon in its own fat over moderate heat, stirring constantly, until crisp, about 5 minutes. Add the shredded radicchio and cook until it wilts, about 3 minutes. Add the rice and stir for 2 minutes to heat well. Add enough boiling stock to cover the rice. Simmer, stirring constantly, gradually adding the rest of the stock so that the rice is always covered with a veil of liquid.

Exactly 14 minutes after adding the first stock, remove the saucepan from the heat. Season with salt and pepper, cover and leave to stand for about 2 minutes.

Transfer to a warm platter and serve immediately.

Risotto agli Scampi

SCAMPI RISOTTO

I sometimes make this risotto with sliced lobster, crabmeat or scallops. If you would like to add colour, sprinkle the risotto with chopped parsley just before serving it. The roast pork in almond sauce on page 106 would complete an elegant luncheon menu.

SERVES 6

90 g / 3 oz / 6 tbsp unsalted butter

450 g / 1 lb raw scampi or large prawns or shrimp, peeled

salt and pepper

1.2 litres / 2 pints / 5 cups fish stock (page 216)

2 tbsp chopped onion

450 g / 1 lb / 2 cups arborio rice

120 ml / 4 fl oz / ½ cup whipping cream

In a frying pan melt 15 g / ½ oz / 1 tbsp butter. Add the scampi and sauté over moderate heat for 2 minutes. Season with salt and pepper. Set aside.

Heat the stock and keep it at a low boil.

In a medium-size saucepan melt the rest of the butter over low heat. Add the onion and cook until translucent, about 5 minutes. Increase the heat to moderate, add the rice and stir until well heated, about 2 minutes. Add 3 ladles of stock. Simmer, stirring constantly, gradually adding the rest of the stock so that the rice is always covered with a veil of liquid. After 12 minutes stir in the scampi and cream. Exactly 14 minutes after adding the first stock, remove the saucepan from the heat. Season with salt and pepper, cover and leave to stand for 2 minutes.

Transfer to a warm platter and serve immediately.

Risotto alle Verdure

VEGETABLE RISOTTO

I vary the vegetables according to the seasons. In winter I replace the peas and beans with sliced globe artichokes, bulb fennel, celery or broccoli. In spring, when I am at Coltibuono, I use nettles because they are delicious with rice. The vegetables can also be sautéed in a little butter before adding them to the rice. To follow, try the baked wrapped sea bream on page 107.

SERVES 6

1.2 litres / 2 pints / 5 cups light chicken stock (page 216)

120 g / 4 oz / 1 stick unsalted butter

1 medium-size onion, finely chopped

2 carrots, diced

450 g / 1 lb / 2 cups arborio rice

120 ml / 4 fl oz / ½ cup dry white wine

180 g / 6 oz / 1¼ cups shelled fresh or frozen peas

180 g / 6 oz green beans, diced

90 g / 3 oz / ¾ cup freshly grated Parmesan cheese

2 tbsp chopped fresh flat-leaf (Italian) parsley

salt and pepper

Heat the stock and keep it at a low boil. In a heavy saucepan melt half the butter. Add the onion and carrots and sauté over low heat until translucent, about 2 minutes. Raise the heat to moderate, add the rice and stir until well heated. Add the white wine and cook until it evaporates. Simmer, gradually adding the stock so that the rice is always covered. Stir constantly. After 10 minutes, add the peas and green beans. Cook for 4 minutes.

Remove the saucepan from the heat. Add the rest of the butter and stir in the Parmesan and parsley. Season to taste. Cover and allow to rest for 2 minutes. Arrange on a warm platter and serve.

● **Red Radicchio Risotto** ●

FRESH VS DRIED PASTA

Although in Italy we make a distinction between home-made fresh egg pasta which can, of course, be dried, and commercial dried pasta, fresh pasta is in no way considered superior. In fact, far more dried pasta is used than fresh. Fresh pasta is particularly popular in Emilia Romagna and Piemonte where it is served with buttery sauces, while dried pasta is served with sauces based on olive oil. At one time dried pasta was used mostly in central and southern Italy, but since olive oil became so much in demand all over Italy, this distinction no longer exists. In recipes, quantities of dried pasta will be less than those for fresh because fresh home-made pasta, even when dried, is heavier than commercial dried pasta.

SUCCESS WITH PASTA

Pasta must be cooked in abundant salted water, without oil or anything else, and must be served *al dente*, meaning tender but firm to the bite. Pasta continues to cook even after it has been removed from the heat, so it should be drained as quickly as possible. It is a mistake, however, to rinse it under cold running water because it gets slippery and loses a lot of flavour. Obviously cooking times vary according to the shape and size of the pasta and the brand used. When buying pasta make sure you choose imported Italian pasta, because it is always made of hard wheat and does not overcook as easily as other varieties.

● **Tagliatelle Mould** ●

Sformato di Tagliatelle

TAGLIATELLE MOULD

Linguine are a good substitute for tagliatelle, and the mould can be surrounded by the Milanese tomato sauce on page 157.

SERVES 6

3 litres / 5 pints / 3 quarts milk

450 g / 1 lb tagliatelle

45 g / 1½ oz / 3 tbsp unsalted butter, at room temperature + extra for the pan

3 eggs, size 5 (US medium), separated

salt and pepper

a pinch of grated nutmeg

90 g / 3 oz / ¾ cup freshly grated Parmesan cheese

Bring the milk to the boil in a large saucepan. Add the tagliatelle and cook until *al dente*. Drain the tagliatelle, saving 180 ml / 6 fl oz / ¾ cup of the milk. Transfer the pasta to a bowl and immediately toss it with the butter. Leave it to cool.

In a bowl beat the egg whites until stiff. In another bowl whisk the yolks and gradually whisk in the reserved milk. Season with salt, pepper and nutmeg.

Pour the egg yolk sauce over the tagliatelle, add the Parmesan and toss well. Gently fold in the beaten egg whites.

Butter a 23-cm / 9-inch springform pan and fill it with the tagliatelle mixture. Bake in a preheated 180°C / 350°F / gas 4 oven until the top is golden, about 40 minutes.

Remove from the oven and leave to cool for a few minutes, then insert a knife around the edges to loosen the tagliatelle mould. Lift off the side of the pan, slide the mould on to a platter and serve immediately.

Soufflé di Tagliatelle

TAGLIATELLE SOUFFLE

This soufflé can be made with easy-to-find dried tagliatelle, although home-made tagliatelle are always better. It is important to make sure you do not overcook the pasta because it is later baked in the soufflé. It can be followed by the chicken roasted in bay leaves on page 110.

SERVES 6

300 g / 10 oz dried tagliatelle, or 450 g / 1 lb fresh home-made tagliatelle (page 217)

60 g / 2 oz / 4 tbsp unsalted butter, at room temperature

4 eggs, separated

240 g / 8 oz / 1 cup ricotta cheese

salt and pepper

Bring a large pot of salted water to the boil and cook the tagliatelle until just before they are *al dente*. Drain and mix with the butter. Allow to cool.

In a bowl beat the egg yolks with the ricotta. Season with salt and pepper. Stir the egg mixture into the tagliatelle.

In another bowl beat the egg whites until stiff. Fold them into the mixture. Butter a deep 23-cm / 9-inch soufflé dish. Pour in the tagliatelle mixture and bake in a preheated 200°C / 400°F / gas 4 oven for about 30 minutes or until the soufflé is well risen and slightly golden on top. Serve immediately.

COOKING PASTA

To cook pasta use a deep, fairly narrow pot and a great deal of water. Do *not* add oil to the cooking water! The proportions are 1 litre / 1¾ pints / 1 quart of water for each 100 g / 3½ oz of pasta. (This would mean 5 litres / 8 pints / 5 quarts of water for 500 g / 1 lb 2 oz of pasta.) Bring the water to the boil over high heat. As soon as it boils, add coarse sea or kosher salt – an abundant quantity for dried pasta and, as it absorbs more liquid, less for fresh. When the water returns to a fast boil put the pasta in. Never break spaghetti or linguine because they were purposely made long and should be cooked and eaten that way. Stir the pasta with a long-handled, preferably wooden, spoon and cover the pot. When the water starts boiling again, remove the lid and continue cooking until the pasta is *al dente* or firm to the bite. I would like to be able to give you specific cooking times, but even Italian brands vary tremendously, so check the cooking times suggested on the package.

Pasta should not remain in its cooking water a moment more than necessary. As soon as it is *al dente*, turn it into a colander and shake well. Transfer the pasta to a warmed serving bowl. Immediately pour on most of the sauce, or a few tablespoons of olive oil, and toss well to prevent the pasta from sticking together. Spoon the rest of the sauce on top of the pasta without stirring again. For a cold pasta salad, transfer the drained pasta to a cooled serving dish.

Sometimes, in order to add flavour to pasta, particularly spaghetti, as soon as it is drained it is transferred to a frying pan containing the hot sauce, with a few tablespoons of the cooking water, and stirred occasionally while it cooks for a couple more minutes. When you intend doing this, boil the pasta for a much shorter time and drain it when it is still quite stiff, or 'standing' as the Neapolitans say, because the longer pasta cooks the softer it becomes. Pasta for a salad should also be undercooked – 1 minute less than if serving it hot.

Spaghetti alla Crema di Finocchio

SPAGHETTI WITH FENNEL PUREE

As an alternative, this sauce can also be made with sweet peppers as well as with boiled broccoli. Fennel and broccoli are so strongly flavoured, they require no herbs.

SERVES 6

2 medium fennel bulbs, divided into quarters

120 ml / 4 fl oz / ½ cup extra virgin olive oil

salt

600 g / 1¼ lb spaghetti

Blanch the fennel in boiling salted water for about 10 minutes. Drain and transfer to a blender or food processor. Add the oil and process until the mixture turns into a purée. Season with a little salt.

Bring a large pot of salted water to the boil. Add the spaghetti and cook until *al dente*.

Drain and transfer to a warm serving bowl. Pour over the fennel sauce, toss well and serve immediately.

Spaghetti al Filetto di Pomodoro

SPAGHETTI WITH RAW TOMATO

Pasta served at room temperature can be delicious, as long as it is not mixed with too many ingredients. Tomato and basil are more than enough. We often have this for lunch in the summer, followed by beef steaks with gorgonzola sauce (page 93).

SERVES 6

6 large ripe tomatoes, peeled, seeded and diced

salt and pepper

600 g / 1¼ lb spaghetti

120 ml / 4 fl oz / ½ cup extra virgin olive oil

18 fresh basil leaves

Sprinkle the tomatoes with salt and leave to drain in a colander for about 30 minutes.

Bring a large pot of salted water to the boil. Add the spaghetti, stir and cook until *al dente*. Drain the spaghetti quickly and transfer it to a large bowl. Add the olive oil and tomatoes and toss well.

Check the seasoning. Leave to cool to room temperature.

Using your fingers, tear the basil into small pieces and sprinkle it over the pasta. Mix well.

This dish can be prepared 2 hours in advance, as long as it is kept at room temperature.

Spaghetti al Rosmarino

SPAGHETTI WITH OIL AND ROSEMARY

Any pasta can be served with this sauce – spaghetti, penne, rigatoni or even fresh tagliatelle. The sauce is prepared while the pasta is cooking. Fresh rosemary is available throughout the year, and it keeps in the refrigerator for at least a week. Follow with brains with brown butter and capers (page 94).

SERVES 6

600 g / 1¼ lb spaghetti

120 ml / 4 fl oz / ½ cup extra virgin olive oil

3 garlic cloves, chopped

3 tbsp chopped fresh rosemary

salt and pepper

Bring a large pot of salted water to the boil. Add the spaghetti, stir once with a wooden spoon and cook until *al dente*.

Meanwhile, pour the oil into a small frying pan, add the garlic and rosemary and sauté over low heat until the garlic is translucent.

Drain the pasta as soon as it is cooked. Transfer it to a warm bowl, add the hot sauce and toss well. Season with salt and pepper to taste and serve at once.

● Buckwheat Tagliatelle with Green ●
Beans (p. 58)

SERVING PASTA

Originally pasta was essentially a first course, but our eating habits have changed in recent years and pasta is now sometimes served as a main course, either before or after a salad or cooked vegetables, but never at the same time or on the same plate. In Italy we like having extra grated Parmesan cheese at table, served separately in a bowl, so we can sprinkle it over pasta with certain sauces.

Unless it is in soup, pasta should always be served in large well-heated bowls using a spoon and a fork, not tongs. Pasta is never cut with a knife: the side of a fork is used instead. To eat spaghetti correctly, a little should be rolled around the prongs of a fork, absolutely without the aid of a spoon. But as this is an acquired skill, I avoid serving spaghetti to foreign guests, simply having short pasta such as penne or rigatoni instead.

Tagliatelle alla Crema di Cipolle

TAGLIATELLE WITH CHEESE AND ONION SAUCE

For a more delicate flavour, soak the sliced onions in water for about 1 hour. (This will make them less pungent.) Then drain and pat dry with paper towels. The onion cream can also be enriched with diced ham. To follow you can serve the baked salmon slices with fennel and lemon on page 121.

SERVES 6

600 g / 1¼ lb onions, sliced

120 g / 4 oz / 1 stick butter

240 ml / 8 fl oz / 1 cup whipping cream

450 g / 1 lb dried tagliatelle, or
600 g / 1¼ lb fresh home-made tagliatelle
(page 217)

120 g / 4 oz fontina cheese, grated

salt and pepper

Put the onions in a saucepan with the butter, cover and cook over very low heat for about 20 minutes, stirring frequently, until the onions are soft and barely golden. Gradually stir in the cream. Pour the onion mixture into a blender or food processor and blend to a smooth sauce. Pour back into the saucepan.

Bring a large pot of salted water to the boil. Add the tagliatelle and cook until al dente.

Meanwhile, reheat the sauce. Add the cheese and stir until melted. Season to taste.

Drain the pasta and transfer to a serving dish. Pour over the sauce, toss lightly and serve at once.

Tagliatelle di Grano Saraceno

BUCKWHEAT TAGLIATELLE WITH GREEN BEANS

Buckwheat is used mostly in Valtellina, a beautiful mountain region north of Milan. Like wholewheat flour, it contains less starch than white wheat flour so if the pasta is rolled too thinly it tends to break. Buckwheat flour is available in health food stores. This recipe can also be made with white wheat flour. As it is a fairly rich dish, I suggest that afterwards you serve the pea and tomato mould (page 76).

SERVES 6

150 g / 5 oz / 1½ cups buckwheat flour

150 g / 5 oz / 1¼ cups plain (all-purpose) flour

3 eggs, size 1 (US extra large)

1 large potato, peeled and cut into julienne

150 g / 5 oz green beans

120 g / 4 oz / 1 stick unsalted butter

90 g / 3 oz / ¾ cup freshly grated Parmesan cheese

1 tbsp poppy seeds (optional)

Heap the flours on a board. Make a well in the centre and break in the eggs. Using a fork, gently break them up, then, with a circular motion, gradually work the flour into the eggs until it is all well incorporated and a dough has formed. Knead the dough until smooth and elastic, about 10 minutes (see page 199).

Divide the dough into four pieces and, using a pasta machine, roll out into strips, about 2 mm / 1/16 inch thick. Leave the sheets of pasta to dry for a few minutes, then cut them into noodles about 1 cm / ½ inch wide and 20 cm / 8 inches long.

Bring a large pot of salted water to the boil. Add the potato and beans and boil for about 5 minutes. Add the tagliatelle and cook until they rise to the surface.

Meanwhile, melt the butter over low heat.

Drain the pasta and vegetables and arrange on a warm platter. Add the Parmesan and melted butter, toss well and sprinkle with the poppy seeds, if using. Serve at once.

Tagliatelle alle Spezie

TAGLIATELLE WITH MIXED SPICES

For this recipe I generally use dried tagliatelle, although I sometimes prepare it with home-made pasta. To make a change, you can also use this recipe with spaghetti or linguine. To follow you could prepare the veal chops with lemon sauce on page 120.

SERVES 6

60 g / 2 oz / ½ cup walnut pieces

1 tbsp sugar

1 tbsp mixed ground cinnamon, nutmeg and cloves

450 g / 1 lb dried tagliatelle or 600 g / 1¼ lb fresh home-made tagliatelle (page 217)

120 g / 4 oz / 1 stick butter, softened

salt and pepper

In a blender grind the walnuts. Add the sugar and spices and blend well.

Bring a large pot of salted water to the boil. Add the tagliatelle and cook until al dente.

Drain well and transfer to a warm serving dish. Add the butter, spice mixture and seasoning. Toss well and serve immediately.

Timballi di Capellini

SMALL ANGEL HAIR MOULDS

These small moulds make an excellent first course for a fairly formal dinner. I usually serve them on individual dishes and surround them with the spinach and nutmeg sauce on page 158.

SERVES 6

30 g / 1 oz dried porcini mushrooms

225 g / 8 oz angel hair (fine spaghetti)

90 g / 3 oz / 6 tbsp butter, at room temperature, + extra for the moulds

120 ml / 4 fl oz / ½ cup whipping cream

90 g / 3 oz / 1 cup fine dry breadcrumbs (page 132)

180 g / 6 oz / 1½ cups freshly grated Parmesan cheese

salt and pepper

Soak the mushrooms in lukewarm water to cover for 30 minutes.

Bring a large pot of salted water to the boil. Add the angel hair and cook just until *al dente*. Drain and transfer to a bowl. Add the butter and toss well.

Drain and chop the mushrooms. In a small saucepan combine them with the cream and cook over moderate-low heat for about 5 minutes.

Butter 6 individual timbale or dariole moulds or custard cups, each 120–140 ml / 4–5 fl oz capacity, and sprinkle with the breadcrumbs.

Stir the mushroom and cream sauce into the pasta, add the Parmesan cheese and seasoning and mix well. Divide the pasta mixture among the moulds, pressing down lightly. (The moulds can be stored in the refrigerator for a few hours before baking.)

Bake in a preheated 180°C / 350°F / gas 4 oven for about 20 minutes. Turn out onto individual dishes and serve.

Timballo di Rigatoni in Crosta

SWEET AND SAVOURY RIGATONI PIE

This classic Neapolitan dish has many variations. Instead of chopped meat, you can use miniature meatballs. Or, if you would prefer a vegetarian dish, dress the rigatoni with abundant tomato and white sauces. As it is a very substantial dish, follow with the salad with balsamic vinegar on page 136.

SERVES 8

For the pastry

400 g / 14 oz / 3½ cups flour

30 g / 1 oz / 2½ tbsp sugar

200 g / 7 oz / 14 tbsp unsalted butter, in small pieces

4 tbsp milk

1 egg yolk

a pinch of salt

beaten egg yolk for glazing

For the filling

20 g / ⅔ oz dried porcini mushrooms

120 g / 4 oz / 1 stick unsalted butter

150 g / 5 oz lean boneless beef topside (rump), cut into 1-cm / ½-inch pieces

150 g / 5 oz lean boneless veal, cut into 1-cm / ½-inch pieces

1 tbsp whole white peppercorns

1 bay leaf

1 carrot, chopped

1 onion, chopped

2 celery stalks, chopped

240 ml / 8 fl oz / 1 cup dry white wine

salt and pepper

2 chicken livers

30 g / 1 oz / ¼ cup flour

450 ml / ¾ pint / scant 2 cups milk

300 g / 10 oz rigatoni

60 g / 2 oz / ½ cup freshly grated Parmesan cheese

2 hard-boiled eggs, chopped

120 g / 4 oz uncooked sweet Italian sausage, casings removed and crumbled

120 g / 4 oz mozzarella cheese, diced

In a food processor bowl fitted with the metal blade, combine all the pastry ingredients, except the egg yolk for glazing. Process until just mixed. (Or, make the dough by hand.) Remove the dough and knead it by hand for a couple of minutes. Shape into a ball, wrap and chill for about 2 hours.

To make the filling, soak the porcini in warm water for 30 minutes. Drain, squeeze out excess liquid and chop.

In a large frying pan heat 30 g / 1 oz / 2 tbsp butter. Add the beef and veal and sauté over moderate heat, stirring frequently, until brown, about 10 minutes. Add the peppercorns, bay leaf and chopped vegetables. Sauté until the onion is translucent, just a few more

minutes. Stir in the white wine and mushrooms, cover and simmer very gently over low heat for about 1½ hours or until the meat is tender but still intact. While the meat sauce is cooking, check it occasionally and, when necessary, add a little water to keep it moist. In all you will probably need about 240 ml/8 fl oz/1 cup. Adjust seasoning and remove the bay leaf.

Slice the chicken livers. In a small frying pan heat 15 g/½ oz/1 tbsp of butter. Add the chicken livers and sauté over high heat for just a few minutes. Season with salt and pepper. Set aside.

In a saucepan melt 30 g/1 oz/2 tbsp of butter over moderate heat. Add the flour and stir until well blended. Stirring constantly, gradually add the milk and bring to the boil. Boil until you have a fairly runny sauce, about 5 minutes.

Bring a large pot of salted water to the boil. Add the rigatoni and cook until it is still quite firm (about 6 minutes). Drain the pasta in a colander and turn it into a bowl. Toss well with the rest of the butter and the Parmesan cheese.

In a large bowl combine the meat sauce, the contents of the chicken liver pan, the chopped eggs, sausage, mozzarella, white sauce and rigatoni. Mix very well.

Bring the pastry dough to room temperature. Divide into two pieces, one two-thirds larger than the other. On a lightly floured work surface roll out the larger piece of dough until it is about 3 mm/⅛ inch thick. Use to line a 23-cm/9-inch springform pan. Fill it with the meat and rigatoni mixture. Smooth the surface. Roll out the rest of the dough to make a lid and cover the top. Trim, seal and crimp the edges. Prick the surface with a fork so that steam can escape. Brush with beaten egg yolk.

Bake in a preheated 180°C/350°F/gas 4 oven until the pastry is golden, about 45 minutes. Remove from the oven and leave to cool for a couple of minutes, then remove the side of the pan. Transfer to a platter and serve.

● **Sweet and Savoury Rigatoni Pie (p. 59)** ●

Torta di Riso e Spinaci

RICE AND SPINACH MOULD

This is a very attractive and easy dish to serve because it involves no last-minute preparation. This recipe can also be used for a luncheon dish by baking the rice in a ring mould and filling the centre with savoury lemon sauce (page 154). It can be followed by the Swiss chard rolls on page 139.

SERVES 6

60 g/2 oz/⅓ cup raisins

900 g/2 lb fresh spinach leaves

100 g/3½ oz/7 tbsp unsalted butter + extra for the pan

1 medium-size onion, chopped

60 g/2 oz pancetta, chopped

480 ml/16 fl oz/2 cups light meat stock (page 216)

300 g/10 oz/1⅓ cups arborio rice

3 eggs

90 g/3 oz/¾ cup freshly grated Parmesan cheese

60 g/2 oz/⅔ cup pine nuts

salt and pepper

6 tbsp fine dry breadcrumbs (page 132)

Soak the raisins in water to cover for about 30 minutes. Drain and reserve. Blanch the spinach in boiling salted water for about 2 minutes. Drain, squeeze dry and chop.

In a medium-size saucepan melt half the butter over very low heat. Add the onion and pancetta and sauté very gently until the onion is translucent, about 5 minutes. Add the spinach, stir well and cook for about 5 more minutes to blend the flavours.

Bring the stock to the boil, add the rice and cook for 12 minutes without stirring. Pour the rice on to a board and spread it out with a spatula, to stop it cooking any further.

Beat the eggs in a bowl. Add the rice, the spinach mixture and Parmesan and stir vigorously. Mix in the raisins, pine nuts and the rest of the butter. Season with salt and pepper.

Butter a 20-cm/8-inch springform pan and sprinkle it with the breadcrumbs. Pour in the rice mixture and smooth the surface. (If necessary, it can be kept chilled for a few hours before baking.)

Bake in a preheated 180°C/350°F/gas 4 oven for about 20 minutes or until the blade of a knife inserted in the middle comes out hot. Allow to cool slightly, then turn out on to a platter and serve.

STANDBY INGREDIENTS

It is a good idea to keep in stock a few supplies for making pasta and rice dishes at the last minute. Obviously canned tomatoes, dried porcini mushrooms, capers in vinegar, anchovy fillets in oil, canned tuna fish, dried chili peppers, garlic and onions all keep well, as do fine dry breadcrumbs. Dried oregano and tarragon retain their pungent flavour. You will find that a chunk of Parmesan cheese, tightly wrapped, will keep in the refrigerator for a couple of months.

Vermicelli alle Vongole

VERMICELLI WITH CLAMS

There are innumerable recipes for clam sauce, but I have chosen this one because the oil and garlic are barely cooked, giving the sauce a very fresh flavour. This dish could be followed by fried eggs with mozzarella (page 84).

SERVES 6

1.5 kg / 3¼ lb clams

3 garlic cloves, finely chopped

120 ml / 4 fl oz / ½ cup extra virgin olive oil

grated zest of 1 lemon

600 g / 1¼ lb vermicelli

salt and pepper

2 tbsp chopped fresh flat-leaf (Italian) parsley

Bring a large pot of salted water to the boil. Meanwhile, scrub and drain the clams. Place them in a large wide pan over moderate heat. Cover and cook until all the clams have opened. Remove the clams with a slotted spoon and keep them warm. Strain the clam liquid through a fine sieve to get rid of any sand. Pour the strained liquid into a large pan and add the garlic, oil and lemon zest.

Add the pasta to the boiling water and cook until *al dente*. Drain the pasta and add to the pan with the garlic mixture. Sauté on moderate heat, stirring frequently, for a couple of minutes. Season to taste.

Sprinkle with the parsley and toss well. Pour into a serving dish with the clams and serve at once.

Zuppa di Patate

POTATO AND HERB SOUP

This is a typical Genoese soup with all the wonderful flavours of Ligurian herbs – a perfect prelude to veal roll in tomato sauce (page 104).

SERVES 6

4 tbsp extra virgin olive oil

1 medium-size onion, sliced

90 g / 3 oz pancetta, chopped

3 garlic cloves, finely chopped

1.2 kg / 2¾ lb boiling potatoes, peeled and diced

salt and pepper

1 tbsp dried oregano

1.5 litres / 2½ pints / 1½ quarts light chicken stock (page 216)

2 tbsp chopped fresh parsley

2 tbsp chopped fresh basil leaves

2 tbsp chopped fresh chives

Heat the oil in a fairly deep saucepan. Add the onion, pancetta and garlic and sauté gently over low heat for about 5 minutes, until translucent.

Add the potatoes and season with salt, pepper and oregano. Stirring occasionally, cook for a further 20 minutes to allow the potatoes to absorb the flavours.

Add the stock, bring to the boil and simmer gently over low heat for about 10 minutes.

Add the parsley, basil and chives. Stir well, pour into a soup tureen and serve.

Zuppa di Patate e Carciofi

ARTICHOKE AND POTATO SOUP

When choosing artichokes, make sure they are firmly closed. If the leaves are open they are old.

SERVES 6

900 g / 2 lb globe artichokes

juice of 1 lemon

4 tbsp extra virgin olive oil

1 medium-size onion, finely chopped

900 g / 2 lb potatoes, peeled and thinly sliced

300 g / 10 oz plum tomatoes, peeled and chopped (or use canned Italian ones)

1 tsp dried oregano

1.5 litres / 2½ pints / 1½ quarts light meat stock (page 216)

salt and pepper

Remove the pointed spikes and hard outer leaves from the artichokes as well as the furry chokes. Cut the artichoke bottoms into slices and immediately drop into a bowl of water, to which the lemon juice has been added, to prevent them turning black.

Heat the oil in a deep saucepan. Add the onion and sauté gently, stirring constantly, on low heat until translucent, about 5 minutes. Add the drained artichokes and the potatoes. Stirring occasionally, cook uncovered over low heat for 10 minutes so that the flavours amalgamate. Add the tomatoes, oregano and stock and stir well. Cover the pot and simmer gently for 1 hour.

Season to taste with salt and pepper. Pour into a soup tureen and serve.

● **Artichoke and Potato Soup** ●

I Piatti di Mezzo

— Middle Courses —

While I was growing up, and even during the first few years after I was married, it was customary at the family evening meal as well as at more formal supper parties to serve a dish between the first and the main course. This was called a PIATTO DI MEZZO, an in-between dish. It was never part of the mid-day meal, whose two or three courses were already quite enough, but was only served in the evening, when the fare tended to be lighter. A typical supper menu then might have consisted of a soup, a PIATTO DI MEZZO, a fish or meat course accompanied by a vegetable or salad, and fruit to finish.

The traditional repertoire of recipes for PIATTI DI MEZZO was wide and varied. It included moulded dishes called SFORMATI; meat and vegetable pies with different forms and names like PASTICCI, TORTE and CROSTATE; diverse renderings of the versatile egg such as soufflés and FRITTATE; and some deep-fried foods as well. I think we were able to take those heavier meals of yester-year in our stride because we moved around more in those days. Our daily routines were less sedentary. Of course, it helped that there was often a family cook to prepare all those courses as well as someone to serve them and someone else to take care of all the dirty dishes afterwards.

Times may have changed but many of those traditional PIATTI DI MEZZO have survived. Today they turn up on my table as the main course. Because of the place they characteristically held at a meal, as an 'in-between' dish, I find them ideal for a light luncheon or supper. They do not overwhelm the appetite and are especially tasty. Also, due to their former social context, a custom of the upper classes, these dishes tend to be elegant and pleasing to the eye.

Of all the types of PIATTI DI MEZZO, the SFORMATO, or mould, is perhaps the most classic. Traditional recipes for this dish are usually quite rich, typically calling for game, sweetbreads and the like. I prefer the many varieties of vegetable moulds. You can use globe artichokes, carrots, green beans, bulb fennel, mushrooms, fresh peas, spinach and courgettes (zucchini) or any congenial and colourful combination of these.

● Savoury Rice and Leek Pie (p. 82) ●

These moulds are easy to prepare beforehand and can be put in the oven to bake at the last minute. Once the vegetables are cooked all you have to do is put them through a food mill, bind them together with a white sauce and eggs, and pour into the mould. It is most important that the vegetables be puréed to the right consistency, which I would describe as subtly coarse. They should keep some of their texture. I achieve this by using an Italian utensil called a SETACCIO, which is a kind of sieve through which you mash the vegetables with a meat pounder. You can also chop them very finely with a MEZZALUNA, but that takes a lot of time and effort. A MOULI-LEGUMES does the job nicely. A blender or food processor should not be used because it would reduce the vegetables to an undesirable creamy consistency.

The mould should be buttered and coated with breadcrumbs or grated Parmesan cheese. For baking you can set the mould in a BAGNO-MARIA, a water bath, which will keep the crust soft and moist. Without this, the crust will bake to a fine crunchy gold.

*T*here are many creative ways to garnish these vegetables moulds for presentation at your table. If you use a ring mould, you can surround it and fill the centre with sprigs of fresh herbs or an accompanying sauce. Recently I attended an elegant dinner party where the hostess had placed a vegetable ring mould in the corner of a large rectangular plate and had filled the hole with fresh green beans in such a way that they overflowed on to the platter. I have since tried this 'fountain effect' with success using fresh asparagus and another time small spring peas.

Perhaps the most popular PIATTO DI MEZZO to have made the transition to a main course is the TORTA DI VERDURA, a vegetable pie. I particularly favour this dish because it can be rendered in so many different ways. On informal occasions I make a sweet pastry base (PASTA FROLLA) and leave the pie open on the top. For parties and formal entertaining, I encase the filling in puff pastry, PASTA SFOGLIA, and it immediately becomes a pie worthy to 'set before the queen'. If you want to enrich the vegetable filling, add a thickened white sauce, or for additional flavour and texture use ricotta cheese.

The cheese soufflé is another traditional PIATTO DI MEZZO that can be served as a light and elegant main course for guests. I learned from my mother's cook, who was from the Veneto, how to 'italianize' the basic recipe a bit by using a base of semolina-polenta and even mashed potatoes instead of the classic white sauce.

Timing is an important consideration when you serve a soufflé. Since they take about 25–30 minutes to cook, I put them on my menu only when I also want to include a first course. In that way I wait until all my guests have arrived and are well into their drinks and conversation. Then, about 10 minutes before we are ready to go to the table I put the *soufflé in the oven to bake. By the time we have sat down and enjoyed the first course, about 25–30 minutes later, the soufflé is ready to serve.*

*B*ecause PIATTI DI MEZZO *originated as family fare (they were never served in restaurants), there are many recipes that make good use of left-overs. Among these, croquettes are my family's favourite. I make them with left-over potatoes, pieces of cheese, bits of rice, slices of polenta (see Chapter 2, I PRIMI), as well as with scraps of chicken and other meats. I also purée left-over vegetables, roll them in egg and breadcrumbs, and deep-fry them very lightly in oil. An especially tasty variation on this theme are little balls of ricotta cheese sautéed in olive oil. Since these croquettes should be fried at the very last minute and then brought immediately to the table, they are not very convenient to serve when you have guests, unless you have help in the kitchen. For family suppers the job of fast-fry cook was one my youngest son used to enjoy when he was a teenager.*

Another favourite family fast-food adapted from a traditional PIATTO DI MEZZO makes use of day-old bread. In Italy, bread has always been considered sacred, a symbol of the gift of life, and wasting it is sinful. So we have many recipes, especially in Tuscany, for using up bread that has gone stale. A simple one is to dip slices in milk, layer them with cheese and prosciutto or maybe mushrooms, and bake in the oven until the cheese melts. Another is to arrange little squares of bread with pieces of cheese and bits of anchovy on skewers and bake in the same way.

Finally, for a light luncheon I often serve a selection of cold vegetable moulds. You can play with colours from the deep purple of beetroot, the bright red of tomatoes and orange of carrots to the fresh green of peas and beans. Or you can mix cooked and diced peas, green beans, carrots and beetroot, the ingredients of the classic INSALATA ALLA RUSSA, with some aspic to hold them in shape, for a lovely marbled effect. These moulds are so colourful in themselves that you won't even need a centrepiece to decorate your table.

Crocchette di Patate

POTATO CROQUETTES WITH HAM AND MOZZARELLA

For a meal based on fish I sometimes make these croquettes with a few anchovy fillets instead of the ham. The mozzarella and anchovies make a very interesting combination.

SERVES 6

600 g / 1¼ lb boiling potatoes

120 ml / 4 fl oz / ½ cup warm milk

3 eggs

salt and pepper

120 g / 4 oz mozzarella cheese, diced

120 g / 4 oz cooked ham, finely chopped

60 g / 2 oz / ½ cup flour

180 g / 6 oz / 1¾ cups fine dry breadcrumbs (page 132)

extra virgin olive oil for deep-frying

Cook the potatoes, in their skins, in boiling water until tender. Drain and peel, then return to the pan and mash, adding the warm milk. Stir over low heat for a couple of minutes. Allow to cool.

In a bowl combine the mashed potatoes and 1 lightly beaten egg. Season

MIDDLE COURSES

I Piatti di Mezzo were served at dinner after the first course and before the main course. Nowadays they are often served as first courses and sometimes as main courses instead of meat or fish. You will find that, with a salad, several of them are a perfect lunch and others would make an excellent brunch.

with salt and pepper and mix thoroughly. Take a little of the mixture in one hand, put some mozzarella and some ham into the centre, and form a shape about 5 cm / 2 inches long and 2.5 cm / 1 inch wide, enclosing the cheese and ham. Continue until all the ingredients are used. Chill.

Beat the remaining eggs. Put the flour on one plate and the breadcrumbs on another. Lightly dredge the croquettes in the flour, shaking off any excess. Dip them into the beaten egg, then roll in the breadcrumbs.

In a deep wide pan heat the oil to 180°C / 350°F. Add the croquettes a few at a time and fry until golden on all sides. Drain on paper towels and serve very hot.

Crostoni di Mozzarella

BAKED MOZZARELLA ON TOAST

This is a quick and easy substitute for pizza when you are in a hurry, and is especially loved by children. I often do it for my grandsons when they come to visit. It could be followed by grilled wrapped trout (page 122).

SERVES 6

6 slices of coarse-textured white bread

2 tbsp extra virgin olive oil

6 Italian plum tomatoes, peeled

6 baby mozzarella cheeses or 6 thick slices of mozzarella

6 anchovy fillets in oil, drained

1 tbsp chopped fresh parsley

Line a baking sheet with foil.

Sprinkle the bread with olive oil and arrange it on the baking sheet. Cut the tomatoes into strips and drain them well.

OPENING SCALLOPS

If you buy scallops in their shells you can open them by putting them on a hot charcoal grill. Any that don't open spontaneously can be forced open by sticking the point of a knife between the shells. Remove the scallops with their coral roe and soak them in cold water for about 10 minutes to get rid of any sand.

Arrange a whole mozzarella, or slice, on each slice of toast and surround it with strips of tomato. Top the cheese with an anchovy fillet.

Transfer the baking sheet to a pre-heated 180°C / 350°F / gas 4 oven and bake until the mozzarella starts to melt, about 10 minutes.

Sprinkle with chopped parsley and serve at once.

Crostoni alla Pancetta e Cappesante

PANCETTA-WRAPPED SCALLOPS ON TOAST

Smoked bacon can be used instead of pancetta, and the scallops can be replaced by peeled raw prawns or shrimp. For a main course, serve these with spinach with raisins and pine nuts (page 145).

SERVES 6

18 shelled scallops

18 thin slices of pancetta

6 slices of coarse-textured bread

1 tbsp extra virgin olive oil

I prefer to toast coarse-textured country bread, but if it is not available, this is the one time sliced bread can be used instead. If you brush it lightly with extra virgin olive oil before toasting it in the oven you will find it has a better flavour. The bread should not be too well toasted because when too dark it is bitter.

Crostoni di Radicchio

RED RADICCHIO ON TOAST

*O*n winter evenings, after a bowl of soup, we often have this for a family supper. For a richer dish, top each toast with a fried egg. Red radicchio can be replaced by chopped spinach, Swiss chard or sliced onion.

SERVES 6

6 small heads of red radicchio

60 g / 2 oz / 4 tbsp unsalted butter

salt and pepper

6 slices of country bread

6 thin slices of Gruyère or emmenthal cheese

Bring a large saucepan of salted water to the boil. Add the radicchio and blanch it for 2 minutes. Drain and dry on paper towels.

---

1 tbsp chopped fresh parsley

a pinch of chili powder (optional)

Roll up each scallop in a slice of pancetta and secure with a wooden cocktail stick. Heat a heavy frying pan over moderate heat, then add the wrapped scallops. Cook, turning once or twice, until the pancetta is crisp on all sides, about 10 minutes.

● **Pancetta-Wrapped Scallops on Toast** ●

Meanwhile, spread the bread slices on a baking sheet and toast in a preheated 180°C/350°F/gas 4 oven until golden, about 5 minutes.

Brush the toast with the olive oil. Arrange 3 scallops on each slice of toast and sprinkle with parsley and a little chili powder, if you like. Arrange on a warm platter and serve piping hot.

In a large frying pan, melt 45 g/
1½ oz/3 tbsp butter over moderate heat.
Add the radicchio and sprinkle with salt
and pepper. Cover the pan and lower the
heat. Cook for about 5 minutes.

Spread the bread with the rest of the
butter. Toast in a preheated 180°C/
350°F/gas 4 oven until golden.

Arrange the toast on a heatproof
platter. Place the radicchio on the toast
and top each with a slice of cheese.
Return to the oven and bake until the
cheese is melted, about 5 minutes.
Season with pepper and serve immediately.

Frittata di Pomodori

TOMATO OMELETTE

When baking tomatoes, I make a
few extra so that we can have this
omelette the next day. In summer I serve
it with fried vegetables such as courgette
(zucchini) flowers or the fried courgettes
(zucchini) in mint sauce (page 147).

SERVES 6

---

3 eggs

---

2 tbsp chopped fresh parsley

---

salt and pepper

---

1 tbsp extra virgin olive oil

---

6 baked Parmesan tomatoes (page 142)

In a bowl lightly whisk the eggs with the
parsley and seasoning.

In a 15-cm/6-inch non-stick frying
pan, heat the oil. Pour in the eggs to
make a layer about 1 cm/½ inch thick.
Arrange the tomatoes, face up, on the
eggs. Cook over moderate heat,
occasionally poking the eggs with a
wooden fork, until they are well set.
Lower the heat and cook for a further 2
minutes. Slide the omelette on to a
platter and serve.

Frittata di Spaghetti

SPAGHETTI OMELETTE

Traditionally we use any left-over
pasta to make a *frittata*. I suggest you
make a little extra when you prepare the
linguine with tuna sauce on page 158 or
the spaghetti with oil and rosemary on
page 56. The penne with gorgonzola
cream on page 44 also makes a delicious
omelette. Serve hot or at room temperature.

SERVES 6

---

3 eggs

---

*300 g/10 oz left-over spaghetti or other
pasta with sauce*

---

salt and pepper

---

1 tbsp extra virgin olive oil

In a deep bowl beat the eggs lightly. Add
the pasta and stir well so that the eggs
stick to the pasta. Season with salt and
pepper.

In a 15-cm/6-inch non-stick frying
pan heat the oil. Pour in the egg mixture
and cook over moderate heat, poking
the mixture occasionally with a wooden

FRITTATE

I think you will find it quite easy
to make *frittate*, the thick open-
faced Italian omelettes, if you have
a good-quality non-stick frying pan.
Frittate are generally about
2 cm/¾ inch thick. Although the
eggs must set, they should never be
dry inside. If you are adding a just-
cooked ingredient to the egg, make
sure it is cool before you mix it in
or the egg will start to cook. Before
cooking your omelette heat the pan
well and when it is hot brush it lightly
with a little oil or butter. Then you
will have no trouble with sticking.

spoon. After about 5 minutes, lift the
omelette with a spatula; if it has a golden
crust, cover the pan with a plate and
turn the omelette over on to it. Slip the
omelette back into the pan with the
uncooked side down and cook until that
side is firm, about 2 minutes. When
ready the eggs should be well set but not
dry.

Frittata di Tagliatelle alla Ricotta

TAGLIATELLE AND RICOTTA OMELETTE

Use either dried tagliatelle or left-
overs. I often do the latter, making
tagliatelle with mixed spices (page 58).

SERVES 6

---

*180 g/6 oz dried tagliatelle and
60 g/2 oz/4 tbsp melted butter, or
300 g/10 oz cooked tagliatelle with sauce*

---

3 eggs

---

120 g/4 oz/½ cup ricotta cheese

---

1 tbsp chopped fresh sage

---

salt and pepper

---

1 tbsp extra virgin olive oil

---

30 g/1 oz/2 tbsp unsalted butter

If using dried tagliatelle, cook them in a
large pot of boiling salted water until *al
dente*. Drain and toss with the melted
butter. (The pasta can be refrigerated for
up to 12 hours.)

In a bowl, beat the eggs lightly. Add
the pasta, ricotta and sage. Season with
salt and pepper and toss well.

In a 30-cm/12-inch non-stick frying
pan heat the oil with the unsalted butter.
Pour in the egg mixture and, occasionally
poking the mixture with a wooden fork,

● Spaghetti Omelette ●

cook over moderate heat until the eggs have almost set. Cover the pan with a plate and turn the omelette over on to it. Slip the omelette back into the pan with the uncooked side down. Cook until that side is golden, about 3 minutes.

Slide the omelette on to a warm platter and serve immediately.

Gelatina di Finocchio

SAVOURY ORANGE AND FENNEL ASPIC

I find the transparency of aspic very elegant, so at dinner parties I set it in individual moulds and serve it garnished with the feathery fennel tops.

SERVES 6

---

6 oranges

---

1 lemon

---

1 egg white

1½ tbsp powdered unflavoured gelatine

---

3 fennel bulbs

---

salt and pepper

● **Savoury Orange and Fennel Aspic** ●

Squeeze the oranges and the lemon and pour the juice into a medium-size saucepan. Beat the egg white until stiff and add it to the juice. Stirring constantly, bring the juice slowly to the boil over low heat. Remove from the heat and strain the clarified juice through muslin or a very fine sieve into a bowl.

Sprinkle the gelatine over the warm juice and stir until dissolved.

Remove the tough outer leaves from the fennel. Wash, dry and cut it into julienne. Stir the fennel into the juice and season with salt and pepper.

Pour the mixture into a mould or 6 individual moulds and, as soon as it is cold, refrigerate for at least 3 hours.

Turn out on to a platter to serve.

Gelatina in Forma

COLD TOMATO RING

If you would like to serve this tomato ring as a main course, fill the centre with boiled scampi, prawns or shrimp dressed with home-made mayonnaise (page 217) and surround it with shredded green salad leaves.

SERVES 6

900 g / 2 lb ripe Italian plum tomatoes, peeled, seeded and chopped

1 tsp sugar

salt and pepper

2 tbsp finely chopped fresh chives

1 tbsp balsamic vinegar

3 tbsp powdered unflavoured gelatine

extra virgin olive oil

In a medium-size saucepan, combine the tomatoes, sugar and a little salt and pepper. Cook over moderate heat for 30 minutes.

Add the chives, stir well and remove from the heat. Add the balsamic vinegar. Sprinkle the gelatine over the tomato mixture and stir until it has dissolved. Purée the mixture in a blender or food processor.

Lightly oil a 20-cm/8-inch ring mould. Pour in the tomato mixture and refrigerate for at least 3 hours.

Turn out on to a platter to serve.

Pasticcio di Cipolle al Prosciutto

BREAD, ONION AND HAM PIE

In Italy we have an infinite variety of recipes using bread. Sometimes they call for stale bread, sometimes for fresh. I prefer to use coarse-textured bread but at a pinch an ordinary white loaf will do. Serve cream of chickpea soup (page 28) before this pie and follow with the prune meringue tart on page 187.

SERVES 6

3 tbsp extra virgin olive oil

6 large onions, thinly sliced

salt and pepper

6 large slices of coarse-textured bread, each about 1 cm / ½ inch thick

240 ml / 8 fl oz / 1 cup milk

4 eggs, size 5 (US medium)

a pinch of grated nutmeg

unsalted butter for the dish

180 g / 6 oz cooked ham, chopped

90 g / 3 oz / ¾ cup freshly grated Parmesan cheese

In a frying pan, heat the oil. Add the onions and, stirring frequently, cook them over low heat until translucent, about 10 minutes. Season with salt and pepper.

Soak the bread in the milk until it is well absorbed, about 10 minutes. Drain and squeeze dry. Beat the eggs with a little salt and the nutmeg.

Butter a large, shallow ovenproof dish. Arrange the bread in the bottom in a single layer. Cover the bread with the onion. Scatter the ham on top and then sprinkle with the Parmesan. Top with the beaten eggs, spreading evenly.

Bake in a preheated 180°C/350°F/gas 4 oven until golden, about 50 minutes. Serve piping hot.

Pasticcio di Pane e Mozzarella

BREAD, EGG AND MOZZARELLA PIE

Although this is essentially a very simple country dish, it can be served in several ways. Cooked in individual moulds it becomes quite an elegant first course.

SERVES 6

unsalted butter for the dish

450 ml / ¾ pint / scant 2 cups milk

180 g / 6 oz sliced white crustless bread (12 slices)

210 g / 7 oz mozzarella cheese, thinly sliced

6 anchovy fillets in oil, drained and halved lengthwise

6 eggs

salt and pepper

3 tbsp freshly grated Parmesan cheese

Butter a deep 18-cm/7-inch soufflé dish.

Put the milk in a shallow dish, dip in the bread just to moisten it, and layer in the soufflé dish. Top with the slices of mozzarella and the anchovies.

In a bowl, whisk the eggs for about 3 minutes, until fluffy. Season with salt and pepper and add the Parmesan cheese. Pour into the soufflé dish.

Bake in a preheated 200°C/400°F/gas 6 oven until well risen and golden, about 30 minutes. If using 6 individual moulds, bake for only 12 minutes. Serve at once.

Pizzelle al Pomodoro

SMALL FRIED PIZZAS WITH TOMATO SAUCE

Occasionally, we have a large batch of these for brunch or lunch, served with broccoli with pancetta and garlic (page 128) and goat's cheese in extra virgin olive oil (page 168). We serve the *pizzelle* with a very cold dry white wine or champagne and finish with a basket of mixed fruit.

SERVES 6

1½ tbsp dried yeast, or 1 tbsp fresh (compressed) yeast

180 g/6 oz/1½ cups flour + 2 tbsp

salt

extra virgin olive oil for deep-frying

500 ml/16 fl oz/2 cups Neapolitan tomato sauce (page 158)

Combine the yeast and 120 ml/4 fl oz/½ cup lukewarm water and leave to dissolve and start to foam, about 10 minutes.

In a large bowl, combine the flour, a pinch of salt and the yeast mixture. Stir with a wooden spoon until a soft dough is formed. Knead on a floured surface until smooth and elastic, about 10 minutes. Roll the dough into a ball, place in a floured bowl and cover with a cloth. Leave to rise in a warm place until the dough has doubled in size, about 2 hours.

Punch the dough to knock out air. Divide it into pieces and shape each into a log about 2.5 cm/1 inch thick. Cut the logs into 2.5-cm/1-inch pieces. On a floured board, flatten the pieces of dough with a rolling pin into discs about 3 mm/⅛ inch thick. Leave to rise for about 30 minutes.

In a deep wide pan heat the oil to 180°C/350°F. Fry the pizzas, a few at a time, until puffed and just golden. Remove with a slotted spoon and drain on paper towels.

Transfer to a warm platter and serve with the tomato sauce in a sauceboat.

Polenta Verde

POLENTA AND SPINACH MOULD

Although this dish requires a lot of stirring, if you are fond of polenta it is well worth trying. Follow with a fairly light main course such as chicken roasted in bay leaves (page 110).

SERVES 6

900 g / 2 lb fresh spinach leaves

120 g / 4 oz / 1 stick unsalted butter

1 garlic clove

270 g / 9 oz / 2 cups yellow cornmeal

salt and pepper

In a large saucepan, bring salted water to the boil. Add the spinach, cook over moderate heat for 3 minutes, drain and squeeze out excess water, and chop finely.

In a medium-size saucepan melt 15 g / ½ oz / 1 tbsp butter over low heat. Add the garlic and cook until translucent. Add the spinach and, stirring, cook for 3 minutes. Remove the garlic and set the spinach aside.

In the large saucepan bring 1.5 litres / 2½ pints / 1½ quarts water to the boil. Pour in the cornmeal in a steady stream, whisking constantly. Cook for 40 minutes, stirring frequently. Remove from the heat and add the rest of the butter and the spinach. Season with salt and pepper. Stir well. Pour the mixture into a wet mould or bowl. Press down gently. Unmould on to a platter and serve hot.

COOKING POLENTA AND SEMOLINA

*T*o cook polenta or semolina, the proportions in weight are five to one: five parts of boiling water to one of flour. Add the semolina or polenta in a slow steady stream, whisking constantly to avoid the formation of lumps. Semolina and polenta both take a long time to cook and a lot of stirring with a wooden spoon. Fortunately a parboiled variety is now available which cooks in a few minutes.

● **Polenta and Spinach Mould** ●

Sfogliata di Prosciutto all'Uva

HAM AND CHEESE TART WITH GRAPES

W hen I make pastry I often prepare several batches and freeze them, already rolled, for emergencies. Try to find seedless grapes; otherwise cut the grapes in half, remove the seeds and arrange them in the pastry case face down. I suggest you follow this with pork chops in mustard sauce (page 100).

SERVES 6

240 g / 8 oz puff pastry (⅓ recipe quantity on page 219)

30 g / 1 oz / 2 tbsp unsalted butter

30 g / 1 oz / ¼ cup flour

300 ml / ½ pint / 1¼ cups milk

1 tbsp Marsala wine

120 g / 4 oz / 1 cup freshly grated Parmesan cheese

● **Ham and Cheese Tart with Grapes** ●

salt and pepper

120 g / 4 oz cooked ham, chopped

a small bunch of white or green grapes, about 300 g / 10 oz

Roll out the pastry dough and use to line a 23-cm / 9-inch flan or tart pan with a removable bottom. Prick the pastry case all over with a fork and cover the bottom with dried beans. Bake in a preheated 180°C / 350°F / gas 4 oven for 20 minutes. Remove the beans and leave to cool.

Meanwhile, prepare the white sauce. In a saucepan melt the butter over moderate heat. Add the flour and stir for a couple of minutes. Add the milk, stirring constantly. Bring to the boil and boil for 1 minute. Remove the sauce from the heat and stir in the Marsala and cheese. Season with salt and pepper.

Sprinkle the ham over the bottom of the pastry case. Add the sauce and smooth the surface. Arrange the grapes over the top. Return to the oven and bake until just golden, about 10 minutes.

Sformato di Formaggio

HOT CHEESE MOULD

This dish can also be made in the shape of a loaf using a loaf pan of the same dimensions. It could be served after the cream of chickpea soup on page 28 and then followed by the Vin Santo sorbet on page 192.

SERVES 6

60 g / 2 oz / 4 tbsp unsalted butter + extra for the pan

90 g / 3 oz / ¾ cup freshly grated Parmesan cheese + 3 tbsp

60 g / 2 oz / ½ cup flour

500 ml / 16 fl oz / 2 cups milk

90 g / 3 oz / ¾ cup grated Gruyère or emmenthal cheese

4 eggs

salt

a pinch of grated nutmeg

Butter a 20-cm/8-inch ring mould and coat it with 3 tbsp Parmesan.

In a saucepan melt the butter over low heat. Add the flour and stir with a wooden spoon until all the flour is absorbed. Gradually add the milk, stirring constantly, then bring to the boil and cook until the sauce is thick and comes away from the sides of the pan. Stir in the rest of the Parmesan and the Gruyère. Remove the saucepan from the heat and allow to cool.

Whisk the eggs for about 3 minutes, until fluffy. Stirring, add the eggs a little at a time to the cheese sauce. Season with salt and nutmeg.

Transfer the mixture to the mould and smooth the top. Place the ring mould in a larger pan containing about 2.5 cm/1 inch water. Bake in a preheated 180°C/350°F/gas 4 oven for 50 minutes.

Remove from the oven and allow to stand for 5 minutes. Turn out on to a warm platter to serve.

Sformato di Patate e Cipolle

POTATO AND ONION MOULD

As a main course serve this with the Bolognese meat sauce on page 152 or prepare individual servings as a first course for a formal luncheon. The vegetables can be prepared well in advance, but keep them in a cool place without chilling.

SERVES 6

900 g / 2 lb boiling potatoes

45 g / 1½ oz / 3 tbsp unsalted butter + extra for the dish

2 large onions, thinly sliced

180 g / 6 oz / 1½ cups freshly grated Parmesan cheese

4 eggs, separated

salt and pepper

90 g / 3 oz / 1 cup fine dry breadcrumbs (page 132)

Cook the potatoes, in their skins, in boiling water until tender. Drain and peel, mash and leave to cool completely.

In a large frying pan melt the butter over moderate heat. Add the onions and, stirring frequently, cook until just golden. Remove from the heat and allow to cool.

To the mashed potatoes add the Parmesan and the egg yolks. Season with salt and pepper and stir very well. Mix in the onions. In a bowl, beat the egg whites until stiff. Fold them carefully into the potato mixture.

Butter a 20-cm/8-inch round ovenproof dish. Coat with the breadcrumbs. Transfer the potato mixture to the dish and smooth the top.

Bake in a preheated 180°C/350°F/gas 4 oven until golden, about 50 minutes. Serve at once, in the dish.

Sformato di Piselli al Pomodoro

PEA AND TOMATO MOULD

For a change, I sometimes serve this mould with a sauce made from boiled puréed courgettes (zucchini) or fennel instead of tomatoes, seasoned with olive oil. Serve after the lemon risotto on page 51.

SERVES 6

450 g / 1 lb / 3 cups shelled fresh peas

60 g / 2 oz / 4 tbsp unsalted butter + extra for the mould

1 tsp sugar

salt and pepper

VEGETABLE MOULDS

There are two methods for preparing vegetable moulds. The classic method is to mix the vegetable purée with béchamel sauce, but the new way is to mix it only with egg so that the flavour of the vegetable is more pronounced. In both cases the mould is usually baked in a bain-marie or water bath for about 50 minutes.

4 egg yolks and 2 eggs

240 ml / 8 fl oz / 1 cup light tomato and oil sauce (page 155)

Blanch the peas in boiling salted water for 3 minutes. Drain, transfer to a bowl of iced water. Drain when cold.

In a frying pan melt the butter. Add the peas and season with the sugar, salt and pepper. Sauté over low heat until soft, about 10 minutes. Purée the peas in a blender. Add the egg yolks and whole eggs and blend well.

Butter a 23-cm/9-inch ring mould and pour in the pea mixture. Place the mould in a large roasting pan containing 2.5 cm/1 inch of water. Bake in a preheated 180°C/350°F/gas 4 oven for about 50 minutes.

Before serving, warm the tomato sauce in a bowl set in a large pan of simmering water. Turn out the mould on to a warm platter. Pour the sauce over it and serve immediately.

Sformato di Piselli alle Zucchine

VEGETABLE RING WITH GREEN SAUCE

This subtly flavoured vegetable ring is very versatile. It can also be served as a first course or as a side dish with artichokes stuffed with mozzarella (page 128). Mashed carrots can be a good substitute for peas.

SERVES 6

30 g / 1 oz / 2 tbsp unsalted butter + more for the mould

30 g / 1 oz / ¼ cup flour

240 ml / 8 fl oz / 1 cup milk

salt and pepper

450 g / 1 lb / 3 cups shelled fresh peas

4 eggs, beaten

120 g / 4 oz cooked ham, diced

2 tbsp fine dry breadcrumbs (page 132)

210 g / 7 oz courgettes (zucchini)

120 ml / 4 fl oz / ½ cup whipping cream

90 g / 3 oz / ¾ cup freshly grated Parmesan cheese

In a saucepan, melt the butter over low heat. Add the flour and stir with a wooden spoon until all the flour is absorbed. Gradually add the milk, stirring constantly, then bring to the boil and cook until the sauce is thick and comes away from the sides of the pan.

Add the peas to a saucepan of boiling salted water and cook until tender, 6–10 minutes depending on size. Drain.

● Hot Cheese Mould ●

● **Pea and Tomato Mould (p. 76), with** ●
Tomato Cream Mousse

Spuma di Pomodoro

TOMATO CREAM MOUSSE

There is a much-quoted Italian saying that translates as, 'Our eyes must have their share', so I often prepare this pretty dish on summer evenings. It may be garnished with the aspic given below or, more simply, with diced tomatoes dressed with a little oil, vinegar and chopped fresh basil. If you are having a buffet, serve it with the ham mousse on page 79 and a selection of omelettes and vegetable moulds, each with a different main ingredient.

SERVES 6

For the mousse

900 g / 2 lb very ripe tomatoes, peeled and chopped

salt and pepper

1 garlic clove

30 g / 1 oz / ½ cup fresh basil leaves

1 tbsp chopped fresh chives

2 tbsp balsamic vinegar

1½ tbsp powdered unflavoured gelatine

120 ml / 4 fl oz / ½ cup whipping cream

For the aspic

240 ml / 8 fl oz / 1 cup light chicken stock (page 216)

1½ tbsp powdered unflavoured gelatine

6 tbsp chopped fresh parsley

In a bowl, combine the white sauce, eggs and ham. Season with salt and pepper. Add the peas and stir well.

Butter a 20-cm/8-inch ring mould and sprinkle with the breadcrumbs. Pour in the pea mixture. Place the mould in pan containing 5 cm/2 inches of hot water. Transfer to a preheated 180°C/350°F/gas 4 oven and bake for 50 minutes.

Blanch the courgettes (zucchini) in boiling salted water for 3 minutes. Drain and slice. In a processor, combine the courgettes (zucchini), cream and cheese until blended. Season with salt and pepper. Pour into a pan and heat without boiling. Turn out the mould on to a platter. Pour over the sauce and serve.

To prepare the mousse, put the tomatoes in a colander, sprinkle them with salt and leave to drain for about 30 minutes.

In a blender, purée the tomatoes with the garlic, basil, chives, balsamic vinegar, salt and pepper until creamy.

In a saucepan, heat half the purée without allowing it to boil. Remove from the heat and sprinkle on the gelatine. Stir until dissolved. Stir in the rest of the purée and leave to cool to room temperature.

In a bowl, whip the cream until stiff. Fold it into the tomato purée. Pour into a 20-cm/8-inch ring mould and refrigerate for at least 4 hours.

To prepare the aspic, heat the stock in a saucepan, but do not boil. Remove from the heat and sprinkle on the gelatine. Stir until dissolved. Leave to cool. When at room temperature, stir in the chopped parsley. Pour into a rectangular dish about 30 x 15 cm/12 x 6 inches. Leave to set in the refrigerator for at least 2 hours.

To serve, wrap a warm cloth around the outside of the mould and turn it out on to a platter. Dice the aspic and heap some in the middle of the tomato ring. Arrange the rest around it.

This dish may be prepared in advance and kept in the refrigerator for several hours.

Spuma di Prosciutto

HAM MOUSSE

When using this recipe as a middle course, serve it plain. Otherwise it is as delicious as it is pretty surrounded with shredded rocket (arugula) or watercress.

SERVES 6

240 ml / 8 fl oz / 1 cup light meat stock (page 216)

1½ tbsp powdered unflavoured gelatine

3 eggs, size 5 (US medium), separated

240 ml / 8 fl oz / 1 cup whipping cream

240 g / 8 oz cooked ham, finely minced (ground)

salt and pepper

In a small saucepan heat the stock until it is hot but not boiling. Sprinkle the gelatine over it and stir until dissolved. Leave to cool.

Lightly whisk the egg yolks. Beat the egg whites until stiff peaks form. In another bowl, whip the cream until stiff.

In a large bowl, combine the cold stock, ham, egg yolks and whipped cream. Fold in the egg whites. Season with salt and freshly ground pepper. Transfer the mixture to a wet 20-cm/8-inch ring mould. Refrigerate for at least 3 hours. Just before serving, wrap a warm cloth around the outside of the mould and turn it out on to a cold plate.

Timballo di Scamorza

CHEESE PIE

This dish, although very popular in the Naples area, is practically unknown in the rest of Italy.

SERVES 6

450 g / 1 lb loaf of white bread

2 tbsp milk

6 eggs

salt and pepper

45 g / 1½ oz / 3 tbsp unsalted butter + extra for the pan

450 g / 1 lb scamorza cheese, thinly sliced

Remove the crust from the bread and cut it into fairly thin slices. In a bowl, whisk the milk into the eggs and season lightly with salt and pepper. Soak the slices of bread in the egg and milk mixture until the liquid has been completely absorbed.

Butter a 20-cm/8-inch springform pan or soufflé dish. Being careful not to leave any gaps, arrange a layer of bread in the bottom of the pan. Cover it with a layer of cheese. Continue making layers until all the ingredients are used, finishing with a layer of bread. Dot the top with the butter.

Bake in a preheated 180°C/350°F/ gas 4 oven until golden, about 50 minutes. Remove the side of the pan and slide the pie on to a platter. Or leave in the soufflé dish. Serve immediately.

Torta di Asparagi

ASPARAGUS TART

Because we all love asparagus, whenever I make this tart I save the stalks and cooking water for soup or risotto. In spring I sometimes serve this as a luncheon dish with the soufflé omelette with herbs on page 83.

SERVES 6

1 recipe quantity short pastry dough (page 218)

1.2 kg / 2½ lb fresh asparagus

15 g / ½ oz / 1 tbsp butter + extra for the pan

salt and pepper

120 g / 4 oz / 1 cup finely grated Gruyère or emmenthal cheese

120 g / 4 oz cooked ham, thinly sliced

3 eggs, size 5 (US medium), beaten

180 ml / 6 fl oz / ¾ cup whipping cream

6 tbsp grated Parmesan cheese

Lightly butter a 23-cm/9-inch flan or tart pan with a removable bottom. Roll out the pastry dough and use to line the pan. Refrigerate.

Wash the asparagus and cut off the bottom of the stalks if they are woody. If necessary, scrape lightly with a vegetable peeler. Tie into bundles of about 5 spears each.

Bring a deep pot of salted water to the boil. Add the asparagus and cook for 8 to 10 minutes, depending on size. Drain and cut off the green tips. Set aside.

In a frying pan, melt the butter over low heat. Add the asparagus tips and sauté gently for 3 minutes. Season with salt and pepper.

Sprinkle half the Gruyère cheese over the bottom of the pastry case. Cover with sliced ham and arrange the asparagus on top.

In a bowl, mix the beaten eggs with the cream, the rest of the Gruyère cheese and a pinch of salt. Pour the mixture over the asparagus. Sprinkle with the Parmesan. Transfer the tart to a preheated 180°C/350°F/gas 4 oven and bake for about 40 minutes. Serve hot.

Torta di Cipolla

ONION TART

For a lighter dish you can also use globe artichokes or bulb fennel instead of onions.

SERVES 6

240 g / 8 oz / 2 cups flour

salt and pepper

120 g / 4 oz / 1 stick unsalted butter + extra for the pan

4 tbsp extra virgin olive oil

900 g / 2 lb onions, finely chopped

3 eggs, lightly beaten

a pinch of grated nutmeg

6 anchovy fillets in oil, drained

Mound the flour on the work surface and sprinkle with a pinch of salt. Make a hollow in the middle of the flour and add the butter in small pieces. Using the tips of your fingers, lightly blend the butter and flour together until the mixture has the consistency of fine crumbs. When all the flour is absorbed, add 2 tbsp cold water and mix as quickly as possible to a soft dough. Wrap the dough and allow it to rest in the refrigerator for about 1 hour.

In a heavy frying pan heat the oil. Add the onions and, stirring frequently, cook over very low heat until translucent. Season with salt and pepper and leave to cool completely.

Lightly butter a 23-cm/9-inch flan or tart pan with a removable bottom. Line it with the pastry dough. Stir the eggs and nutmeg into the onions. Spoon the mixture into the pastry case and spread evenly. Cut the anchovy fillets into narrow strips and arrange them in a lattice over the onion filling.

Bake in a preheated 180°C/350°F/gas 4 oven for about 30 minutes. Serve hot.

Torta alla Genovese

BAKED LAYERS OF ANCHOVIES AND SWISS CHARD

This Genoese dish is excellent at lunch. The anchovies can be replaced by filleted fresh sardines.

SERVES 6

1.2 kg / 2½ lb Swiss chard

6 tbsp extra virgin olive oil + extra for the dish

2 medium-size onions, chopped

salt and pepper

3 eggs, size 5 (US medium), beaten

600 g / 1¼ lb fresh anchovies

1 tbsp chopped fresh parsley

2 tbsp fine dry breadcrumbs (page 132)

1 tsp dried oregano

Carefully wash the Swiss chard and remove any tough stalks. In a large pot bring 2.5 cm/1 inch of salted water to the boil. Add the Swiss chard and cook for about 3 minutes. Drain, squeeze out any excess water and chop very finely.

Heat half the oil in a large frying pan. Add the onions and cook over low heat until translucent. Add the chopped Swiss chard and continue to cook over very low heat for 10 minutes, stirring occasionally. Season with salt and pepper. Remove from the heat and transfer to a bowl. Stir in the eggs and set aside.

Rinse the anchovies and dry them on paper towels. Split them in half and remove the heads, tails and backbones.

Oil a 23-cm/9-inch ovenproof dish. Make a layer of the Swiss chard mixture on the bottom, then cover with a layer of anchovies. Continue making layers, finishing with a layer of anchovies, until all the ingredients are used. Sprinkle with the parsley, breadcrumbs and oregano. Pour over the rest of the oil.

Bake in a preheated 180°C/350°F/gas 4 oven for 30 minutes. Serve piping hot.

● **Onion Tart** ●

Torta di Patate

POTATO AND MOZZARELLA PIE

Potato dishes are generally associated with northern climes, but this recipe comes from Naples where it is usually served as a first course.

SERVES 6

1.2 kg / 2½ lb boiling potatoes

60 g / 2 oz / 4 tbsp unsalted butter + extra for the pan

salt and pepper

4 eggs

60 g / 2 oz / ⅔ cup fine dry breadcrumbs (page 132)

210 g / 7 oz mozzarella cheese, sliced

6 anchovy fillets in oil, drained (optional)

Cook the potatoes, in their skins, in boiling salted water until tender. Drain and peel, then mash the potatoes.

In a medium-size saucepan, warm the mashed potatoes over low heat. Stir in the butter and season with salt and pepper. Allow the mashed potatoes to dry slightly. Remove from the heat and leave to cool a little, then stir in the eggs, one at a time.

Lightly butter a 23-cm / 9-inch spring-form pan and coat with breadcrumbs. Spoon half the potato mixture into it. Cover with the sliced mozzarella and anchovy fillets. Cover with the rest of the potatoes.

● **Fried Eggs with Mozzarella (p. 84)** ●

Bake in a preheated 180°C / 350°F / gas 4 oven for about 1 hour, covering the top with foil after 30 minutes.

Remove the side of the pan, slide the pie on to a serving platter and serve immediately.

Torta di Riso e Porri

SAVOURY RICE AND LEEK PIE

Gruyère or emmenthal cheese can be used instead of Parmesan, and onions instead of leeks, although they obviously do not have the same delicate flavour.

SERVES 6

6 large leeks

450 g / 1 lb / 2 cups arborio rice

4 eggs, beaten

90 g / 3 oz / ¾ cup freshly grated Parmesan cheese

salt

30 g / 1 oz / 2 tbsp unsalted butter + extra for the pan

60 g / 2 oz / ⅔ cup fine dry breadcrumbs (page 132)

Cut the roots and green tops off the leeks. Wash thoroughly. Bring a large saucepan of salted water to the boil, add the leeks and cook for 15 minutes. Drain, chop and set aside.

Bring a saucepan of salted water to the boil. Add the rice and cook for 12 minutes. Drain and rinse under cold water to prevent further cooking.

In a mixing bowl, combine the rice, chopped leeks, eggs, Parmesan and salt to taste. Stir well.

Lightly butter a 23-cm / 9-inch spring-form pan and sprinkle well with the breadcrumbs. Pour in the rice mixture and dot with the butter. Bake in a pre-heated 180°C / 350°F / gas 4 oven until golden, about 20 minutes.

Remove the side of the pan, slide the pie on to a platter and serve immediately.

EGG DISHES

*Y*ou will find several egg dishes in this section because in Italy we never have eggs for breakfast. An Italian breakfast consists of a cup of coffee with a slice of bread and jam; there are those who just have coffee at home and a brioche later in the morning. Light lunches or suppers often consist of an egg dish with raw or cooked vegetables followed by fruit.

Tortino alle Erbe

SOUFFLE OMELETTE WITH HERBS

In the summer, when the whole family is at Coltibuono, we have innumerable guests. So, because many of these vegetable dishes are excellent served at room temperature, I often make a variety of the most colourful ones and serve them as a buffet. They are followed by local cheeses and an array of summer fruit.

SERVES 6

6 eggs, separated

salt and pepper

60 g / 2 oz / ½ cup flour

300 ml / ½ pint / 1¼ cups milk

2 tbsp chopped fresh parsley

2 tbsp chopped fresh tarragon

2 tbsp chopped fresh basil

1 tbsp chopped fresh chives

extra virgin olive oil for the dish

In a bowl whisk the egg yolks with a little salt and pepper. Gradually sift in the flour, stirring constantly to avoid the formation of lumps. Add the milk and the chopped herbs. Beat the egg whites until stiff and carefully fold them into the mixture.

Lightly oil a 20-cm / 8-inch round ovenproof dish. Pour in the mixture and transfer to a preheated 180°C / 350°F / gas 4 oven. Bake until puffed up and golden, about 30 minutes.

Serve either hot and puffy or at room temperature, when the soufflé omelette will have flattened.

Tortino alla Piemontese

BAKED MASHED POTATOES WITH EGGS

This is a useful dish because it can be prepared ahead of time and the eggs added just before it is put in the oven. For a light dinner, serve after a soup such as ricotta dumplings in broth (page 39).

SERVES 6

900 g / 2 lb potatoes

salt

120 g / 4 oz / 1 cup freshly grated Parmesan cheese

60 g / 2 oz / 4 tbsp unsalted butter + extra for the dish

120 ml / 4 fl oz / ½ cup warm milk

6 eggs

6 anchovy fillets in oil, drained

Cook the potatoes, in their skins, in boiling salted water until tender. Drain and peel, then mash them. First beat in the Parmesan and half the butter, then gradually beat in the milk. Return to the saucepan over low heat and stir for a few minutes.

Lightly butter a 23-cm / 9-inch round ovenproof dish. Transfer the potato purée to it. Smooth the surface and, using a spoon, make six hollows in the potato. Transfer to a preheated 180°C / 350°F / gas 4 oven and bake for 40 minutes.

Remove the dish from the oven. Break a white of egg into each hollow, reserving the yolk. Dot with the rest of the butter and bake for 5 more minutes.

Put a yolk on each egg white. Roll the anchovies and gently place on top of the yolks. Return to the oven and bake for a further 2 minutes.

Serve very hot.

Uova alla Mozzarella

FRIED EGGS WITH MOZZARELLA

When we are all at Coltibuono, and Romola, our precious family help, brings us fresh eggs laid by her own hens, we have this for supper. It is such a family favourite that I have a dozen small earthenware pans. Generally we serve this with the grilled mixed vegetables on page 146, sometimes followed by the mascarpone and coffee dessert on page 183.

SERVES 6

300 g / 10 oz mozzarella cheese

3 tbsp extra virgin olive oil

6 fresh eggs

6 anchovy fillets in oil, drained and cut in half lengthwise

6 tbsp Neapolitan tomato sauce (page 158)

1 tbsp dried oregano

salt and pepper

Cut the mozzarella into 6 equal slices, discarding the 2 rounded ends.

Divide the olive oil among 6 frying pans and heat over moderate heat. Add a slice of mozzarella to each pan. Break one egg over each slice of mozzarella and cross 2 anchovy fillets on top of the eggs. Add 1 tbsp of tomato sauce to each pan and sprinkle with oregano, pepper and very little salt.

Cook over very low heat until the eggs are just set. Serve immediately.

Uova in Tazza

BAKED EGGS WITH HAM AND CHEESE

When I prepare this dish, which is perfect for a dinner, I use the egg whites for a sweet soufflé or meringue dessert. The whites can be kept in the refrigerator for a couple of days.

SERVES 6

15 g / ½ oz / 1 tbsp unsalted butter + extra for the moulds

240 ml / 8 fl oz / 1 cup whipping cream

6 egg yolks

salt

6 thin slices of cooked ham, finely chopped, about 120 g / 4 oz

120 g / 4 oz Gruyère or emmenthal cheese, coarsely grated

Lightly butter 6 individual moulds or custard cups. Pour a little cream into each one. Slide a yolk on to the cream in each mould and sprinkle with a little salt. Add the ham and cheese. Cover with the rest of the cream and dot with the butter.

Transfer to a preheated 180°C/ 350°F/gas 4 oven. Bake for 8 minutes and serve at once.

STUFFED VEGETABLES

Stuffed baked vegetables are another Italian classic. Basic stuffing consists of breadcrumbs or milk-soaked bread with chopped herbs, a little of the vegetable to be stuffed and Parmesan cheese, all bound with an egg. Aubergines (eggplants), sweet peppers, tomatoes, onions, cabbage and courgettes (zucchini) can be stuffed, and I hope you will enjoy being inventive by adding other things to the basic stuffing.

Zucchine Ripiene al Prosciutto

COURGETTES (ZUCCHINI) STUFFED WITH HAM

When I serve this as a main course, a simple Milanese tomato sauce (page 157) is passed around separately.

SERVES 6

6 medium-size courgettes (zucchini)

3 eggs

3 tbsp fine dry breadcrumbs (page 132)

3 tbsp freshly grated Parmesan cheese

15 g / ½ oz / 1 tbsp unsalted butter, melted

180 g / 6 oz cooked ham, chopped

salt and pepper

2 tbsp extra virgin olive oil

Bring a saucepan of salted water to the boil. Add the courgettes (zucchini) and cook for 5 minutes. Drain and pat dry. Cut off and discard both ends of the courgettes (zucchini). Using an apple corer, scoop out the pulp from the centres, leaving both ends intact, to make the hollow of a boat.

In a bowl beat the eggs. Add the breadcrumbs, Parmesan, butter and chopped ham. Mix well. Transfer the mixture to a small frying pan. Stirring constantly, cook over low heat until the mixture thickens slightly. Remove from the heat and season with salt and pepper.

Stuff the courgettes (zucchini) with the mixture. Pour the oil and 2 tbsp water into an ovenproof dish and arrange the courgettes (zucchini) in it. Bake in a preheated 180°C/350°F/gas 4 oven for about 20 minutes.

● **Courgettes Stuffed with Ham** ●

I Secondi

MAIN OR SECOND COURSES

*T*he main course of the traditional Italian meal is called IL SECONDO, not because it is of secondary importance but simply because it follows the first course. That said, however, I do think it is characteristic of the Italian way of eating that the main course is both qualified and quantified by what has gone before it. In other words, we do not serve those huge and heavy dishes of meat and potatoes or whatever that characterize the principal course in other culinary traditions.

With regard to meat dishes, let me put my prejudices on the table at the start. I am practically a vegetarian, not by philosophy nor even so much for health reasons, but simply out of personal preference. In general, Italians as a nation have never been big meat-eaters, at least not until very recently. With the exception of one or two regions in the north, the country does not have terrain suitable for grazing large herds of cattle.

Meat is expensive and until well after the Second World War Italy was a poor country. There was a period following the war when eating meat twice a day was a sign of new affluence and gave a sense of well-being — cholesterol apart. No longer. Occasionally I have eliminated the meat course from the menu of my cooking classes altogether, concentrating instead on various types of first courses and vegetable dishes — with only an occasional protest, usually from some of the men who make up for this privation at dinner that evening. However, I always — or almost always — serve meat to my guests and I have many recipes that successfully tempt me to put my prejudice aside and enjoy them as well.

*P*erhaps due to the scarcity of the larger cuts of beef and veal in former times, our culinary tradition is rich in recipes that use to full advantage the smaller pieces of meat, such as sweetbreads, tripe, tongue, liver and kidney. I have learned over the years, however, that mine is not a taste shared by the majority of my students, so I omit these recipes from my classes.

Traditionally every farm had chickens and rabbits, at least one pig, and some sheep, and all of these eventually arrived on the table, and into recipe books in a variety of

● **Rabbit with Olives (p. 96)** ●

delicious dishes. Italians have always been avid hunters so game of all sorts — small birds, hare and wild boar — have never been lacking in the larder nor are they in this book.

Perusing collections of Italian recipes I sometimes feel that Italians really do not like the taste or even the look of meat unless it is transformed by mixing it with other ingredients. For this reason I think that if any meat dish deserves the title 'king of our kitchen' it would be POLPETTONE, meatloaf. Undoubtedly this will come as a surprise to many. I have the impression that in other countries meatloaf is considered a rather mundane dish, but not so in Italy. We have dozens of different ways to prepare it and every family has its favourite.

If POLPETTONE be king, POLPETTE, meat patties, are royal descendants. This is another flavourful family dish that can be elegant as well as economical. These Italian-style hamburgers can also be grilled with herbs, layered with cheese, or sautéed and served with a hot chilli pepper or sweet mint sauce.

Next in the Italian hierarchy of meat dishes I would place ARROSTI ARROTOLATI, rolled roasts, especially made from breast of chicken, turkey and veal. These are filled with a mixture that usually contains sausage, salami, omelette and greens. When they are sliced to serve they reveal a lively swirl of colours.

There is a distinctively Italian way of cooking the larger cuts of white meat. I braise or roast veal, lamb, chicken and rabbit very slowly, starting practically at room temperature and raising the heat gradually, adding just enough white wine to keep the meat moist so that all the fat has time to dissolve. The outside turns a dark, almost burnt brown and the inside remains tender. I have found that for most of my students it requires an act of faith to proceed in this way, accustomed as they are to nouvelle cuisine methods of undercooking, but they become convinced when they taste the results. In order to obtain a delicious sauce to accompany the meat all I have to do is simply skim off the fat and deglaze the rich cooking juices that have accumulated at the bottom of the pan. I never add flour.

Roast beef is the exception to this rule of slow cooking. I roast it at a high temperature and remove it from the oven while still AL SANGUE, rare and juicy. For an Italian touch before roasting I pierce the piece of meat in the centre and insert rosemary and garlic.

I always serve meat already carved and arranged on a large white platter, surrounded by one or two suitable vegetables simply sautéed in butter. I would never present the meat on its platter alone.

Although Italy enjoys several thousand miles of coastline and is surrounded by some of the richest waters of the Mediterranean, fish is not a common national dish. It remains very much a regional speciality, even in these days of refrigerated transport and freezing. Instinctively, Italians want their food to be fresh and therefore prefer to feast on fish when they are at the sea and can buy it at markets along the wharf when the boats come in with the day's catch, or at least eat it at a seaside restaurant where they are sure the proprietor does the same.

Of course, to enjoy really fresh fish means that you must eat specific fish in specific places. On our northern shores where there are vast expances of sandy sea, species such as SOGLIOLA (sole), CODA DI ROSPO (monk-fish) and ROMBO (turbot) are plentiful. Where the coastline is rocky, TRIGLIA (red mullet), ORATA (gilt-head bream), and DENTICE (dentex, similar to sea bass) are among the most highly prized specimens. Tuna and swordfish abound in the waters off the island of Sicily, while the island of Sardinia is practically the only place where you can still trap ARAGOSTA (spiny lobster). Fortunately this delicacy can be transported fresh since it can survive at least a couple of days in tanks. From north to south cooks compose highly seasoned fish stews made mostly of left-over pieces from that day's market.

*S*imilar to the Italian predilection for the small tasty bits and pieces of meat is their love for tiny fish like ALICI (fresh anchovies), eaten raw after they have been marinated for several hours in lemon juice, and for the crustaceans, prawns and shrimp, as well as for the small members of the octopus family – SEPPIE (cuttlefish), CALAMARI (squid) and MOSCARDINI (a minuscule curled octopus).

In the interior of the country very little fish is consumed, except in the large cities that have fish markets and specialized restaurants. For this reason, although I love fish, I very seldom include recipes for it in my classes since we live in an area where fresh fish is not easily found.

Agnello ai Carciofi

BRAISED LAMB WITH ARTICHOKES

The slow cooking makes the lamb very succulent, and the tartness of the wine gives it an excellent flavour. It can be prepared well ahead of time and gently heated before serving with potatoes with rosemary (page 141).

SERVES 6

900 g / 2 lb boneless lamb

6 tbsp extra virgin olive oil

2 garlic cloves, chopped

240 ml / 8 fl oz / 1 cup dry white wine

salt and pepper

6 globe artichokes

juice of 1 lemon

Cut the lamb into 4- to 5-cm/1½- to 2-inch cubes.

In a flameproof casserole heat half the oil with half the garlic and cook over low heat until the garlic is translucent. Add enough lamb just to cover the bottom of the casserole and brown it on all sides over moderate heat, about 10 minutes.

MEAT-EATING IN ITALY

I Secondi are the main courses. They are meat and fish dishes or made from offal (variety meats) which we Italians particularly enjoy. We are not fond of red meat, except for the Tuscans with their famous Florentine steaks. They are essential to Sunday lunch and you can smell them cooking as you walk through the mountain villages at noon. The most popular meats are chicken, pork, lamb, liver, kidneys and tripe.

Remove it. Add the rest of the oil and garlic to the casserole and brown the remaining lamb.

Return all the lamb to the casserole. Pour in the wine and season with salt and pepper. Cover and cook over low heat for about 30 minutes.

Meanwhile, prepare the artichokes. Fill a bowl with cold water and add the lemon juice. Cut off the tough outer leaves and dig out the chokes. Drop immediately into the lemon water to prevent the artichokes from discolouring. One by one, drain the artichokes and slice them lengthwise, and then drop them into the casserole. Season with salt and pepper and stir well.

Cover the casserole again and cook very gently, turning the meat occasionally, for 20 minutes. If necessary, add a little water from time to time to keep the cooking juices moist.

Arrange on a platter and serve piping hot.

Arista di Maiale al Finocchio

ROAST PORK IN FENNEL SAUCE

The fresh flavour of the fennel sauce goes very well with pork. However, in summer, when fennel is out of season, I substitute courgette (zucchini) skins prepared in the same way. You can use whole courgettes (zucchini), but when the sauce is made just with the skins, it is a beautiful green. Serve with the baked Parmesan tomatoes on page 142.

SERVES 6

2 tbsp chopped fresh rosemary

4 garlic cloves, chopped

1 tsp ground black pepper

1 tsp fennel seeds

salt

1 loin of pork, chined (cut between the backbone and meat), weighing 1.8 kg / 4 lb

60 g / 2 oz / 4 tbsp unsalted butter

2 tbsp extra virgin olive oil

1 fennel bulb, sliced

120 ml / 4 fl oz / ½ cup milk

240 ml / 8 fl oz / 1 cup white wine

Mix together the rosemary, garlic, pepper, fennel seeds and salt to taste. Stuff this mixture between the meat and the bone. Tie the meat and bone together with a kitchen string.

In a roasting pan, melt 15 g/½ oz/ 1 tbsp butter with the olive oil over low heat. Add the meat and transfer to a pre-heated 180°C/350°F/gas 4 oven. Roast for about 1½ hours, basting occasionally.

Meanwhile, in a small saucepan melt 1 tsp butter. Add the sliced fennel, salt to taste and a little water. Cover and cook over low heat until tender, about 10 minutes.

Pour the contents of the saucepan into a blender with the rest of the butter and the milk. Process until very smooth.

When the meat is ready, discard the chine bone (backbone), carve and arrange the slices on a warm platter. Keep warm.

Pour off the fat from the roasting pan. Deglaze the cooking juices with the white wine over moderate heat, scraping the pan well. Bring to the boil and cook for a couple of minutes. Add the fennel sauce and stir well. Pour the sauce through a sieve over the meat and serve piping hot.

● **Roast Pork in Fennel Sauce** ●

Arrosto di Maiale con le Prugne

ROAST PORK WITH PRUNES

I occasionally wrap the prunes in bacon instead of pancetta because it adds a subtle smoky aroma. Serve with braised red cabbage with apples (page 132).

SERVES 6

18 pitted prunes

240 ml / 8 fl oz / 1 cup dry white wine

2 tbsp extra virgin olive oil

15 g / ½ oz / 1 tbsp unsalted butter

1 boned loin of pork, about 1.2 kg / 2½ lb

18 thin slices of pancetta

salt and pepper

Soak the prunes in the wine for about 1 hour.

Heat the oil and butter in a roasting pan. Add the pork and brown it over high heat for about 10 minutes, turning a couple of times. Transfer the pan to a preheated 180°C/350°F/gas 4 oven and, turning and basting frequently, roast for 2 hours.

Meanwhile, drain the prunes, reserving the wine. Wrap a slice of pancetta around each prune and secure with a wooden cocktail stick.

About 10 minutes before the pork is ready, add the prunes to the roasting pan.

Remove the pork and prunes from the pan and keep warm. Skim off the fat from the cooking juices and deglaze with the wine, scraping the pan well. Cook over moderate heat for about 5 minutes or until well reduced. Season with salt and pepper.

Carve the pork and arrange the slices on a warm platter. Spoon the cooking juices over the meat and arrange the pancetta-wrapped prunes on the platter.

SIMPLE PAN SAUCES

Unlike the French, who make elaborate sauces separately to go with their roast meats, we serve them with a sauce made from the natural juices accumulated while the meat cooks. The best pans for this are made of heavy aluminium because the meat is inclined to stick to them. When the roast is removed, the pan is moved to the top of the stove. A little white wine is added and the pan is deglazed by scraping with a wooden spoon. When the wine is reduced, the sauce is strained and served in a sauceboat.

Arrosto agli Spinaci

SPINACH AND VEAL ROLL

A very elegant meat roll. Serve with carrots in cream and mushroom sauce (page 131).

SERVES 6

600 g / 1¼ lb fresh spinach leaves

3 tbsp freshly grated Parmesan cheese

1 egg

a pinch of grated nutmeg

salt and pepper

600 g / 1¼ lb boned breast of veal, cut in a single slice

120 g / 4 oz cooked ham, sliced

15 g / ½ oz / 1 tbsp unsalted butter

2 tbsp extra virgin olive oil

1 garlic clove

6 fresh sage leaves

240 ml / 8 fl oz / 1 cup dry white wine

Wash the spinach and put it in a saucepan. Cook briefly, covered, on moderate heat in the water clinging to the leaves. Drain and leave to cool, then squeeze dry and chop finely.

In a bowl combine the chopped spinach, Parmesan and egg. Season with nutmeg, salt and pepper. Mix well.

Open a pocket in the veal, cutting from one side horizontally, not going to the end. Fill the meat with the spinach mixture. Cover the spinach with a layer of ham. Carefully roll up the veal and secure with kitchen string. Season lightly with salt and pepper.

In a roasting pan over low heat melt the butter with the oil. Add the garlic and sage leaves and cook until the garlic is just translucent. Remove it from the pan. Add the veal roll, turn up the heat to moderate and brown the roll on all sides.

Pour half the wine over the meat. Cover the pan, lower the heat and cook for 60 minutes, basting the meat occasionally. Uncover the pan and cook for a further 30 minutes, allowing the meat to take on more colour.

Transfer the veal roll to a warm platter and keep warm. Pour the rest of the wine into the pan and deglaze the cooking juices, scraping the pan well.

Slice the meat and arrange on the warm platter. Coat with the cooking juices and serve immediately.

FREEZING MEAT

If you want to freeze meat it is better to do so after it has been cooked because raw meat loses a lot of its juices while thawing and so becomes tough. Stews freeze very well, but roast meat tends to dry out. Thaw at room temperature and then just heat the stew, otherwise you might overcook it.

Bistecche al Gorgonzola

BEEF STEAKS WITH GORGONZOLA BUTTER

This butter has a strong flavour that goes very well with beef. For a milder flavour, use a sweet cheese such as goat's cheese with fresh chopped chives instead of gorgonzola.

SERVES 6

60 g / 2 oz / 4 tbsp unsalted butter

3 tbsp gorgonzola cheese

1 tsp sweet paprika

1 tbsp chopped fresh flat-leaf (Italian) parsley

1 tbsp lemon juice

6 slices of beef fillet (tenderloin), about 180 g / 6 oz each

salt

Using a wooden spoon cream half the butter with the gorgonzola, paprika, parsley and lemon juice. Place the mixture in a piping bag with a medium nozzle. Set aside.

In a large frying pan heat the rest of the butter. Add the slices of beef and cook for about 2 minutes on each side on high heat. Season with a little salt.

Arrange the steaks on a warm serving dish and pipe a rosette of gorgonzola butter on to each one. Serve immediately.

● Spinach and Veal Roll ●

Brasato al Chianti

BEEF BRAISED IN CHIANTI

In Tuscany beef is braised in Chianti with the addition of a few porcini mushrooms and tomato. It is very flavoursome, so traditionally it is served with juniper-flavoured lentils (page 140).

SERVES 6

1 piece of beef rump or topside (top round), 1.2 kg / 2½ lb

3 medium-size carrots, sliced

3 small onions, sliced

3 celery stalks, sliced

a handful of fresh parsley

3 bay leaves

1 tbsp juniper berries

1 tsp white peppercorns

3 whole cloves

1 bottle of Chianti Classico Riserva

10 g / ⅓ oz dried porcini mushrooms (or use shiitake)

15 g / ½ oz / 1 tbsp butter

1 tbsp extra virgin olive oil

salt

3 ripe plum tomatoes, peeled and chopped

Put the meat in a deep bowl. Add the sliced vegetables, the parsley, bay leaves, juniper berries, peppercorns, cloves and wine. Leave to marinate for 24 hours, turning the meat over occasionally.

Soak the mushrooms in 240 ml / 8 fl oz / 1 cup lukewarm water for at least 30 minutes. Remove the mushrooms and strain the water through a fine sieve to get rid of any sand. Set aside.

Remove the meat and pat it dry. In a flameproof casserole heat the butter and oil. Add the meat and brown it on all sides over moderate heat.

Remove the vegetables and flavourings from the marinade and add them to the casserole. Add 480 ml / 16 fl oz / 2 cups of the wine. Season and bring to a slow simmer over low heat. Add the mushrooms and tomatoes.

Cover the casserole and transfer it to a preheated 180°C / 350°F / gas 4 oven. Cook for about 3 hours, alternately adding wine or the water from the mushrooms so that the meat and vegetables are kept constantly very moist.

Remove the beef and slice it. Transfer it to a warm platter and keep warm. Put the vegetables and cooking juices through a food mill. Reheat on moderate heat until the excess liquid has completely evaporated and the sauce has thickened. Season the sauce and spoon it over the sliced meat. Serve immediately.

Carré di Vitello ai Funghi

ROAST VEAL WITH MUSHROOMS

Italian men do not do the carving, so I generally ask the butcher to bone and roll the meat and to give me the bones. I put them in the roasting pan with the meat because they add a great deal of flavour to the sauce. This is rather a special dish that I generally serve with the potatoes with rosemary on page 141.

SERVES 6

10 g / ⅓ oz dried porcini mushrooms

2 tbsp extra virgin olive oil

1 tbsp fresh thyme leaves

60 g / 2 oz bacon

1 piece of boned veal for roasting, about 1.2 kg / 2½ lb, rolled (bones reserved)

salt and pepper

30 g / 1 oz / 2 tbsp unsalted butter

120 ml / 4 fl oz / ½ cup dry white wine

Soak the mushrooms in water for 30 minutes. Drain and squeeze out excess liquid. Strain the liquid through a fine sieve and reserve for a rice dish or soup.

In a small frying pan heat half the oil. Add the mushrooms and cook over moderate heat for about 3 minutes. Remove from the heat, season and sprinkle with the thyme. Finely chop the mushrooms and bacon together to reduce to a paste.

Using a larding needle, make a hole through the entire length of the meat. Fill it with the bacon and mushroom paste. Season with salt and pepper.

In a roasting pan heat the butter and the rest of the oil over moderate heat. Add the meat and the bones and brown on all sides. Transfer the pan to a preheated 180°C / 350°C / gas 4 oven. Roast for 1½ hours, basting occasionally.

Remove the meat to a serving plate and keep warm. Discard the bones. Put the roasting pan over moderate heat. Add the wine and deglaze the cooking juices, scraping the pan well.

Untie the roast and cut it into slices. Pour the cooking juices over the sliced meat and serve at once.

SERVING I SECONDI

Meat and fish are always served whole with only a small part carved, so the rest will still be warm when it is served a second time. The vegetables are served on the same dish. The same type of service is used for a buffet. Everyone helps himself to the amount he wants, because it is considered very bad manners to leave something on your plate.

Cervella al Burro e Capperi

BRAINS WITH BROWN BUTTER AND CAPERS

Although many Europeans consider brains a great delicacy, most Americans seem to regard them with suspicion. I have, however, made several converts and this is a good way to break the ice. Serve with the fried courgettes (zucchini) in mint sauce on page 147.

SERVES 6

900 g / 2 lb calves' brains

1 tbsp lemon juice

1 tbsp white wine vinegar

120 g / 4 oz / 1 cup flour

90 g / 3 oz / 6 tbsp unsalted butter

2 tbsp capers in vinegar, drained

salt and pepper

Put the brains in a bowl. Cover with cold water and add the lemon juice. Leave to soak for about 30 minutes.

Drain and rinse under cold running water. Using a sharp knife carefully remove the outer membrane. Rinse off any blood. Transfer to a saucepan. Cover with fresh cold water and add the vinegar. Simmer gently for 10 minutes.

Drain and rinse the brains under cold water to cool. Pat dry. Cut the brains into fairly thick slices. Dredge them lightly in the flour.

In a large frying pan heat the butter on moderate heat until it turns golden. Add the brains and sauté for about 2 minutes on each side. Transfer to a warm serving dish.

Add the capers to the pan and stir for a minute or two. Season to taste. Pour the butter and capers over the brains and serve at once.

Cinghiale in Dolceforte

WILD BOAR IN SWEET AND SOUR CHOCOLATE SAUCE

This is a traditional Christmas recipe that has been prepared in Florence since the Renaissance. In fact, some cooks still add little pieces of candied orange and lemon peel. The recipe is perfect for wild boar because the sauce disguises its strong gamey flavour. You should allow it to marinate for 24 hours.

SERVES 6

1.8 kg / 4 lb wild boar leg or shoulder, boned and cut into serving pieces

2 carrots, sliced

2 celery stalks, sliced

2 medium-size onions, sliced

1 tsp black peppercorns

1 bottle of Chianti Classico or other good red wine

salt

120 g / 4 oz / 3/4 cup raisins

120 g / 4 oz pitted prunes

4 tbsp extra virgin olive oil

1 tbsp juniper berries

2 bay leaves

90 g / 3 oz / 7 tbsp sugar

4 garlic cloves, chopped

120 ml / 4 fl oz / 1/2 cup red wine vinegar

90 g / 3 oz bittersweet chocolate, grated

60 g / 2 oz / 2/3 cup pine nuts

In a large bowl combine the meat, half the sliced carrots, celery and onions, the peppercorns and the wine. Season with salt and leave to marinate for 24 hours, turning occasionally.

Soak the raisins and prunes in water to cover for 30 minutes; drain.

Remove the meat from the marinade and pat it dry. Strain the marinade and set aside both the vegetables and the liquid.

In a shallow saucepan heat the olive oil until it starts to discolour. Add the meat and brown it on all sides for about 10 minutes on moderate heat. Add the vegetables from the marinade together with the remaining sliced vegetables, the juniper berries and 1 bay leaf. Stir over low heat for a couple of minutes. Add half the liquid from the marinade. Lower the heat, cover the saucepan and simmer very gently, turning the meat occasionally, for about 3 hours or until the meat is tender, adding the rest of the marinade gradually. Remove from the heat and allow to cool, then remove any fat that rises to the top.

Transfer the meat to a platter. Discard the bay leaf. Put the remaining contents of the pan through a food mill to chop very coarsely. Return the sauce to the saucepan and, if too liquid, reduce it over low heat until fairly thick. Add the meat to the sauce and warm over very low heat.

In a small saucepan melt the sugar with the garlic, remaining bay leaf and 1 tbsp water. Cook until golden brown. Add the vinegar and chocolate and cook over very low heat for just a few minutes, stirring well, to melt the chocolate and reduce the vinegar.

Add the chocolate mixture, raisins, prunes and pine nuts to the wild boar saucepan and stir very well. Simmer gently for 10 minutes before serving.

Coda di Rospo alla Mostarda

MONKFISH IN MUSTARD SAUCE

Fish almost always has a delicate taste and should not be cooked in too many fancy ways. Simply grilled or boiled, with fresh lemon juice and a little extra virgin olive oil, is usually the best treatment. But sometimes little things can be added. Serve this dish with the baked medley of vegetables on page 147.

SERVES 6

2 tbsp extra virgin olive oil

6 slices of monkfish, 240 g / 8 oz each

5 tbsp finely chopped fresh chives

salt and pepper

3 tbsp capers in vinegar, drained

2 tbsp dry mustard

240 ml / 8 fl oz / 1 cup dry white wine

In a shallow flameproof casserole, heat the oil and arrange the fish slices in it. Sprinkle with the chives and a little salt and pepper. Scatter over the capers.

Dissolve the mustard in the wine and pour over the fish.

Transfer the dish to a preheated 180° C/350° F/gas 4 oven and bake for 20 minutes, carefully turning the fish over once.

Arrange the fish on a warm platter. Reduce the cooking juices, pour them over the fish and serve piping hot.

Coniglio Marinato

MARINATED RABBIT

The same recipe can be made with chunks of veal or beef, or even hare in the hunting season. If you want a thicker sauce, push the vegetables through a food mill with the marinade instead of straining it. This is excellent with tagliatelle with mixed spices (page 58).

SERVES 6

1 medium-size carrot, sliced

1 medium-size onion, sliced

1 celery stalk, sliced

4 tbsp extra virgin olive oil

2 bay leaves

2 whole cloves

1 small sprig of fresh thyme

½ bottle of dry red wine

120 ml / 4 fl oz / ½ cup wine vinegar

1 tsp black peppercorns

1.8 kg / 4 lb rabbit, in serving pieces

15 g / ½ oz / 1 tbsp unsalted butter

salt

In a bowl combine the carrot, onion, celery, 2 tbsp of the oil, the bay leaves, cloves, thyme, wine, vinegar and peppercorns. Add the rabbit and leave to marinate overnight.

Drain and dry the rabbit. Reserve the marinade.

In a large flameproof casserole heat the butter and the rest of oil. Add the rabbit and season with salt. Cook over moderate heat until golden brown, about 10 minutes. Add 240 ml / 8 fl oz / 1 cup

of the marinade to the casserole, cover and continue cooking over low heat for about 1½ hours. Add the rest of the marinade from time to time.

Arrange the rabbit on a platter and keep warm. Strain the marinade, return it to the casserole and boil to reduce to about 6 tbsp. Pour the marinade over the rabbit and serve.

Coniglio alle Olive

RABBIT WITH OLIVES

Chicken can be cooked in the same way, but it is fattier and less tasty.

SERVES 6

1.8 kg / 4 lb rabbit, in serving pieces

3 tbsp flour

3 tbsp extra virgin olive oil

3 garlic cloves, chopped

2 small carrots, sliced

1 celery stalk, sliced

salt and pepper

240 ml / 8 fl oz / 1 cup dry white wine

210 g / 7 oz green or black olives, stoned

Dredge the rabbit lightly with the flour. In a large frying pan heat the oil over moderate heat. Add the rabbit and brown all over, about 10 minutes. Add the garlic, carrots and celery and cook for a few minutes longer.

Season with salt and pepper.

Pour the wine over the rabbit and add the olives. Cover and cook over low heat for about 1½ hours, occasionally adding a little water, if necessary, to keep the cooking juices moist.

Arrange the rabbit on a platter, spoon on the sauce and the olives and serve.

Coniglio con Patate

SAUTÉED RABBIT WITH POTATOES

If you don't like rabbit, use chicken instead and cook for a shorter time. At lunch first serve spaghetti with oil and rosemary (page 56), or omelette strips in broth (page 26) for dinner.

SERVES 6

240 ml / 8 fl oz / 1 cup extra virgin olive oil

900 g / 2 lb potatoes, peeled and diced

2 tbsp chopped fresh rosemary

salt and pepper

1.8 kg / 4 lb rabbit, in serving pieces

120 g / 4 oz / 1 cup flour

15 g / ½ oz / 1 tbsp unsalted butter

240 ml / 8 fl oz / 1 cup dry white wine

Heat all but 2 tbsp of the oil in a heavy frying pan. Add the potatoes and rosemary. Turning occasionally, cook over moderate heat until golden. Drain on paper towels, sprinkle with salt and set aside. Pour the oil from the pan.

Lightly dredge the pieces of rabbit with flour. Heat the rest of the oil and the butter in the frying pan. Add the rabbit and, turning occasionally, cook over moderate heat until golden brown, about 10 minutes. Season with salt and pepper and add the wine. Cover and cook on low heat until the rabbit is tender and all the liquid has evaporated, about 1½ hours.

Add the potatoes to the rabbit. Stir and cook, uncovered, over moderate heat for a few minutes.

Arrange on a warm platter and serve.

Coniglio in Salsa di Mele

RABBIT IN APPLE SAUCE

Sometimes I make this rabbit more oriental, simply by adding some curry powder or perhaps grated horseradish to the apple sauce. Horseradish is very easy to grow in the kitchen garden in a climate that is not too dry.

SERVES 6

2 tbsp extra virgin olive oil

1 carrot, sliced

1 celery stalk, sliced

1 medium-size onion, sliced

1 garlic clove, chopped

1.8 kg / 4 lb rabbit, in serving pieces

1 tbsp chopped fresh sage

1 tbsp chopped fresh rosemary

salt and pepper

2 cooking apples

2 whole cloves

15 g / ½ oz / 1 tbsp butter

120 ml / 4 fl oz / ½ cup dry white wine

juice of 1 orange

In a roasting pan heat the oil. Add the carrot, celery, onion and garlic and spread them on the bottom of the pan. Put the rabbit pieces on top and sprinkle with the chopped herbs. Season with salt and pepper.

Transfer to a preheated 200°C/400°F/gas 6 oven and bake for 15 minutes, turning the pieces twice. Lower the temperature to 160°C/325°F/gas 3, pour 120 ml / 4 fl oz / ½ cup of water over the rabbit and bake for a further 1½ hours. Turn and baste the rabbit occasionally, adding more water if necessary to keep the cooking juices always moist.

Meanwhile, peel and core the apples and cut them into large chunks. Put them in a small saucepan with 2 tbsp water, the cloves and butter. Cover and cook over very low heat for about 15 minutes. When they are tender, remove the cloves and mash well or purée in a blender.

Remove the rabbit from the roasting pan and keep it warm. Strain the cooking juices into a saucepan and add the wine and orange juice. Stir in the apple purée. Cook over low heat for about 10 minutes, stirring frequently.

Arrange the rabbit on a warm platter and spoon the sauce over it. Serve immediately.

Cosciotto di Agnello alle Acciughe

ROAST LEG OF LAMB WITH ANCHOVIES

If you are roasting older lamb, cook it at 160°C/325°F/gas 3 for at least 2 hours or it will be tough. The lamb will improve if you gradually add about 120 ml / 4 fl oz / ½ cup of dry white wine to the cooking juices after the first hour.

SERVES 6

3 garlic cloves

6 anchovy fillets in oil, drained

3 tbsp capers in vinegar, drained

1 leg of lamb, about 1.8 kg / 4 lb

15 g / ½ oz / 1 tbsp unsalted butter

2 tbsp extra virgin olive oil

pepper

Chop the garlic, anchovies and capers together. Make several incisions in the lamb with a small pointed knife and fill them with the mixture.

Melt the butter with the oil in a roating pan and heat well. Add the leg of lamb and cook over moderate heat until golden all over, about 10 minutes. Season with pepper. Transfer to a preheated 180°C/350°F/gas 4 oven and, basting frequently, roast for about 1½ hours.

When ready, transfer to a warm serving plate and carve at the table.

LONG SLOW ROASTING

*T*o achieve a good glaze the meat has to be roasted, either in the oven or on top of the stove, for a fairly long time so that it darkens. We are not fond of underdone white meat. Pork, lamb and chicken are cooked for at least 1½ hours and large pieces of meat even longer. The sauce is always served separately because roasts are crisp outside and would soon get soggy with sauce on them.

● **Leg of Lamb with Mint and Thyme** ●

Cosciotto di Agnello alla Menta

LEG OF LAMB WITH MINT AND THYME

*U*ntil fairly recently we used to roast lamb in a wood-burning bread oven, which resulted in it being crisp on the outside and tender within. Whenever possible we still roast this way because electric and gas ovens seem to change the flavour. Serve the lamb with sliced baked potatoes with rosemary (page 141).

SERVES 6

1 leg of lamb, about 1.8 kg / 4 lb

2 tbsp fresh thyme leaves, or 1 tbsp dried thyme

2 tbsp chopped fresh mint, or 1 tbsp dried mint

5 garlic cloves

120 g / 4 oz pancetta

salt and pepper

15 g / ½ oz / 1 tbsp unsalted butter

2 tbsp extra virgin olive oil

240 ml / 8 fl oz / 1 cup dry white wine

Slit the meat with a sharp knife at about 7.5-cm/3-inch intervals, but leave it attached to the bone. Chop the herbs, garlic and pancetta together. Season with salt and pepper. Push this stuffing into the slits in the lamb. Tie the meat together with kitchen string.

In a roasting pan heat the butter and oil. Add the lamb and transfer to a pre-heated 180°C/350°F/gas 4 oven. Roast until the outside is crisp and golden, about 1½ hours.

Remove the lamb from the pan and keep warm. Deglaze the pan juices with the wine over moderate heat, scraping the pan well. Boil to reduce slightly.

Carve the meat and arrange on a warm platter. Spoon on the sauce and serve at once.

Costolette alle Erbe

HERBED VEAL CHOPS

Herbs mixed with breadcrumbs make a very tasty crust for veal chops. Veal can be rather expensive, so I also make this dish with boneless chicken breasts, slit in half and flattened, or slices of turkey breast. This recipe goes well with winter salad with walnuts (page 138).

SERVES 6

2 eggs, size 5 (US medium)

salt

4 tbsp chopped mixed fresh rosemary, oregano, thyme and sage

180 g / 6 oz / 2 cups fine dry breadcrumbs (page 132)

6 veal chops, cut about 2.5 cm / 1 inch thick, 240 g / 8 oz each

240 g / 8 oz / 2 sticks unsalted butter

1 lemon

In a soup plate lightly whisk the eggs with a pinch of salt. In another dish mix the chopped herbs and breadcrumbs together. First dip the chops in the egg, then in the breadcrumbs, coating well on all sides.

In a large frying pan heat half the butter on moderate heat. Add 3 chops and cook until golden on both sides, about 5 minutes. Remove and drain on paper towels. Keep hot. Add the rest of the butter and cook the rest of the chops.

Arrange the chops on a warm platter, garnish with wedges of lemon and serve immediately.

SERVING SALADS WITH MAIN COURSES

If salad is served with meat or fish, it is put on to a separate small plate beside the dinner plate because it would soon become limp if it came into contact with hot food. Salad is only served with meat without sauces, such as breaded veal escalopes (scaloppine) or grills. Generally speaking, salad is not served with fish because its flavour is considered too strong to go with salad.

Costolette al Limone

VEAL CHOPS WITH LEMON SAUCE

For an equally delicious but less expensive version of this recipe, use pork chops or chicken breasts. Serve with grape, cheese and apple salad (page 139).

SERVES 6

6 veal chops, about 240 g / 8 oz each

120 ml / 4 fl oz / ½ cup extra virgin olive oil

grated zest and juice of 3 lemons

salt and pepper

2 tbsp chopped fresh parsley

Without touching the bone, gently flatten the meat with a pounder.

In a bowl whisk together the oil, half the lemon juice and a little salt and pepper to make a marinade. Arrange the chops in a shallow dish and pour the marinade over them. Marinate the chops for about 2 hours, turning occasionally.

Heat 3 tbsp of the marinade in a large frying pan. Add the drained chops and cook over moderate heat until golden, about 5 minutes on each side. Transfer the meat to a platter and keep warm.

Pour the rest of the lemon juice into the pan and stir over low heat. Add the lemon zest and parsley and, stirring constantly, cook for a couple of minutes.

Spoon the hot sauce over the chops and serve immediately.

Costolette al Pomodoro e Basilico

BREADED VEAL SCALOPPINE WITH TOMATO AND BASIL

Served cold, this is excellent on a buffet with tuna and bean salad (page 137). The cold tomato and basil make an interesting contrast with the hot meat. The scaloppine can also be prepared well ahead of time, the tomato added at the last minute, and served cold.

SERVES 6

6 large ripe tomatoes, peeled and seeded

salt and pepper

2 eggs

6 veal escalopes (scaloppine), 150 g / 5 oz each, or 12 half the size, pounded

180 g / 6 oz / 2 cups fine dry breadcrumbs (page 132)

120 g / 4 oz / 1 stick unsalted butter

3 tbsp chopped fresh basil

3 tbsp extra virgin olive oil

1 tbsp white wine vinegar

Dice the tomatoes, sprinkle with salt and leave to drain in a colander for about 30 minutes.

In a soup plate lightly whisk the eggs with a little salt and pepper. One by one, dip the veal slices in the egg. Dredge well with the breadcrumbs.

In a large frying pan melt the butter over moderate heat. Fry the veal until golden on one side, then turn and fry the other side for a total of about 5 minutes. Remove carefully from the pan and drain on paper towels.

While the veal is being fried, transfer the tomato to a bowl. Sprinkle with basil,

dress with oil and vinegar and toss well.

Arrange the veal on a serving plate and allow to cool. Put part of the dressed tomato in the middle of each one and serve.

Costolette alla Senape

PORK CHOPS IN MUSTARD SAUCE

Generally speaking, pork chops are tender only when they are cooked quickly. They can be served with Swiss chard rolls (page 139).

SERVES 6

2 tbsp extra virgin olive oil

6 pork chops, about 240 g / 8 oz each

2 tbsp Dijon mustard

120 ml / 4 fl oz / ½ cup dry white wine

1 tbsp wine vinegar

salt and pepper

1 tbsp chopped fresh flat-leaf (Italian) parsley

In a large wide frying pan or flameproof casserole heat the oil. Add the chops and brown on both sides over moderate heat for about 5 minutes. Remove and arrange them on a serving plate. Keep warm. Pour off the fat from the pan.

In a cup stir the mustard, wine and vinegar together. Over low heat add the mustard mixture to the pan. Stir well with a wooden spoon and add salt and pepper to taste. Cook until well reduced on moderate heat.

Pour the sauce over the chops, then sprinkle with parsley and serve at once.

● **Breaded Veal Scaloppine with Tomato and Basil** ●

Faraona alle Pesche

ROAST GUINEA FOWL WITH PEACHES

I usually serve this dish with the sliced potato and spinach roll (page 144). The poor relation, chicken with canned peaches, can serve in an emergency.

SERVES 6

---

6 loose-stone (freestone) peaches

---

2 tbsp lemon juice

---

a pinch of grated nutmeg

---

1 guinea fowl, about 1.8 kg / 4 lb, trussed

---

1 tbsp chopped fresh rosemary

---

1 tbsp chopped fresh sage

---

salt and pepper

---

90 g / 3 oz pancetta, sliced very thin

---

15 g / ½ oz / 1 tbsp unsalted butter

---

2 tbsp extra virgin olive oil

---

120 ml / 4 fl oz / ½ cup dry white wine

---

2 tbsp brandy

Blanch the peaches in boiling water, then peel them. Cut in half and remove the stones. Sprinkle the hollows with lemon juice and nutmeg. Arrange on a baking sheet and bake in a preheated 180°C/350°F/gas 4 oven for about 20 minutes. Remove and set aside.

Sprinkle the guinea fowl with the herbs mixed with a little salt and pepper and wrap it in the thin slices of pancetta. Set in a pan with the butter and oil and roast in the oven for 1½ hours.

Transfer the guinea fowl to a serving dish. Keep warm. Skim off the fat and put the roasting pan over low heat. Add the white wine and deglaze. Add the brandy and allow the alcohol to evaporate. Add the peaches and heat well.

● **Roast Guinea Fowl** ●
with Peaches

Arrange the peaches around the guinea fowl and pour the deglazed cooking juices over it.

Fegato alla Salsa di Cipolle

LIVER IN ONION SAUCE

This dish is excellent served with a simple polenta (page 219). Serve it in a mound in the middle of a platter with the liver and sauce surrounding it.

SERVES 6

---

90 g / 3 oz / 6 tbsp unsalted butter

---

450 g / 1 lb onions, thinly sliced

---

240 ml / 8 fl oz / 1 cup dry white wine

---

salt and pepper

---

120 ml / 4 fl oz / ½ cup single (light) cream

---

grated zest of 1 orange

---

900 g / 2 lb calves' liver, sliced about
5 mm / ¼ inch thick

In a frying pan melt half the butter. Add the onions and half the wine and season with salt and pepper. Cover and cook over low heat for about 30 minutes.

Pour the contents of the pan into a blender. Add the rest of the wine and process until a purée is formed. Return the purée to the pan and add the cream and orange zest. Stirring constantly, cook over low heat for about 3 minutes. Keep warm.

Heat the rest of the butter in another frying pan. Add the sliced liver and sauté over high heat on both sides for 3 minutes. The liver should be slightly pink inside. Season with salt and pepper. Arrange the liver on a warm platter, cover with the onion sauce and serve immediately.

Filetti di Pesce con Carciofi

FISH FILLETS WITH ARTICHOKES

When artichokes are out of season I use leeks instead to make this dish. Serve with the artichokes stuffed with mozzarella on page 128.

SERVES 6

juice of 1 lemon

6 globe artichokes

3 tbsp extra virgin olive oil

salt and pepper

unsalted butter for the dish

6 fillets of red snapper, plaice or sole, 180 g / 6 oz each, skinned

1 tbsp chopped fresh flat-leaf (Italian) parsley

Fill a bowl with cold water and add the lemon juice. Prepare the artichokes by cutting off the spikes, removing the tough outer leaves, and digging out the chokes. Slice finely lengthwise and drop immediately into the bowl of lemon water to prevent discoloration.

Drain the sliced artichokes and dry them on paper towels. In a frying pan heat the oil. Add the artichokes, cover and cook over low heat for about 5 minutes. Remove the pan from the heat and season the artichokes with salt and pepper.

Butter an ovenproof dish and arrange the fish fillets in it in one layer. Butter a sheet of foil and cover the dish with it. Transfer to a pre-heated 200°C/400°F/gas 6 oven and bake for 8 minutes.

Remove the dish from the oven and arrange the artichokes on top of the fish. Cover again and return to the oven to bake for 5 minutes longer.

Sprinkle with parsley and serve.

Filetti di Sogliola alla Crema

FILLETS OF SOLE IN CREAM SAUCE

This is an elegant party dish that I would serve surrounded with a lemon risotto (page 51) and spinach with raisins and pine nuts (page 145).

SERVES 6

15 g / ½ oz / 1 tbsp unsalted butter + extra for the dish

120 g / 4 oz button mushrooms, thinly sliced

120 ml / 4 fl oz / ½ cup dry white wine

12 large raw prawns or shrimp

6 fillets of sole, about 240 g / 8 oz each

salt and pepper

120 ml / 4 fl oz / ½ cup whipping cream

1 tbsp chopped fresh parsley

In a small frying pan melt the butter over moderate heat. Add the mushrooms and sauté for a few minutes. Set aside.

In a small saucepan bring the wine to the boil. Add the prawns or shrimp, return to the boil and cook for 3 minutes, turning them once. Drain, reserving the cooking liquid. Peel the prawns or shrimp and set aside.

Butter an ovenproof dish and arrange the sole fillets in it. Add the cooking liquid from the prawns. Season with salt and pepper. Cover the dish with a piece of buttered foil and transfer to a pre-heated 200°C/400°F/gas 6 oven. Bake for 10 minutes.

Arrange the prawns or shrimp on top of the sole fillets. Cover them with the mushrooms and spoon the cream on top. Return to the oven, uncovered, and bake for 3 or 4 minutes longer.

Sprinkle with the parsley and serve immediately.

Filetti di Sogliola alle Zucchine

SOLE FILLETS WITH COURGETTES (ZUCCHINI) AND TOMATO

This dish is even enjoyed by people who are not very keen on fish. The same recipe can be used for slices of fresh tuna.

SERVES 6

4 tbsp extra virgin olive oil

1 medium-size onion, thinly sliced

4 medium-size ripe tomatoes, peeled and diced

450 g / 1 lb small courgettes (zucchini), thinly sliced

salt and pepper

1 tbsp capers in vinegar, drained

120 g / 4 oz / ⅔ cup green olives, stoned and halved

900 g / 2 lb fillets of sole

Pour 1 tbsp of oil into a wide shallow pan. Add the onion in a single layer and cook over low heat for 3 minutes. Cover the onion with half the tomato. Add all the sliced courgettes (zucchini) and season with salt and pepper. Add 2 tbsp oil, the capers and olives. Cover and continue to cook over low heat for a further 15 minutes.

Arrange the fillets of sole on top of the vegetables and cover them with the rest of the tomato. Sprinkle with the remaining oil and season lightly. Cover with a lid and cook for a further 8 minutes.

Arrange carefully on a warm platter and serve immediately.

Filetto di Maiale alla Mostarda

PORK LOIN WITH MUSTARD

This elegant dish can be prepared ahead of time and popped in the oven for the final cooking when your guests arrive. As it is already carved, a lot of time is saved when serving. On special occasions I sandwich thin slices of goose liver and white truffles between the slices of pork, creating a truly sensational dish. I suggest you start with the jellied consommé on page 27.

SERVES 6

a large piece of caul fat

15 g / ½ oz / 1 tbsp unsalted butter

1 tbsp extra virgin olive oil

1 boned loin of pork, about 1.2 kg / 2½ lb

6 large Savoy cabbage leaves or equivalent Swiss chard

3 tbsp Dijon mustard

salt

120 ml / 4 fl oz / ½ cup white wine

Soak the caul for 30 minutes in a bowl of water. Drain.

In a roasting pan heat the butter and oil over moderate heat. Add the pork and brown evenly on all sides, about 10 minutes. Remove the meat from the pan and leave to cool completely.

Bring a saucepan of salted water to the boil and blanch the cabbage leaves or Swiss chard. Drain, refresh and pat dry with paper towels.

Slice the pork and spread each slice with a little mustard. Season with a little salt and press the slices together again so the loin has its original shape. On a board spread out the caul and cover it with half the blanched cabbage or chard leaves. Place the meat in the centre and cover with the remaining leaves. Carefully wrap the leaves and caul around the pork. Tie together lengthwise with kitchen string.

Return the wrapped pork to the pan and roast in a preheated 180°C/ 350°F/gas 4 oven for 20 minutes.

Remove the meat from the pan and keep warm. Pour off the excess fat and deglaze the juices with the white wine, scraping the pan. Stirring constantly, reduce a little over moderate heat.

Untie the meat and arrange on a platter. Cover with the sauce and serve immediately, slicing into the cabbage.

● **Sole Fillets with Courgettes (Zucchini) and Tomato, Fish Fillets with Artichokes** ●

Gallettine alla Menta

BEEF PATTIES WITH MINT AND ORANGE

These simple beef patties look soph- isticated enough to be served for an improvised lunch surrounded by spiced onions (page 135).

SERVES 6

2 slices of coarse-textured white bread, crusts removed

240 ml / 8 fl oz / 1 cup milk

900 g / 2 lb lean minced (ground) beef

1 egg

1 small onion, finely chopped

2 tbsp chopped fresh mint, or 1 tbsp dried mint

salt and pepper

2 tbsp extra virgin olive oil

15 g / ½ oz / 1 tbsp unsalted butter

6 slices of peeled seedless orange

Soak the bread in the milk for about 10 minutes. Drain and squeeze dry.

In a bowl combine the beef, bread, egg, onion and mint. Season with salt and pepper. Using your hands, mix together very well. Roll the meat into 6 balls and press them between the palms of your hands to flatten them.

In a frying pan with a heatproof handle heat the oil and the butter. Add the beef patties and brown on both sides over the high heat for about 2 minutes on each side. Place a slice of orange on each patty and transfer the pan to a preheated 200°C/400°F/gas 6 oven. Bake for 2 minutes.

Transfer to a warm platter and serve.

MEATLOAF AND MEATBALLS

Meatloaf and meatballs are immensely popular and there is a variety of both. I don't think any cook prepares them in quite the same way twice. Prosciutto or cooked ham, sausage or mortadella are often added to the meat, as well as milk-soaked bread to lighten it. There is nearly always a little grated Parmesan and often herbs or spices. Both meatloaf and meatballs are cooked slowly, often with a little wine or milk to soften them.

Granatine al Marsala

MEAT PATTIES IN MARSALA SAUCE

Except for the Tuscans, who eat enor- mous T-bone steaks, Italians are not fond of beef. This is probably why they have dozens of versions of the meatloaf and meatball. I like to accompany this one with small onions in yellow pepper sauce (page 136).

SERVES 6

2 slices of coarse-textured white bread, crusts removed

240 ml / 8 fl oz / 1 cup milk

900 g / 2 lb lean minced (ground) beef

2 eggs, size 5 (US medium)

90 g / 3 oz / ¾ cup freshly grated Parmesan cheese

180 g / 6 oz cooked ham, finely chopped

salt and pepper

90 g / 3 oz / 6 tbsp unsalted butter

3 tbsp chopped fresh rosemary

120 g / 4 oz / 1 cup flour

120 ml / 4 fl oz / ½ cup dry Marsala wine

Soak the bread in the milk for 10 minutes. Squeeze out any excess milk and crumble the bread.

In a bowl combine the beef, eggs, Par- mesan, bread and ham. Season with salt and pepper. Mix until very well blended.

Using a wooden spoon, cream half the butter until soft and stir in the chopped rosemary. Divide the meat and rosemary butter into 12 portions. Press a portion of rosemary butter into the middle of each portion of meat and roll into a ball. Press to flatten and dredge the patties with a little flour, shaking off the excess.

In a frying pan heat the rest of the butter. Cook the patties for 2 minutes on each side. Add the Marsala, lower the heat and cook for a further 5 minutes, carefully turning the patties once.

Arrange the patties on a warm platter, coat with the sauce and serve at once.

Involtini al Pomodoro

VEAL ROLLS IN TOMATO SAUCE

Served with the mushroom risotto on page 51 or the potato and onion mould (page 76), this is a useful dish for guests because the veal rolls can be prepared well in advance and reheated in their sauce.

SERVES 6

180 g / 6 oz cooked ham, chopped

1 tbsp chopped fresh rosemary

● **Beef Patties with Mint and Orange,** ●
Veal Rolls in Tomato Sauce

*18 thin veal escalopes (scaloppine), about
600 g / 1¼ lb total*

15 g / ½ oz / 1 tbsp unsalted butter

2 tbsp extra virgin olive oil

2 tbsp flour

360 ml / 12 fl oz / 1½ cups dry white wine

*600 g / 1¼ lb plum tomatoes, peeled and put
through a food mill*

salt and pepper

Combine the ham with the chopped
rosemary. Flatten the slices of veal with
a meat pounder. Lay the slices of veal flat.
Divide the ham and rosemary mixture
among them, putting it in the middle.
Roll up the veal and secure with wooden
cocktail sticks.

In a large frying pan heat the butter
and oil over moderate heat. Add the veal
rolls and brown all over for about 10
minutes. Sprinkle with the flour and add
the wine, stirring well. Continue
cooking until most of the wine has evaporated. Add the tomatoes, season with
salt and pepper and stir. Cover the pan,
lower the heat and simmer gently for
about 20 minutes.

Transfer the veal rolls to a warm
serving platter, spoon over the sauce and
serve.

Maiale alle Mandorle

ROAST PORK IN ALMOND SAUCE

This method of roasting makes the
pork very tender, and the milk and
almonds add a very subtle flavour.

SERVES 6

*1 loin of pork, about 1.8 kg / 4 lb, chined (cut
between the backbone and the meat)*

90 g / 3 oz prosciutto, chopped

4 tbsp chopped blanched almonds

3 tbsp fine dry breadcrumbs (page 132)

salt and pepper

10 fresh bay leaves

butter for the pan

1 small onion, chopped

360 ml / 12 fl oz / 1½ cups milk

Make small incisions in the meat and stuff
them with the chopped prosciutto.
Process the almonds and breadcrumbs in
a blender with salt and pepper to taste
and spread all over the pork. Arrange
the bay leaves between the meat and the
chine bone (backbone). Tie the meat and
bone together very firmly.

Place the pork in a buttered pan and
roast in a preheated 180°C/350°F/gas
4 oven for 1½ hours. Lower the temperature to 160°C/325°F/gas 3, add the
onion and milk to the pan and roast a
further 1 hour. Take out the meat and
carve it, discarding the bone. Arrange
the slices on a platter and keep warm.

Pour the entire contents of the pan
into a blender, scraping carefully. Purée
and, if too thick, add more milk to make
a smooth sauce. Heat in a small saucepan,
stirring constantly. Coat the sliced meat
with the sauce and serve at once.

Manzo al Prezzemolo

BOILED BEEF IN PARSLEY SAUCE

This sauce is also excellent on boiled
chicken, hard-boiled eggs, asparagus, and globe artichokes. I usually make
a double quantity, to serve with the beef
as well as one of the vegetables and some
simply boiled rice (see page 50), to make
a whole meal. I would also serve the
strained broth in cups, or keep it frozen
for another use.

SERVES 6

*1 piece of topside (top round) of beef, about
1.2 kg / 2½ lb*

1 onion

1 carrot

1 celery stalk

15 g / ½ oz / 1 tbsp unsalted butter

2 tbsp flour

juice of 1 lemon

2 egg yolks, beaten

2 tbsp chopped fresh parsley

salt

In a large saucepan bring 3 litres/
5 pints/3 quarts of salted water to the
boil. Add the beef with the peeled onion,
carrot and celery. As soon as the water
returns to the boil, turn down the heat
as low as possible. Skim the scum from
the surface, then cover and simmer very
gently for about 3 hours.

Remove the beef from the broth and
keep warm. Strain the broth.

In a heavy saucepan melt the butter
over moderate heat and stir in the flour.
Gradually add 240 ml/8 fl oz/1 cup of
the broth, stirring constantly. Add the
lemon juice. Bring to the boil and
simmer for about 2 minutes. Off the heat

add the egg yolks and parsley and mix well. Check the salt.

Slice the meat, arrange on a platter and spoon over the sauce. Serve very hot.

Medaglioni all'Arancia

VEAL MEDALLIONS WITH ORANGE

As the veal has to be cooked at the last minute, I prepare the orange ahead of time. I like to start with the rice ring with tarragon mayonnaise on page 26.

SERVES 6

1 orange

60 g / 2 oz / 4 tbsp unsalted butter

6 slices of veal fillet (tenderloin), 150 g / 5 oz each

salt and pepper

4 tbsp brandy

Using a vegetable peeler remove the zest from the orange and cut it into very fine julienne. Blanch in boiling water for a couple of minutes. Drain and set aside.

Remove all the white pith from the orange. Cut 6 slices from the widest part, each about 1 cm / ½ inch thick.

In a frying pan melt half the butter over moderate heat. Add the veal slices and cook for 2 minutes. Season with salt and pepper. Turn and cook the other side for 2 minutes.

Pour off the cooking fat. Add the brandy, the rest of the butter in small pieces and the orange rind julienne. Cover with a lid and cook for about 2 minutes on low heat.

Arrange the veal medallions on a warm serving plate. Put a julienne of orange on each medallion. Pour the sauce over the meat and serve immediately.

Orata in Cartoccio

BAKED WRAPPED SEA BREAM (PORGY)

The fish can be cleaned ahead of time and chilled for a couple of hours before cooking it. The sauce can also be prepared in advance. Serve with cardoons flavoured with anchovies (page 129).

SERVES 6

6 medium-size ripe tomatoes, peeled and diced

salt and pepper

1 sea bream (porgy), about 1.8 kg / 4 lb

30 g / 1 oz / 2 tbsp unsalted butter

2 tbsp chopped fresh flat-leaf (Italian) parsley

4 tbsp extra virgin olive oil

juice of 1 lemon

Sprinkle the diced tomatoes with salt and leave to drain in a colander for about 1 hour.

Clean and scale the fish. Rinse under cold running water and pat dry with paper towels.

COOKING FISH IN PAPER

Fish is often cooked in paper or foil because the wrapping keeps it moist and seals the flavours in. Until recently, greaseproof or parchment paper was always used, but fish now appears wrapped in foil. Paper, however, has great advantages because it is porous and, as it expands, it looks more elegant when served. The fish parcel is opened at table to keep in all the aroma until the last moment. Meat is never wrapped because it tends to get tough.

Cream the butter with 1 tbsp parsley and a little salt and pepper. Spread the mixture inside the fish.

Whisk the oil, lemon juice and the rest of the parsley together. Brush a sheet of foil with some of the oil mixture. Place the fish on to the foil and pour the rest of the oil mixture over it. Cover with the tomatoes. Wrap the foil around the fish, sealing well.

Put the wrapped fish in a roasting pan and bake in a preheated 180°C / 350°F / gas 4 oven for about 30 minutes.

Transfer the foil parcel to a platter and open at the table.

Orata al Pomodoro

RED SNAPPER WITH TOMATO SAUCE

SERVES 6

3 tbsp balsamic vinegar

4 tbsp extra virgin olive oil

3 sprigs of fresh rosemary

1 red snapper, weighing about 2.1 kg / 4½ lb, cleaned

salt and pepper

900 g / 2 lb plum tomatoes, peeled, or drained canned tomatoes, chopped

Mix the vinegar with the oil. Dip the sprigs of rosemary in the mixture and put them into the cavity of the fish. Add a sprinkle of salt and pepper.

Brush a baking dish with the remaining oil and vinegar mixture. Lay the fish in the dish, cover with the chopped tomatoes and sprinkle with salt and pepper. Cook in a preheated 180°C / 350°F / gas 4 oven until the flesh of the fish will flake easily when tested with a fork, about 30 minutes. Brush it often with the drippings.

Arrange the fish on a platter and serve.

Pesce al Finocchio

MACKEREL FILLETS WITH FENNEL

You can use fish fillets of any kind for this recipe. I usually like to serve this just with baked potatoes, but you could try the small onions with grapes on page 135.

SERVES 6

4 tbsp extra virgin olive oil

6 mackerel fillets, 240 g / 8 oz each

salt and pepper

120 ml / 4 fl oz / ½ cup dry white wine

1 tbsp fennel seeds

1 tbsp fine dry breadcrumbs (page 132)

45 g / 1½ oz / 3 tbsp unsalted butter

juice of ½ lemon

lemon quarters for serving

a small bunch of fresh parsley

Pour the oil into a pan large enough to hold all the fillets. Arrange the fillets in the pan and season them with salt and pepper. Add the wine and sprinkle with the fennel seeds. Cook over moderate heat for about 10 minutes.

Carefully remove the cooked fillets and arrange them on a serving dish. Keep warm. Stir the breadcrumbs, butter and lemon juice into the cooking juices and simmer for a couple of minutes. The sauce should not be too thick.

Spoon the sauce over the fillets. Garnish with the lemon quarters and parsley and serve at once.

Palombe allo Spiedo

PIGEONS ON THE SPIT

When cooked over charcoal, squab pigeons are very tasty, but their meat tends to dry even when wrapped in bacon, so they need to be brushed with oil very frequently. If using a spit in an oven, preheat it to 180°C / 350°F / gas 4.

SERVES 6

3 young wood pigeons (squabs), preferably wild

9 fresh sage leaves

3 thin slices of pancetta

120 ml / 4 fl oz / ½ cup extra virgin olive oil

salt

240 ml / 8 fl oz / 1 cup good red wine

● **Mackerel Fillets with Fennel** ●

1 tbsp red wine vinegar

6 slices of wholewheat bread, toasted

Fill the pigeons with the sage leaves and wrap them in the pancetta slices. Thread the pigeons on to a spit.

Place a roasting pan in the coals to collect the juices that fall from the birds. Set the spit in place and cook, occasionally brushing the birds with a little olive oil.

After 30 minutes, season the birds with a little salt and add the wine and vinegar to the cooking juices. While the spit is turning, the wine will bubble and slowly reduce. Cook for a further 30 minutes.

When the pigeons are ready, cut them in half. Place half a pigeon on each slice of toast and arrange on a warm platter. Stir the cooking juices well and spoon over the pigeons. Serve at once.

Pesce Spada Marinato

GRILLED MARINATED SWORDFISH

The fish requires very little grilling because it half-cooks in the lemon juice as it absorbs the flavours of the marinade. Other fish steaks such as tuna or salmon can be grilled in the same way, as can small whole fish like trout or red mullet. In the latter case, I put a sprig of fresh mint inside each fish. Boiled potatoes are the perfect accompaniment, because you can dress them with the rest of the marinade.

SERVES 6

juice of 3 lemons

120 ml / 4 fl oz / ½ cup extra virgin olive oil

2 tbsp chopped fresh mint

6 swordfish steaks, about 180 g / 6 oz each

salt and pepper

In a bowl whisk the lemon juice, olive oil and chopped mint together.

Arrange the swordfish slices in a large shallow dish, in one layer. Sprinkle with salt and pepper and pour the marinade over the fish. Cover and marinate for at least 6 hours, turning carefully once or twice.

Cook over charcoal or under a very hot grill (broiler) for 3 minutes on each side. Arrange on a warm serving dish, sprinkle with half the marinade and serve.

Petti di Pollo all'Uva

CHICKEN BREASTS WITH GRAPES

In autumn, when the garden is full of ripe grapes, we quite often have this dish. The slight acid in the grapes seems to bring out the flavour of the chicken, which I serve with potatoes with tuna and chives (page 141).

SERVES 6

450 g / 1 lb white or green seedless grapes

45 g / 1½ oz / 3 tbsp butter

2 tbsp extra virgin olive oil

6 chicken breasts (breast halves)

1 medium-size carrot, chopped

1 small onion, chopped

1 celery stalk, chopped

1 tbsp chopped fresh parsley

salt and pepper

120 ml / 4 fl oz / ½ cup dry white wine

juice of ½ lemon

Peel the grapes. If they are large, cut them in half.

In a frying pan heat the butter and oil. Add the chicken breasts and, turning occasionally, cook over high heat for about 10 minutes. After the first 5 minutes add the chopped carrot, onion, celery and parsley.

Season with salt and pepper. Lower the heat and add the white wine, lemon juice and grapes. Continue cooking, covered, until the wine has evaporated and the sauce thickened, about 20 minutes.

Arrange the chicken breasts on a warm serving plate, pour the sauce and grapes over them and serve immediately.

● **Chicken Breasts with Grapes** ●

Petto di Tacchino all'Arancia

TURKEY BREAST WITH ORANGE JUICE

When I prepare this quick and easy dish for a more elegant dinner, I add caramelized orange zest to the sauce. To make this, cut the pared zest of one orange into narrow strips and caramelize in 90 g / 3 oz / 7 tbsp sugar, melted over moderate heat in a small saucepan until golden. Drain the zest and add it to the sauce with the butter after flaming the brandy.

SERVES 6

boneless piece of turkey breast, about 900 g / 2 lb

salt and pepper

90 g / 3 oz / 6 tbsp unsalted butter, softened

juice of 2 oranges

juice of $\frac{1}{2}$ lemon

3 tbsp brandy, warmed

Roll the turkey breast and tie it up firmly. Sprinkle liberally with salt and pepper and brush with some butter.

In a flameproof casserole melt 30 g / 1 oz / 2 tbsp butter over moderate heat. Add the turkey and, turning frequently, cook until slightly golden, about 10 minutes.

Pour the orange and lemon juices over the turkey breast. Continue cooking, covered, over very low heat for about 50 minutes, turning the turkey a couple of times.

Remove the turkey from the pan and keep warm. Pour the warm brandy into the pan and set it alight. Add the rest of the butter and stir the cooking juices well. Season if necessary.

Slice the turkey and arrange on a warm platter. Spoon on the sauce and serve immediately.

Piccioni Ripieni di Pere

PIGEONS STUFFED WITH PEAR

If you don't want to have a first course, serve with the red radicchio risotto on page 52, followed by the lemon tart on page 192. The same recipe can be used for quails, in which case you would need two for each person and the cooking time would be reduced to 1 hour.

SERVES 6

2 slices fresh coarse-textured bread

240 ml / 8 fl oz / 1 cup milk

60 g / 2 oz / 6 tbsp raisins

10 g / $\frac{1}{3}$ oz dried porcini mushrooms

90 g / 3 oz cooked ham, chopped

60 g / 2 oz / $\frac{2}{3}$ cup pine nuts

1 tbsp chopped fresh rosemary

1 tbsp chopped fresh sage

1 egg, size 5 (US medium)

salt and pepper

$\frac{1}{2}$ firm dessert pear

3 young wood pigeons (squabs)

3 thin slices of pancetta, about 30 g / 1 oz total

15 g / $\frac{1}{2}$ oz / 1 tbsp butter

2 tbsp extra virgin olive oil

240 ml / 8 fl oz / 1 cup dry white wine

Soak the bread in the milk for about 10 minutes, then squeeze dry. Soak the raisins in warm water to cover for 30 minutes; drain. Soak the mushrooms in lukewarm water to cover for 30 minutes; squeeze dry and chop.

To make the stuffing, in a bowl combine the raisins, mushrooms, bread, ham, pine nuts, rosemary, sage and egg. Season with salt and pepper. Mix very well. Peel the pear half and cut it into three pieces.

Fill each pigeon with a slice of pear and one-third of the stuffing. Wrap a slice of pancetta around each bird and truss.

In a baking pan heat the butter and oil. Arrange the pigeons in it and transfer to a preheated 180°C / 350°F / gas 4 oven. Roast for 1½ hours, turning the pigeons every 15 minutes and basting occasionally with wine, using half of it.

Remove the pan from the oven. Cut the pigeons in half and arrange on a platter. Keep warm. Over moderate heat deglaze the cooking juices with the rest of the wine, scraping the pan well, and reduce a little. Spoon over the pigeons and serve.

Pollo all'Alloro

CHICKEN ROASTED IN BAY LEAVES

The ancient Romans are said to have cooked poultry in bay leaves and the tradition has been carried on. The chicken will absorb the perfect amount of flavour from the bay leaves.

SERVES 6

1 roasting chicken, about 1.8 kg / 4 lb

salt and pepper

18 bay leaves, preferably fresh

6 tbsp extra virgin olive oil

● **Chicken Roasted in Bay Leaves,** ●
Chicken with Hazelnut Sauce (p. 112)

Pollo in Casseruola

CASSEROLE OF CHICKEN WITH ONIONS AND CARROTS

This family dish can also be made very successfully with diced veal, sliced globe artichokes and peas. It becomes a one-course meal when served with the red radicchio risotto on page 52.

SERVES 6

1.8 kg / 4 lb chicken, in serving pieces

salt and pepper

6 tbsp extra virgin olive oil

120 g / 4 oz pancetta, thickly cut and diced

480 ml / 16 fl oz / 2 cups dry white wine

3 sprigs of fresh parsley, 2 sprigs of fresh rosemary, 3 bay leaves and 6 fresh sage leaves tied together

600 g / 1¼ lb small onions (pickling or pearl)

3 medium-size carrots, diced

Season the chicken with salt and pepper.

In a flameproof casserole heat half the oil. Add the pancetta and fry on moderate heat for a few minutes. Add the chicken pieces and fry until just golden, about 10 minutes. Add the wine and bunch of herbs. Cover and simmer over low heat for about 50 minutes.

Remove the chicken and boil to reduce the wine to 120 ml / 4 fl oz / ½ cup.

Meanwhile, heat the rest of the oil in a frying pan, add the onions, carrots and salt and pepper to taste and simmer over very low heat for 20 minutes. (You can keep the three ingredients separately in the refrigerator for about 3 hours but reheat, obviously, for longer.)

Return the chicken pieces to the casserole and add the vegetables. Cook for about 5 minutes. Discard the herbs and serve in the casserole.

Season the chicken inside and out with salt and pepper. Pour 1 tbsp oil into the cavity and insert 10 bay leaves. Put 4 bay leaves in between the legs and the body and 4 in between the wings and the body and tie the chicken firmly with a long length of kitchen string.

Pour the rest of the oil into a baking dish. Put the chicken in the dish and transfer to a preheated 180°C/350°F/ gas 4 oven. Basting occasionally, roast for 1½ hours. Turn the chicken four times.

Transfer to a warm serving dish, remove the string and all the bay leaves and serve.

Pollo al Ginepro

ROAST CHICKEN WITH JUNIPER

Although roast chicken seems very banal, it is one of the hardest things to cook successfully because it is so often either raw or dry. Romola, who has been helping me at Coltibuono for the last 30 years, prepares it this way. We generally serve it with the sliced baked potatoes with rosemary on page 141 and a salad with herbs (page 136).

SERVES 6

1 chicken, about 1.8 kg / 4 lb

6 tbsp extra virgin olive oil

1 tbsp chopped fresh rosemary

2 garlic cloves, chopped

5 fresh sage leaves, chopped

2 tbsp juniper berries, crushed

salt and pepper

1 lemon

120 ml / 4 fl oz / ½ cup dry white wine

Brush the chicken well with olive oil. In a small bowl mix the rosemary, garlic, sage and juniper berries with a little salt and pepper. Rub the chicken inside and out with the herb mixture. Put the lemon inside the chicken and truss it.

Pour the rest of the oil into a roasting pan and add the chicken. Transfer to a preheated 180°C / 350°F / gas 4 oven and roast for 1½ hours, basting and turning frequently.

Remove the pan from the oven and transfer the chicken to a hot platter. Keep warm. Skim the fat off the roasting juices, then deglaze with the wine and 2–3 tbsp of water over moderate heat, scraping the pan well. Carve the chicken and arrange on the platter. Pour over the sauce and serve immediately.

Pollo alle Nocciole

CHICKEN WITH HAZELNUT SAUCE

In the Middle Ages hazelnuts, almonds and walnuts were used a great deal in Italy for the preparation of savoury dishes. They totally disappeared for centuries, but recently a few recipes have been revived. I particularly like this combination with chicken.

SERVES 6

210 g / 7 oz / 1½ cups shelled hazelnuts

1.8 kg / 4 lb chicken, in serving pieces

salt and pepper

2 tbsp flour

45 g / 1½ oz / 3 tbsp unsalted butter

120 ml / 4 fl oz / ½ cup dry white wine

4 tbsp light chicken stock (page 216)

120 ml / 4 fl oz / ½ cup milk

Spread the nuts on a baking sheet and toast them in a preheated 180°C / 350°F / gas 4 oven for 5 minutes. Keep your eye on them because they can burn suddenly. Turn the nuts on to a coarse kitchen towel and rub to get rid of their skins while they are still hot. Chop finely and set aside.

POULTRY AND LAMB

Our chickens, guinea fowl and ducks are rather small: they seldom weigh as much as 1.8 kg / 4 lb and usually are about 1.2 kg / 2½ lb. Lamb is slaughtered very young, at about 12 kg / 25 lb, so the meat is very tender. Lamb is considered white meat and so is cooked for a long time. Italians would be very unwilling to eat rare lamb.

Season the chicken with salt and pepper and dredge lightly with flour. In a large frying pan melt the butter. Add the chicken and cook over moderate heat until golden, about 15 minutes. Add the wine and bring to the boil. Lower the heat to a gentle simmer and cover the pan. Cook for about 40 minutes.

Transfer the chicken to a platter and keep warm. Deglaze the cooking juices with the chicken stock, scraping the pan well. Add the milk and hazelnuts and simmer gently for a few minutes.

Spoon the sauce over the chicken and serve immediately.

Pollo al Vin Santo

ROAST CHICKEN IN VIN SANTO

The sweetish wine gives a pleasant and unusual flavour to the chicken.

SERVES 6

1 roasting chicken, about 1.8 kg / 4 lb

salt and pepper

2 tbsp extra virgin olive oil

15 g / ½ oz / 1 tbsp butter

120 ml / 4 fl oz / ½ cup Vin Santo or white vermouth

Truss the chicken and season with salt and pepper, rubbing it in well.

In a roasting pan heat the oil and butter. Add the chicken and cook over high heat until golden on all sides, about 10 minutes. Add half the Vin Santo. Transfer to a preheated 180°C / 350°F / gas 4 oven and roast for 1½ hours.

Remove the chicken from the pan and keep warm. Skim the fat off the roasting juices. Add the rest of the Vin Santo and deglaze over low heat, scraping the pan.

Carve the chicken and arrange the pieces on a warm platter. Pour the sauce over the chicken and serve piping hot.

Polpettine ai Capperi

MEATBALLS WITH CAPERS

The meatballs are quick and easy to make and the capers give them a unique flavour. For a one-course lunch or supper, serve with the aubergine (eggplant) salad on page 128.

SERVES 6

3 slices of coarse-textured white bread, crusts removed

240 ml / 8 fl oz / 1 cup milk

900 g / 2 lb minced (ground) beef

1 egg

1 tbsp chopped fresh chives

1 tbsp chopped fresh marjoram

3 tbsp capers in vinegar, drained

salt and pepper

4 tbsp flour

2 tbsp extra virgin olive oil

15 g / ½ oz / 1 tbsp butter

240 ml / 8 fl oz / 1 cup good red wine

Soak the bread in the milk for about 10 minutes. Drain and squeeze dry.

In a bowl combine the beef, bread, egg, chives, marjoram and capers. Season with salt and pepper. Work with your hands to blend the mixture well. Roll the meat into walnut-size balls. Dredge lightly in flour.

In a frying pan heat the oil and butter over moderate heat. Add the meatballs and brown on all sides, about 10 minutes. Pour in the wine. Lower the heat, cover and cook for a further 10 minutes, turning the meatballs from time to time.

Using a slotted spoon, transfer the meatballs to a warm platter. Boil the cooking juices until well reduced, then spoon over the meatballs. Serve at once.

Polpettone alle Erbe

HERBED PORK AND BEEF LOAF

Adding the milk halfway through the cooking time softens the meatloaf and provides enough sauce to serve it simply with potatoes with rosemary (page 141).

SERVES 6

2 slices of coarse-textured white bread, crusts removed

240 ml / 8 fl oz / 1 cup milk

450 g / 1 lb lean minced (ground) beef

450 g / 1 lb lean minced (ground) pork

120 g / 4 oz mortadella, chopped

1 egg and 1 egg yolk

4 tbsp chopped fresh chives

4 tbsp chopped fresh parsley

1 tbsp chopped fresh basil

1 tbsp chopped fresh marjoram

1 tbsp chopped fresh rosemary

1 bay leaf

salt and pepper

6 paper thin slices of pancetta or bacon

3 tbsp extra virgin olive oil

Soak the bread in the milk for about 10 minutes. Drain, reserving the milk, and squeeze dry.

In a bowl combine the beef, pork, mortadella, bread, egg, egg yolk, chives, parsley, basil, marjoram, rosemary and bay leaf. Season with salt and pepper. Knead well until blended. Shape into a loaf and cover with the pancetta.

Pour the oil into a roasting pan and place the meatloaf in the middle. Transfer to a preheated 180°C/350°F/gas 4 oven and bake, turning twice, for 20 minutes. Strain the milk through a fine sieve and pour into the roasting pan. Cook for 1 hour longer.

Transfer to a serving plate and allow to cool slightly. Meanwhile, boil to reduce the cooking juices. Slice the meatloaf, spoon over the sauce and serve.

PROSCIUTTO

The best known prosciutto comes from Parma and is labelled with a five-pointed ducal crown. Another prime prosciutto comes from San Daniele in Friuli. The prosciutto produced in Tuscany and Umbria is much saltier and not considered nearly as good. Wild boar prosciutto is cured in Tuscany in the area called the Maremma, between Siena and the coast.

Prosciutto Cotto al Miele

SWEET AND SOUR HAM

When I can find it, I use smoked ham for this recipe because it gives it a very subtle flavour. This goes very well with braised red cabbage with apples (page 132).

SERVES 6

30 g / 1 oz / 2 tbsp unsalted butter

6 fairly thick slices of cooked ham, 150 g / 5 oz each

*R*olled roasts are another great Italian favourite. The meat is rolled around anything from a flat omelette to sausagemeat, ham or mortadella to spinach or Swiss chard. The meat mustn't toughen with the slow cooking, so it is generally veal, turkey or chicken breast. Rolled roasts are excellent cold, so they often appear on buffet tables or at summer dinners.

Rolle' di Tacchino al Balsamico

ROLLED TURKEY BREAST IN BALSAMIC SAUCE

The same recipe can be prepared with a slice of veal, or chicken breasts. Depending on the season, I serve this with artichokes stuffed with mozzarella (page 128) or chickpeas with rosemary (page 132).

SERVES 6

---

1 boneless piece of turkey breast, about 400 g / 14 oz

---

120 g / 4 oz uncooked sweet Italian sausage, casing removed and crumbled

---

1 egg, lightly beaten

---

3 tbsp freshly grated Parmesan cheese

---

1 tbsp juniper berries, crushed

---

10 fresh sage leaves

---

120 g / 4 oz mortadella, thinly sliced

---

15 g / ½ oz / 1 tbsp unsalted butter

---

2 tbsp extra virgin olive oil

---

4 tbsp white wine vinegar

---

4 tbsp light meat stock (page 216)

---

6 tbsp good quality honey

In a large frying pan melt the butter over moderate heat. Add the ham slices and cook for 2 minutes on each side. Add the

● **Sweet and Sour Ham (p. 113)** ●

vinegar and stock. Cover the pan and cook over low heat for about 10 minutes.

Spread the honey on the ham, cover again and allow the flavours to blend for a couple more minutes. Transfer to a warm serving platter and serve immediately.

salt and pepper

120 ml / 4 fl oz / ½ cup dry white wine

4 tbsp good balsamic vinegar

Split open the turkey breast and flatten it gently with a meat pounder to 'butterfly' it.

In a bowl combine the sausagemeat, egg, Parmesan and juniper berries. Mix well. Cover the turkey breast with a layer of this mixture, but do not go too near the edges. Arrange the sage leaves on top and place a layer of mortadella over them. Carefully roll up the turkey breast and tie with kitchen string.

Heat the butter and oil in a roasting pan. Put in the turkey breast and season with salt and pepper. Transfer the pan to a preheated 180°C/350°F/gas 4 oven and roast for about 1 hour, turning occasionally and gradually adding the wine and a little water as necessary to keep the cooking juices moist.

Remove the turkey from the pan and keep warm. Add the balsamic vinegar and deglaze over low heat, scraping the pan well.

Slice the turkey and arrange on a warm platter. Spoon over the sauce and serve immediately.

SAUSAGES

*I*n northern and central Italy pork sausages are always sweet, that is without chili pepper or other strong seasoning – just a little black pepper. Occasionally veal is mixed with the pork. Hot spicy sausages flavoured with garlic and fennel are produced in the south.

Salsicce in Crosta

SAUSAGES IN PASTRY

This is an elegant way of serving sausages for dinner. They can be wrapped either in puff pastry or bread dough. The vinegar makes the sausages lighter and less greasy. I like to serve them with the onions stuffed with ham (page 133).

MAKES 12

300 g / 10 oz puff pastry (page 218)

2 tbsp extra virgin olive oil

12 uncooked sweet Italian sausages, about 60 g / 2 oz each

3 tbsp white wine vinegar

1 egg yolk, beaten, to glaze

Roll out the pastry dough until it is very thin, about 2 mm/¹⁄₁₆ inch, and cut it into 15- x 10-cm/6- x 4-inch rectangles.

In a frying pan heat the oil. Add the sausages and cook them over moderate heat for about 3 minutes, turning a couple of times. Pour the fat out of the pan and add the vinegar. Cook until the vinegar has completely evaporated, then leave the sausages to cool.

Place a sausage on each pastry rectangle and wrap them up, sealing the edges. Arrange on a baking sheet. Brush with beaten egg yolk and transfer to a preheated 180°C/350°F/gas 4 oven. Bake until just golden, about 10 minutes.

Serve on a warm platter.

Saraghi in Teglia

SEA BREAM (PORGY) IN WINE WITH PORCINI

'*S*araghi' are a delicate white fish typical of the Mediterranean. This recipe works equally well using sea bream (porgy) or sea bass.

You can keep the water in which the porcini were soaking for use in a soup, sauce, or meat or chicken stock. Strain the water through a fine sieve first. You can also freeze and keep it for many months.

SERVES 6

6 g / ¼ oz dried porcini mushrooms

6 small sea bream (porgy), about 300 g / 10 oz each

1 tbsp white wine vinegar

6 small sprigs of fresh rosemary

3 tbsp flour

45 g / 1½ oz / 3 tbsp butter

6 anchovy fillets in oil, drained

240 ml / 8 fl oz / 1 cup dry white wine

juice of 1 lemon

salt and pepper

2 tbsp chopped fresh parsley

Soak the mushrooms in water to cover for about 30 minutes. Drain, squeeze dry and chop.

Clean and rinse the fish. Pat dry with paper towels. Sprinkle the insides with a few drops of vinegar and insert a sprig of rosemary in each one. Dredge lightly with flour.

Heat the butter in a wide pan large enough to hold all the fish. Cook the fish on each side for 5 minutes. Add the mushrooms and the anchovy fillets. Pour the wine over and cook for a further 3 minutes.

Sprinkle the fish with the lemon juice and season with salt and pepper. Arrange the fish on a warm platter. Stir the parsley into the cooking juices, boil until reduced and spoon over the fish. Serve at once.

SMALL FISH

*W*e eat a lot of what Italians call blue fish – sardines, anchovies and mackerel. In the Mediterranean these fish are very small. Sardines, for example, are never more than 10–13 cm/4–5 inches long. Because they are so small they are always opened and boned. The head is removed but usually the tail is left on. They are often stuffed with herbs and deep-fried.

Sardine Ripiene

BAKED STUFFED SARDINES

*S*tuffed sardines are often breaded and fried in olive oil. They are crisp and delicious. Vary the stuffing by adding chopped anchovy fillets and capers or chopped spinach sautéed in a little oil.

SERVES 6

4 slices of fresh coarse-textured bread, crusts removed

240 ml / 8 fl oz / 1 cup milk

1.8 kg / 4 lb fresh sardines

2 tbsp chopped fresh parsley

1 egg yolk, lightly beaten

90 g / 3 oz / ¾ cup freshly grated Parmesan cheese

1 tsp grated nutmeg

salt and pepper

120 ml / 4 fl oz / ½ cup extra virgin olive oil

● **Cuttlefish Stuffed with Prawns,** ●
Fresh Tuna in Caper Sauce (p. 120)

Soak the bread in the milk for about 10 minutes. Drain and squeeze dry.

Scale the sardines and remove their heads. Slit them open almost to their tails; gut and remove the backbone. Rinse and pat dry.

In a bowl combine the bread, parsley, egg yolk, Parmesan and nutmeg. Season with salt and pepper. Stir well. Divide the mixture among the sardines. Reshape them, overlapping the two flaps, and press to seal in the filling.

Lightly oil an ovenproof dish and arrange the sardines in it. Season with a little salt and pour over the rest of the oil. Transfer to a preheated 200°C/ 400°F/gas 6 oven and bake for about 15 minutes.

Serve piping hot.

Seppie Ripiene di Gamberetti

CUTTLEFISH STUFFED WITH PRAWNS

Cuttlefish can also be stuffed with chopped spinach and a little sausagemeat or with radicchio and crisply fried chopped bacon. They may be prepared about 3 hours ahead of time and cooked at the last minute. Squid can also be used.

SERVES 6

12 cuttlefish, each about 7.5 cm / 3 inches long

3 tbsp fine dry breadcrumbs (page 132)

3 tbsp freshly grated Parmesan cheese

1 egg, beaten

2 tbsp chopped fresh parsley

210 g / 7 oz raw peeled small prawns or shrimp

salt and pepper

120 ml / 4 fl oz / ½ cup extra virgin olive oil

18 large prawns or shrimp in shell, cooked

Pull the tentacles from the cuttlefish; they will come away with the insides. Cut off the tentacles above the eyes. Squeeze out the tough beak from the middle of the tentacles. Remove the thin bone from the sac. Rinse well and dry on paper towels. Chop the tentacles.

In a bowl combine the breadcrumbs, Parmesan, beaten egg, parsley, chopped tentacles and small prawns or shrimp. Stir very well and season with salt and pepper. Stuff the cuttlefish bodies with the mixture, but do not make them too full or they will burst while cooking. Either sew the ends together or thread a wooden cocktail stick through each one to seal.

Oil an ovenproof dish and arrange the cuttlefish in it in one layer. Pour the rest of the oil over them. Transfer to a preheated 180°C/350°F/gas 4 oven and bake for about 20 minutes.

Transfer to a platter and pour the cooking juices over the cuttlefish. Garnish with the prawns or shrimp in shell and serve.

Spezzatino ai Piselli

SAUTE OF VEAL WITH PEAS

I often fill the risotto mould wrapped in prosciutto on page 50 with this veal for a buffet. It tastes as delicious as it looks.

SERVES 6

4 tbsp extra virgin olive oil

1 tbsp chopped onion

600 g / 1¼ lb ripe plum tomatoes, peeled and diced

15 g / ½ oz / 1 tbsp unsalted butter

900 g / 2 lb boned shoulder of veal, cut into 4-cm / 1½-inch cubes

240 ml / 8 fl oz / 1 cup dry white wine

600 g / 1¼ lb / 4 cups shelled fresh peas (or use frozen thawed peas)

salt and pepper

1 tbsp chopped fresh flat-leaf (Italian) parsley

In a flameproof casserole heat 2 tbsp olive oil. Add the onion and cook over low heat until translucent. Add the tomatoes with their juice and continue cooking, covered, over low heat for a further 10 minutes.

In a frying pan heat the butter and the rest of the oil. Add the veal and, stirring frequently, cook over high heat until browned on all sides, about 5 minutes. Add the wine and deglaze the juices, scraping the pan well. Cook for a further 2 minutes.

Transfer the contents of the pan to the casserole and stir. Cover and cook over low heat for 1 hour, gradually adding a little water to keep the tomato sauce slightly moist.

Add the peas and cook for a further 10 minutes. Season to taste.

Pour into a deep dish, sprinkle with the parsley and serve.

Spiedini di Agnello alle Erbe

GRILLED LAMB ON SKEWERS

Wherever there is a flock of sheep there is a recipe for skewered lamb, but this particular one comes from Arezzo. It is essential to marinate the lamb for about 6 hours even though the meat is tender. Lamb is never older than 3 months in Italy; after that it is considered too old and tough to eat.

SERVES 6

3 tbsp white wine vinegar

3 garlic cloves, chopped

3 tbsp chopped fresh mint

2 tbsp chopped fresh rosemary

1 tbsp fresh oregano leaves, or 1 tsp dried oregano

6 tbsp extra virgin olive oil

salt and pepper

900 g / 2 lb boneless lamb, cut into 2.5-cm / 1-inch cubes

6 slices of coarse bread, diced

In a bowl combine the vinegar, garlic, herbs, oil and salt and pepper. Mix well. Add the lamb cubes and stir. Cover and

● **Grilled Lamb on Skewers** ●
**Roast Veal with Herbs
and Lemon Sauce (p. 120)**

leave to marinate for about 6 hours in a cool place, turning the meat from time to time. Thread the meat on to 6 skewers, alternating with the pieces of bread, pushing the pieces close together to avoid drying while cooking.

Lay the skewers over a rectangular pan, so the meat is suspended. Place under a preheated grill (broiler) and cook for 10 minutes, turning frequently and basting with the marinade. Arrange on a platter and serve.

Stinco alle Erbe

ROAST VEAL WITH HERBS AND LEMON SAUCE

Golden and shiny, this is a very elegant roast to present whole at table if the man of the house is a good carver. Be very careful not to let the sauce boil because it is thickened with egg yolk. Try to use all fresh herbs for the stuffing.

SERVES 6

2 tbsp chopped fresh rosemary

1 tbsp chopped fresh thyme

1 tbsp chopped fresh sage

1 tbsp chopped fresh mint

2 garlic cloves, chopped

1 leg of veal, shank end, about 1.8 kg / 4 lb

salt and pepper

2 tbsp flour

15 g / ½ oz / 1 tbsp butter

2 tbsp extra virgin olive oil

*240 ml / 8 fl oz / 1 cup dry white wine
2 egg yolks*

2 tbsp lemon juice

grated zest of 1 lemon

120 ml / 4 fl oz / ½ cup light meat stock (page 216)

2 tbsp chopped fresh flat-leaf (Italian) parsley

In a small bowl combine the herbs, except the parsley, with the garlic and stir well. Using a sharp knife make 3 slits along the length of the meat all the way to the bone. Fill the slits with the mixed herbs and garlic. Tie the meat together firmly with kitchen string. Season with salt and pepper and dredge lightly with flour.

In a roasting pan heat the butter and oil over moderate heat. Add the veal and transfer to a preheated 160°C / 325°F / gas 3 oven. Roast for 4 hours, turning occasionally and gradually adding two-thirds of the wine.

In a bowl combine the egg yolks, lemon juice, zest and stock. Stir well.

Remove the veal from the pan and keep warm. Deglaze the cooking juices with the rest of the wine, scraping the pan well. Add the mixture from the bowl and thicken slightly over very low heat, stirring, making sure that the sauce does not boil or the egg will curdle. Sprinkle with the parsley.

Carve the meat and arrange on a platter. Coat with the sauce and serve piping hot.

Tonno Fresco ai Capperi

FRESH TUNA IN CAPER SAUCE

The caper and anchovy sauce can be prepared ahead of time and reheated. However, the fish steaks should be coated with breadcrumbs just before

frying or they get soggy. This dish cannot be served cold because it must be crisp.

SERVES 6

120 g / 4 oz / 1 cup flour

2 eggs, lightly beaten

180 g / 6 oz / 2 cups fine dry breadcrumbs (page 132)

6 fresh tuna steaks, about 240 g / 8 oz each

salt and pepper

120 ml / 4 fl oz / ½ cup extra virgin olive oil

6 anchovy fillets in oil, drained and chopped

2 tbsp capers in vinegar, drained and chopped

1 tbsp chopped fresh flat-leaf (Italian) parsley

4 tbsp white wine vinegar

120 ml / 4 fl oz / ½ cup dry white wine

15 g / ½ oz / 1 tbsp butter

Put the flour, beaten egg and breadcrumbs in three separate soup plates. Season the fish steaks with salt and pepper. Coat in the flour, shaking off the excess, then dip in the egg and finally coat with the breadcrumbs, pressing them on well. Set aside.

In a small saucepan heat 2 tbsp oil. Add the anchovies, capers, parsley and vinegar. Stir until the liquid has evaporated. Dilute with the white wine and boil to reduce for a few minutes. Stir in the butter. Remove from the heat and keep warm.

In a heavy frying pan heat the rest of the oil. Add the fish steaks and fry on each side for about 2 minutes on moderate heat.

Arrange the fish on a warm serving plate and season with pepper. Dot each steak with the caper sauce and serve at once.

Tonno in Umido

TUNA FISH WITH OLIVES

This is a very tasty family dish that we all love with the polenta on page 219, which turns it into a whole meal.

SERVES 6

---

4 tbsp extra virgin olive oil

---

3 medium-size onions, coarsely chopped

---

600 g / 1¼ lb plum tomatoes, peeled and chopped (or use canned with their liquid)

---

salt and pepper

---

1 tbsp dried oregano

---

180 g / 6 oz / 1 cup green olives, stoned

---

2 tbsp capers in vinegar, drained

---

600 g / 1¼ lb canned tuna fish

Heat the oil in a large frying pan, add the onions and sauté very gently over low heat for about 20 minutes until translucent. Add the tomatoes and season with salt, pepper and oregano. Cover and simmer for a further 20 minutes.

Add the olives, capers and tuna, shaking the pan. Cook for 5 minutes or until there is no excess liquid on the bottom of the pan.

Transfer the tuna and sauce to a warm serving plate and serve at once.

VEGETABLE ACCOMPANIMENTS FOR FISH

There are very few vegetables we consider suitable to serve with fish. These are primarily boiled potatoes, courgettes (zucchini) and carrots. Only very occasionally are other vegetables served, and they would never have strong flavours, as artichokes or asparagus do. Italian fish knives are always silver because steel could spoil the flavour of the fish.

Torta di Alici Gratinate all'Origano

BAKED FRESH ANCHOVIES WITH BREADCRUMBS

You can also prepare this with sardines if you can find very small ones.

SERVES 6

1.2 kg / 2½ lb fresh anchovies

---

3 garlic cloves, finely chopped

---

3 tbsp chopped fresh parsley

---

2 tbsp dried oregano

---

90 g / 3 oz / 1 cup fine dry breadcrumbs (page 132)

---

6 tbsp extra virgin olive oil

---

salt and pepper

---

juice of 2 lemons

Gut the anchovies and remove their heads, tails and backbones. Rinse and place flat on paper towels to dry.

In a cup mix the garlic with the chopped parsley, oregano and breadcrumbs.

Choose an ovenproof dish in which you can make 2 layers of anchovies. Oil the dish and make a layer of anchovies on the bottom. Sprinkle with half the breadcrumb mixture. Season with salt and pepper and sprinkle over half the rest of the oil and lemon juice. Make another layer in the same way.

Transfer the baking dish to a preheated 180°C/350°F/gas 4 oven and bake for 30 minutes.

Allow to cool and serve just warm.

Trance di Salmone al Limone

BAKED SALMON SLICES WITH FENNEL AND LEMON

If you like your vegetables well cooked, fry them in a little oil before baking. The fennel can be replaced by finely sliced globe artichokes or button mushrooms. Follow with the coffee ricotta with honey fingers (page 179).

SERVES 6

---

3 tbsp extra virgin olive oil

---

2 medium-size fennel bulbs, sliced paper-thin

---

salt and pepper

---

6 slices of salmon fillet, about 240 g / 8 oz each

---

240 ml / 8 fl oz / 1 cup dry white wine

---

3 lemons, sliced paper-thin

---

1 tbsp chopped fresh flat-leaf (Italian) parsley

Pour the oil into an ovenproof dish and arrange the fennel slices in it. Season with salt and pepper. Cover with the salmon slices and pour the white wine over the fish. Cover the fish with the lemon slices. Sprinkle with parsley.

Cover the dish with foil, folding it down around the sides. Transfer to a preheated 200°C/400°F/gas 6 oven and bake for 15 minutes.

Carefully transfer the fish, fennel and lemon to a serving platter and keep warm. Pour the cooking juices into a small saucepan and boil to reduce to about 120 ml / 4 fl oz / ½ cup. Pour over the fish and serve immediately.

Orata Fredda al Pomodoro

COLD SEA BREAM (PORGY) IN TOMATO SAUCE

This summer dish can be prepared well in advance. You can substitute sea bream with sardines.

SERVES 6

---

3 tbsp seedless raisins

---

6 small sea bream (porgy), about 300 g / 10 oz each

---

120 ml / 4 fl oz / ½ cup extra virgin olive oil

---

2 medium-size onions, thinly sliced

---

2 tbsp flour

---

salt and pepper

---

4 tbsp dry white wine

---

2 garlic cloves

---

900 g / 2 lb ripe plum tomatoes, peeled and put through a food mill

---

1 tsp dried thyme

---

1 tsp sugar

½ tsp saffron threads (optional)

In a bowl soak the raisins in lukewarm water for about 30 minutes; drain.

Clean and rinse the fish. Pat dry with paper towels.

In a frying pan large enough to hold all the fish, heat 2 tbsp of the oil over moderate heat. Add the onions and cook until translucent. Dredge the fish with flour and put them in the pan. Cook for 5 minutes, then turn the fish over carefully and cook for a further 5 minutes. Season with salt and pepper and pour the wine over the fish. Cook for 2 minutes.

Taking care not to break them, transfer the fish and onions to a serving dish. Leave to cool.

In a medium-size saucepan heat the rest of the oil. Add the garlic and fry until golden. Remove the garlic and add the tomato purée, thyme and sugar. Season with salt and pepper. If using the saffron dissolve it in 2 tbsp warm water and add it to the pan. Stir well and bring to the boil. Cover the pan and cook gently for about 50 minutes to reduce to a fairly thick sauce.

Add the raisins to the tomato sauce. Stir, cover and cook for 2 minutes.

Spoon the sauce over the fish and leave to cool. Serve cold, but not chilled.

Triglie coi Funghi al Cartoccio

WRAPPED RED MULLET WITH MUSHROOMS

Cooking fish in paper or foil is very popular in Italy. The paper keeps in all the flavour and aroma, and if you are dieting you can add little or no oil.

SERVES 6

---

6 red mullet or trout, about 300 g / 10 oz each

---

3 tbsp extra virgin olive oil

---

300 g / 10 oz button mushrooms, thinly sliced

---

salt and pepper

---

6 tbsp dry white wine

---

2 tbsp chopped fresh flat-leaf (Italian) parsley

---

6 slices of pancetta, about 90 g / 3 oz total

Clean and scale the red mullet, then rinse and pat dry.

In a frying pan heat 2 tbsp of oil. Add the mushrooms and sauté over moderate heat for 5 minutes. Season with salt and pepper. Add the wine, sprinkle with the parsley and cook until the wine is evaporated. Remove from the heat.

Brush 6 pieces of greaseproof paper or foil with oil. Each must be large enough to wrap a fish. Fill the mullet with the mushrooms and wrap a slice of pancetta around each fish. Sprinkle with pepper and place a fish in the middle of each piece of foil. Wrap up well so that the juices cannot escape. Arrange the parcels on a baking sheet.

Transfer to a preheated 180°C / 350°F / gas 4 oven and bake for 15 minutes. Arrange the parcels on a platter and serve at once.

Trota al Cartoccio

GRILLED WRAPPED TROUT

The foil keeps in the juices and flavour, making the fish very tender.

SERVES 6

---

3 tbsp extra virgin olive oil

---

12 sprigs of fresh rosemary

---

3 tbsp lemon juice

---

6 trout, about 300 g / 10 oz each, cleaned

---

salt and pepper

Cut out 6 sheets of foil, each large enough to wrap a fish, and brush with oil. Dip 6 rosemary sprigs in the lemon juice, then put one inside each trout. Place the trout on the foil, add the rest of the oil and top with the rest of the rosemary sprigs. Season with salt and pepper. Wrap well and seal. Place the parcels on a preheated hot charcoal grill and cook for 6 minutes on each side.

● **Cold Sea Bream (Porgy) in Tomato Sauce,** ●
Grilled Wrapped Trout

I Contorni

GREENS AND VEGETABLES

I sometimes think I could live solely on fresh greens and vegetables. If they were combined with pasta, I know I could. When my husband and I are at home alone, our usual lunch at least four times a week consists of a couple of raw and boiled vegetables which we season with extra virgin olive oil, salt and freshly ground pepper. And that's it. Now this might not sound very satisfying unless you keep in mind the variety and freshness of Italian vegetables and the quality of the condiments we use to dress them, especially our olive oil. More than anything, it is olive oil that can transform a simple vegetable into a delicious and healthy light lunch.

When I say olive oil I always mean extra virgin olive oil, extracted exclusively from the first cold pressing of hand-picked olives. As far as I am concerned no other kind of oil is worthy of fine food. Of course, this oil is the most expensive, but when you consider that a bottle containing some 75 cl/25 fl oz will be sufficient for dressing about 20 salads, each to serve six persons, it is well worth the money. The advantages it has in flavour are incalculable. It is also a monounsaturated fat, containing no cholesterol, and what price can be put on good health?

M y students often ask how they can distinguish high-quality from low-quality oils. Unfortunately it is difficult to tell a good olive oil from its label. The laws regulating the various categories are too broad to guarantee quality. The term 'extra virgin', which is the highest in the classification, means two things: (1) the oil was produced by mechanical cold, first pressing, that is, no chemicals were added to extract it from the olive; and (2) it has less than one percent acidity.

High acidity is what gives oil an unpleasant fatty taste that coats the palate. An oil that is close to one percent acidity will still taste quite fatty, and the best 'extra virgins' are under 0.5 percent acidity. Be aware, however, that chemically refined oils can be de-acidified by alkaline solutions and then 'rectified' for flavour and colour by the addition of some first-pressed oil.

● Tomatoes with Green Mayonnaise (p. 142) ●

'First pressing' means that the oil comes from the pressing of the fresh fruit, not from a second or even third pressing of the pulp, which can be the case in lesser oils. 'Cold-pressing' indicates the process was carried out without the application of heat, which can damage the oil.

In the last analysis, the only sure proof of a high-quality oil is in the tasting. I find the extra virgin olive oils from Tuscany, especially the ones made in Chianti, are the best to use as a condiment for seasoning salads and vegetables. These oils have a golden green colour and an uniquely fresh, fruity aroma and taste.

*W*hen I dress a salad I add to the extra virgin olive oil only wine vinegar and salt – no garlic or mustard or other seasoning. These, I always think – perhaps somewhat maliciously – are added in other countries to hide the taste of the local olive oil. We say that good vinegar is made from good wine. In the old days practically every household had a little wooden or earthenware barrel for vinegar. My father kept two in the basement of our house in Milan, one for white wine vinegar and one for red. Each contained a 'mother', a skin of bacteria that forms naturally when wine is allowed to oxidize. Whenever he had any left-over wine from the table, he would pour it into these containers and draw off the vinegar as needed from a tap at the bottom. Fine red wine vinegar is aged for at least a couple of years in oak barrels. This adds a roundness to its desirable acidic flavour.

Normally I do not use aromatic vinegars because I prefer to add fresh herbs to the salad itself. If, however, you want to enjoy the taste of a particular herb in your salad during the winter, it is easy to make your own herb vinegars. In summer just add some sprigs of fresh herbs – thyme, mint and tarragon work best – to a bottle of good wine vinegar and leave it to stand for a few weeks. Then filter them out and rebottle the clear herb vinegar.

You should dress a salad just before you are ready to eat it so that the leaves will remain crisp and not become soggy. The usual proportion for the dressing is one part vinegar to four parts of olive oil. Taste a leaf before serving. You will learn that different kinds of greens require more or less oil. Salt should be added to the vinegar, which helps to dissolve it, and lastly the olive oil.

Of course, the most important ingredient of any salad are the greens themselves. I enjoy the luxury of a large kitchen garden at Coltibuono so I can pick greens when they are small, not more than 4-5 cm / 1½-2 inches long, and perfectly tender. I like to mix several varieties of salad greens together with a bouquet of fresh herbs. I would never spoil their delicate taste by adding other vegetables such as carrots and tomatoes.

*D*uring the summer months when tomatoes are at their best, fragrant and fleshy, I serve them as a salad on their own, seasoned with salt and olive oil, but generally no vinegar as the tomatoes are acidic enough. (Sometimes I add a few drops of balsamic vinegar, whose sweetness blends nicely with the natural sweetness of the tomatoes.)

A delicious winter salad can be made of either raw bulb fennel or small raw artichokes. In both cases a little lemon juice added to the olive oil is better than vinegar. In autumn there is nothing better than a salad of raw, wild mushrooms. Sliced, fresh PORCINI (Boletus) are superb simply dressed with olive oil or combined with thin shavings of Parmesan cheese. My favourite wild mushrooms are OVOLI, AMANITA CAESAREA. Alas, their season is short and they are very rare. When the weather is right, OVOLI appear at the same time as the first white truffles. A salad of these two delicacies mixed together is divine.

In all seasons there are vegetables that I steam and serve on their own dressed with lemon juice, a few drops of olive oil, salt and pepper — onions, carrots, broccoli and cauliflower are just a few.

In Italy we incorporate freshly cooked vegetables into several courses of a meal. Restaurants, especially in the south, proudly display entire tables of antipasti dishes made with vegetables, and I have already mentioned how well they work as a topping for pasta. The recipes I give here are for vegetables as the accompaniment to the main course — I CONTORNI, as we call them in Italian, that which is served AROUND the main course on the same platter. These vegetable accompaniments to the meat and fish course also have an aesthetic function at the table. I cannot imagine serving a platter of well-prepared meat by itself. It should be adorned and decorated with a vegetable that not only complements its taste but pleases the eye as well.

Broccoletti alla Pancetta

BROCCOLI WITH PANCETTA AND GARLIC

You can use bacon instead of pancetta. This recipe also makes a very good sauce for spaghetti cooked *al dente*.

SERVES 6

1.2 kg / 2½ lb broccoli, tough stalks removed

salt and pepper

6 tbsp extra virgin olive oil

2 garlic cloves, chopped

90 g / 3 oz pancetta, coarsely chopped

Separate the florets from the tender broccoli stalks and cut the stalks into bite-size pieces. Blanch the stalks for 5 minutes in boiling salted water. Add the florets and cook for a further 3 minutes. Drain and set aside.

In a frying pan heat the oil, add the garlic and sauté for 30 seconds. Add the pancetta and fry over moderate heat until crisp and just golden. Add the blanched broccoli and cook gently for a few minutes, turning once very carefully. Season with pepper, transfer to a warm platter and serve.

PREPARING AUBERGINE (EGGPLANT)

In recipe books one often reads that before being cooked aubergine (eggplant) should be sprinkled with salt to get rid of its bitterness. I never do this because if I want a less sharp flavour I use courgettes (zucchini) instead and, secondly, because when it is fried, instead of becoming crisp it gets soggy. Don't remove the skins: they soften during cooking.

VINEGAR

To make a good dressing always use red wine vinegar and not white. Above all avoid raspberry vinegar which is far too sweet, as well as concentrated vinegars and, for most salads, even balsamic vinegar. The latter is, however, exquisite on meat or fish, strawberries and many cheeses, particularly Parmesan.

Caponata di Melanzane

AUBERGINE (EGGPLANT) SALAD

This is a Sicilian speciality which has a number of variations. It is always served the day after it is cooked and I think you will enjoy it with the breaded veal scaloppine (page 100).

SERVES 6

4 oval aubergines (eggplants), about 900 g / 2 lb total

extra virgin olive oil for deep-frying

3 tbsp extra virgin olive oil

1 onion, chopped

240 ml / 8 fl oz / 1 cup Neapolitan tomato sauce (page 158)

salt and pepper

6 tbsp red wine vinegar

2 tbsp sugar

12 black olives, stoned

2 celery stalks, chopped

2 tbsp capers in vinegar, drained

Trim the ends off the aubergines (eggplants) and cut them into 1-cm/ ½-inch dice. In a heavy pan heat the frying oil. Add the diced aubergine (eggplant) and fry for about 3 minutes. Remove with a slotted spoon and drain on paper towels.

In a saucepan heat 3 tbsp oil, add the onion and, stirring frequently, cook until golden, about 5 minutes. Add the tomato sauce and season with salt and pepper. Stir and remove from the heat.

In another saucepan combine the vinegar, sugar, olives and celery. Stirring occasionally, cook over low heat until the celery is very tender, about 20 minutes. Add the capers, then add the contents of the saucepan to the tomato sauce. Add the aubergine (eggplant) and simmer over low heat for about 15 minutes, stirring frequently.

Spoon on to on a serving plate and, when cool, refrigerate for about 24 hours. Serve at room temperature.

Carciofi con la Mozzarella

ARTICHOKES STUFFED WITH MOZZARELLA

Large artichokes can be tough and so take longer to cook than small ones. For a simpler dish, stuff the artichokes with equal amounts of grated Parmesan and breadcrumbs mixed with a beaten egg. These artichokes go well with the spinach and veal roll on page 92.

SERVES 6

juice of 1 lemon

12 small or 6 large globe artichokes

180 g / 6 oz mozzarella cheese, coarsely chopped

2 tbsp chopped fresh parsley

2 tbsp freshly grated Parmesan cheese

90 g / 3 oz cooked ham, chopped

salt and pepper

3 tbsp extra virgin olive oil

Stir the lemon juice into a bowl of cold water large enough to hold the artichokes. Wash the artichokes, remove only the tough outer leaves and cut off the spikes. Using a wooden spoon, push the leaves apart. Immediately drop the artichokes into the lemon water to prevent discoloration.

Mix together the mozzarella, parsley, Parmesan and ham. Drain the artichokes and season with salt and pepper. Fill the spaces between the leaves with the mozzarella mixture. Stand the artichokes side by side in a shallow pan and sprinkle with a little olive oil.

Pour half a cup of water into the pan. Cover and cook gently for 30 minutes. Transfer to a warm platter and serve.

Cardi Saporiti all'Acciuga

CARDOONS FLAVOURED WITH ANCHOVIES

It is essential to use only the tender inner stalks of cardoon for this dish. Cardoons discolour very easily so they must be kept in water and lemon juice as soon as they are peeled. A little flour is added to the cooking water to keep the vegetable white. This dish goes very well with roast pork in fennel sauce (page 90).

SERVES 6

juice of 2 lemons

2.7 kg / 6 lb cardoons

salt

1 tbsp flour

3 tbsp extra virgin olive oil

1 garlic clove, chopped

6 anchovy fillets in oil, drained

2 tbsp chopped fresh parsley

Stir half the lemon juice into a bowl of cold water large enough to hold the sliced cardoons. Prepare the cardoons by cutting off the hard base, tough outer stalks and the leaves, then scrape the inner stalks with a vegetable peeler and

● Cardoons Flavoured with Anchovies ●

cut them into 8-cm / 3-inch slices, dropping them immediately into the bowl of lemon water to prevent discoloration.

Fill a saucepan with water, add salt and sprinkle the surface with the flour. Add the rest of the lemon juice and bring to the boil. Add the sliced cardoons and simmer gently until tender, about 20 minutes. Drain and dry on paper towels.

In a frying pan heat the oil and garlic over gentle heat. Add the anchovies and mash them with a fork. Add the cardoons and stir to mix. Cover and cook gently for about 5 minutes. Stir in the parsley.

Arrange on a warm platter and serve at once.

Carote alla Panna

CARROTS IN CREAM AND MUSHROOM SAUCE

If you find cream too heavy, use milk, although the flavour will be less delicate. The carrots go well with the sautéed rabbit with potatoes (page 97).

SERVES 6

10 g / 1/3 oz dried porcini mushrooms

30 g / 1 oz / 2 tbsp unsalted butter

1.2 kg / 2 1/2 lb small to medium-size carrots, sliced

juice of 1/2 lemon

a pinch of grated nutmeg

salt and pepper

240 ml / 8 fl oz / 1 cup whipping cream

2 tbsp chopped fresh chives

Soak the mushrooms in warm water for 30 minutes. Remove, squeeze dry and chop. Strain the water through a fine sieve and set aside.

DRESSING INGREDIENTS

An old Italian saying has it that to make a good salad dressing, it requires a philosopher to measure the oil, a miser for the vinegar, a cautious man for the salt and a madman to mix it. Ready-made dressings should be avoided at all costs. Oil and salt are the essentials; herbs and flavoured vinegars vary with the different types of salad. I never decide to add anything until the last minute.

Broccoli with Pancetta and Garlic (p. 128), ● Brussels Sprouts in Lemon Sauce, ● Chickpeas with Rosemary (p. 132)

In a saucepan heat the butter. Add the carrots and, stirring, cook over moderate heat for about 10 minutes. Season with lemon juice, nutmeg, salt and pepper. Add the mushrooms and stir in the cream. Cover the pan and simmer over low heat for about 30 minutes or until the cream is partially reduced. If the sauce is too thick, dilute with a little of the mushroom water.

Sprinkle with chives and serve on a warm platter.

Cavolfiore in Insalata

CAULIFLOWER SALAD WITH OLIVES

Small black olives are best for this salad and they can be bought, canned, in Italian shops. Olives are so popular in Italy that all the street markets have stalls carrying about 20 different varieties. There are sweet and hot olives, large and small ones, in brine or oil, and they come in many colours.

SERVES 6

1 cauliflower, about 1.2 kg / 2 1/2 lb

salt and pepper

180 g / 6 oz / 1 cup stoned black olives

1 tbsp wine vinegar

1 tsp Dijon mustard

4 tbsp extra virgin olive oil

60 g / 2 oz / 1/2 cup coarsely chopped walnuts

Pour enough water into a saucepan to cover the cauliflower stalks but not the florets. Add salt and bring to the boil. Add the cauliflower and cook, covered, until tender, about 15 minutes.

Drain and rinse under cold water. Remove the florets and discard the stalks. Arrange the florets in a salad bowl with the olives.

In a cup dissolve salt to taste in the vinegar with the mustard. Add the oil and mix well.

Pour the dressing over the cauliflower and olives. Toss carefully, then sprinkle with the walnuts and serve.

Cavolini di Bruxelles in Salsa al Limone

BRUSSELS SPROUTS IN LEMON SAUCE

This lemon sauce is also very good with other vegetables, particularly asparagus, fennel bulbs and globe artichokes. Serve the sprouts with sautéed rabbit with potatoes (page 97).

SERVES 6

1.2 kg / 2 1/2 lb Brussels sprouts

30 g / 1 oz / 2 tbsp unsalted butter

2 tbsp flour

240 ml / 8 fl oz / 1 cup light chicken stock (page 216)

salt and pepper

juice of 1 lemon

2 egg yolks

Rinse the sprouts and remove stalks and any wilted leaves. Bring a saucepan of salted water to the boil. Cook the sprouts until just tender, about 10 minutes.

Meanwhile, in a saucepan melt half the butter over moderate heat. Add the flour and stir well. Stirring constantly, gradually add the stock and bring to the boil. Boil for a few minutes. Remove from the heat and season with salt and pepper. Stir in the rest of the butter, the lemon juice and egg yolks.

Drain the sprouts and arrange on a warm platter. Coat with the sauce and serve at once.

Cavolo Rosso alle Mele

BRAISED RED CABBAGE WITH APPLES

Cabbage that has had a touch of frost can be cooked in 40 minutes, but the longer it cooks the better – as long as it is simmered very gently. Serve with roast pork in almond sauce (page 106).

SERVES 6

3 tbsp extra virgin olive oil

1.2 kg / 2½ lb red cabbage or Savoy cabbage, shredded

1 tbsp juniper berries

salt and pepper

4 tbsp red wine vinegar

4 tbsp dry white wine

2 cooking apples, peeled and thinly sliced

In a saucepan heat the oil. Add the cabbage and juniper berries and cook over moderate heat for 10 minutes, stirring occasionally. Season with salt and pepper and sprinkle with the vinegar. Cover and simmer over low heat for about 30 minutes, adding the wine a little at a time to keep the cabbage moist.

Add the apples and cook for a further 20 minutes. Transfer to a warm platter and serve.

Ceci con Rosmarino

CHICKPEAS WITH ROSEMARY

This dish can also be served as a salad at room temperature; sprinkle with rosemary before serving. The chickpeas and onion can be cooked ahead of time and refrigerated for about 8 hours.

SERVES 6

450 g / 1 lb / 2½ cups dried chickpeas

1 medium-size onion

salt and pepper

1 tbsp balsamic vinegar

4 tbsp extra virgin olive oil

1 tbsp chopped fresh rosemary

Soak the chickpeas in water to cover for about 12 hours. Drain.

Bring a saucepan of salted water to the boil. Add the chickpeas and the onion and simmer gently for 30 minutes. Remove the onion and set it aside to cool. Simmer the chickpeas for a further 1 hour.

Meanwhile, chop the onion.

In a cup dissolve salt to taste in the balsamic vinegar, then stir in the oil. Mix well.

Drain the chickpeas and transfer them to a bowl. Add the onion and stir. Pour the dressing over the chickpeas and toss well. Leave to cool until lukewarm then sprinkle with the rosemary.

Cime di Rapa Strascicate

TURNIP LEAVES SAUTÉED WITH GARLIC AND BREADCRUMBS

These turnip tops are delicious with spaghetti cooked *al dente*: toss the spaghetti with the greens and sprinkle with the breadcrumbs.

SERVES 6

6 tbsp extra virgin olive oil

3 garlic cloves, chopped

3 anchovy fillets in oil, drained

a pinch of chili powder

90 g / 3 oz / scant 1 cup fine dry breadcrumbs (see below)

1.2 kg / 2½ lb turnip leaves or other hearty greens (kale, spring greens, etc)

salt and pepper

In a large frying pan heat 3 tbsp of the oil with the garlic. Add the anchovy fillets, sprinkle with the chili powder and cook over low heat, stirring frequently until the anchovies dissolve. Add the breadcrumbs and, stirring constantly, fry until golden. Remove from the pan and set aside.

Meanwhile, bring a saucepan of salted water to the boil. Add the turnip leaves and boil for about 3 minutes. Drain well.

Pour the rest of the oil into the frying pan and heat over moderate heat. Add the turnip tops and, stirring constantly, cook for about 5 minutes. Season with salt and pepper.

Arrange the greens on a warm platter, sprinkle with the breadcrumb mixture and serve immediately.

FINE DRY BREADCRUMBS

Although breadcrumbs are sold in supermarkets, leftover bread can easily be turned into crumbs. Cut the bread into 5-mm/¼-inch slices and spread them on a baking sheet. Dry in a preheated 160°C/325°F/gas 3 oven for about 20 minutes without letting them change colour. Leave the bread to stand for a further 24 hours. Break the bread into pieces and put into a food processor fitted with the metal blade. Process until you have crumbs about the texture of coarse cornmeal. Spread the breadcrumbs on a large plate and leave them to dry further. They may then be stored in an airtight glass jar without any risk of mould.

Cipolle Ripiene al Prosciutto

ONIONS STUFFED WITH HAM

The stuffed onions can be refrigerated for up to 12 hours before baking. Serve with beef patties with mint and orange (page 104).

SERVES 6

2 slices of coarse-textured bread, crust removed

240 ml / 8 fl oz / 1 cup milk

6 large onions

90 g / 3 oz cooked ham, chopped

6 tbsp freshly grated Parmesan cheese

1 egg, lightly beaten

a pinch of grated nutmeg

salt and pepper

unsalted butter for the pan

6 tbsp light meat stock (page 216)

● **Onions Stuffed with Ham** ●

Soak the bread in the milk for about 10 minutes. Drain and squeeze out milk.

Peel the onions, taking care not to damage the outside layers. Bring a saucepan of salted water to the boil. Add the onions and simmer for 15 minutes. Drain and refresh under cold running water. Dry the onions. Cut off about one-quarter of each onion from the stalk end and scoop out the inside, leaving a shell of about 2 layers. Chop the scooped-out onion.

In a bowl combine the chopped onion, ham, Parmesan, soaked bread, egg, nutmeg, salt and pepper. Blend well and use to stuff the onions shells.

Butter a baking pan and arrange the onions in it. Pour over the stock. Transfer to a preheated 180°C / 350°F / gas 4 oven and bake for about 40 minutes, basting frequently to glaze the onions.

Arrange on a warm platter and serve.

Cipolline Glassate al Cioccolato

ONIONS GLAZED WITH CHOCOLATE

I often add 1 tbsp of grated orange zest to this Renaissance dish. The onions give a great lift to the roast pork with prunes on page 92.

SERVES 6

2 tbsp seedless raisins

1.2 kg / 2½ lb small onions (pickling or pearl)

3 tbsp extra virgin olive oil

1 bay leaf

1 tbsp sugar

2 tbsp grated bittersweet chocolate

4 tbsp wine vinegar

salt and pepper

Soak the raisins in water to cover for about 30 minutes.

To peel the onions easily, first blanch them in boiling salted water for 5 minutes; drain.

In a frying pan heat the oil. Add the onions and, stirring frequently, cook over moderate heat until just golden, about 10 minutes.

Add the bay leaf and sprinkle with the sugar and chocolate. Pour over the vinegar and 240 ml/8 fl oz/1 cup water. Stir well, then lower the heat, cover the pan and cook until the liquid has been almost completely absorbed and the onions are soft, about 30 minutes.

Add the drained raisins, stir and cook for a further 2 minutes. Season with salt and pepper.

Transfer to a warm platter and serve at once.

Cipolline alle Spezie

SPICED ONIONS

Spices are used for flavouring in the north-east and south of Italy, but in the rest of the country herbs are more popular. The particular flavour of these onions goes very well with the marinated rabbit on page 96.

SERVES 6

1.2 kg/2½ lb small onions (pickling or pearl)

4 whole cloves

30 g/1 oz/2 tbsp unsalted butter

1 tsp ground cinnamon

1 tsp sugar

salt and pepper

120 ml/4 fl oz/½ cup single (light) cream

● **Small Onions with Grapes** ●

Bring a saucepan of salted water to the boil. Add the onions and blanch for about 5 minutes. Drain and peel. Press a clove into 4 onions.

Melt the butter in the saucepan. Add the onions and sprinkle with the cinnamon and sugar. Season with salt and pepper. Cover the pan and cook over very low heat, shaking the pan frequently, for about 30 minutes.

Remove the cloves and add the cream. Stir and cook for about 5 minutes longer. Serve hot.

Cipolline all'Uva

SMALL ONIONS WITH GRAPES

I completely forgot this recipe for several years and when I started preparing it again it seemed very unusual, and suitable for serving with an asparagus tart (page 79).

SERVES 6

900 g/2 lb small onions (pickling or pearl)

30 g/1 oz/2 tbsp butter

salt and pepper

6 tbsp dry white wine

300 g/10 oz white or green seedless grapes

Bring a saucepan of salted water to the boil. Add the onions and blanch for about 5 minutes. Drain and peel.

Melt the butter in the saucepan. Add the onions and season with salt and pepper. Cover the pan and cook over low heat for about 30 minutes, gradually adding wine as it is absorbed.

Add the grapes and, shaking the pan, cook for a futher 5 minutes. Arrange on a warm platter and serve at once.

Cipolline con Uvetta e Pomodoro

SMALL ONIONS IN TOMATO AND RAISIN SAUCE

I use this recipe for bottling and the onions will keep for up to a year. Serve with mackerel fillets with fennel (page 108).

SERVES 6

1.2 kg/2½ lb small onions (pickling or pearl)

90 g/3 oz/⅔ cup seedless raisins

15 g/½ oz/1 tbsp unsalted butter

2 tbsp extra virgin olive oil

600 g/1¼ lb ripe plum tomatoes, peeled and diced (or use canned)

1 whole clove

salt and pepper

1 tbsp sugar

4 tbsp wine vinegar

Bring a saucepan of salted water to the boil. Add the onions and blanch for about 5 minutes. Drain and peel.

Soak the raisins in water to cover for about 30 minutes.

In a saucepan melt the butter with the oil over moderate heat. Add the onions and, stirring frequently, cook until just golden, about 10 minutes.

Add the tomatoes, clove, salt and pepper and stir to mix. Lower the heat and simmer gently until the onions are soft, about 30 minutes.

In a small saucepan dissolve the sugar in the vinegar and boil for a couple of minutes. Pour the mixture over the onions and add the drained raisins. Stir while the excess liquid evaporates and the mixture heats. Transfer to a warm platter and serve piping hot.

Fagiolini in Salsa di Peperoni

GREEN BEANS IN YELLOW PEPPER SAUCE

The sauce here looks like mayonnaise. It is delicious spooned over spaghetti cooked *al dente*, sprinkled with tomato and basil, and served at room temperature. I suggest you serve the beans with the tomato omelette on page 70.

SERVES 6

1 large or 2 small yellow sweet peppers

6 tbsp extra virgin olive oil

4 tbsp dry white wine

salt

1.2 kg / 2½ lb green beans

2 large ripe tomatoes, peeled, seeded and diced

2 tbsp chopped fresh basil

Place the peppers on the shelf in a preheated 200° C/400° F/gas 6 oven. Bake, turning once, until the skins blister, about 30 minutes. Wrap the peppers in foil and leave them to cool for about 2 minutes, then peel them. Remove the seeds and core and coarsely chop the flesh.

In a blender combine the pepper flesh, oil and wine with a pinch of salt. Purée the mixture until creamy and set aside.

Bring a saucepan of salted water to the boil. Add the beans and cook until just tender, about 5 minutes. Drain and refresh under cold running water.

In a frying pan combine the beans and pepper sauce. Slowly bring to the boil over low heat and cook for a couple of minutes.

Arrange on a warm platter, sprinkle with the tomatoes and basil and serve immediately.

Fricassea di Funghi

MUSHROOMS IN RICH LEMON SAUCE

This is a Genoese speciality. You will find that the rich lemon sauce complements all sautéed vegetables and gives a lift to white meats and fish. Serve with the hot cheese loaf on page 76.

SERVES 6

1.2 kg / 2½ lb fresh porcini or shiitake mushrooms

45 g / 1½ oz / 3 tbsp unsalted butter

salt and pepper

2 tbsp chopped fresh mint, or 1 tbsp dried mint

1 tsp flour

1 egg yolk

juice of 1 lemon

3 tbsp dry white wine

3 tbsp milk

1 tbsp chopped fresh parsley

Trim the mushrooms and wipe them clean, but do not immerse in water. Cut the mushrooms into 5-mm/¼-inch slices.

In a frying pan heat the butter. Add the mushrooms and, stirring frequently, sauté them for about 5 minutes. Season with salt and pepper and sprinkle with the chopped mint. Remove from the heat.

In a cup combine the flour, egg yolk, lemon juice, wine and milk. Stir well to get rid of any lumps. Pour the mixture over the mushrooms and, over low heat, stir the mixture for just a few seconds. The sauce must thicken without boiling or the egg will curdle.

Transfer to a warm platter, sprinkle with the parsley and serve.

Insalata con le Erbe

SALAD WITH HERBS

Naturally other fresh herbs, such as coriander (cilantro) can be used. Lettuce is, however, essential because more strongly flavoured leaves would drown the taste of the various herbs. I generally like to serve this salad with the chicken with juniper on page 112.

SERVES 6

1 soft-leaved lettuce (round or Boston), about 300 g / 10 oz

120 g / 4 oz rocket (arugula)

3 tbsp fresh flat-leaf (Italian) parsley leaves

a handful of fresh dill

a handful of fresh mint leaves

1 tbsp red wine vinegar

salt

4 tbsp extra virgin olive oil

Wash and dry the lettuce. Tear it into bite-size pieces. Wash and dry the rocket (arugula) and cut off any tough stalks. Combine the greens and herbs in a salad bowl.

In a cup dissolve salt to taste in the wine vinegar. Pour over the salad and toss well.

Add the oil, mix well and serve at once.

BEANS

The most popular beans in Italy are cannellini and borlotti. Cannellini are white and fairly small. They play a prominent part in Tuscan cooking, particularly in soups such as ribollita and creamed bean. Borlotti beans when uncooked have red markings, are much larger than cannellini and have a thicker texture. They are used in minestrone soups all over Italy. Fresh beans are put straight into the soup and simmered for about 1½ hours, whereas dried beans must be soaked in water at room temperature for at least 12 hours before cooking. It is a good idea to buy fresh beans at the end of the summer and to shell and freeze them because they will have more flavour than dried beans.

Insalata di Fagioli e Tonno

TUNA AND BEAN SALAD

This is a traditional Tuscan dish to which sliced tomato is occasionally added. Although generally served as an antipasto or first course, it also makes a delightful light lunch, served with onions stuffed with ham (page 133).

SERVES 6

300 g / 10 oz / 1¾ cups dried cannellini, haricot or great northern beans

240 g / 8 oz canned tuna fish, drained

1 small onion, thinly sliced

salt and pepper

4 tbsp extra virgin olive oil

Soak the beans in water to cover for about 12 hours.

Drain the beans and transfer them to a saucepan. Add water to cover by about 2.5 cm / 1 inch. Slowly bring to a gentle simmer, then cover the pan and cook for about 1½ hours over very low heat. Drain off any water that remains.

Transfer the beans to a salad bowl and cool to room temperature. Crumble the tuna over them, add the onion and season with salt and pepper. Sprinkle with the oil and toss delicately.

Serve barely warm or at room temperature.

● **Winter Salad with Walnuts (p. 138), Rocket** ● **(Arugula) and Pear Salad (p. 145)**

Insalata di Noci

WINTER SALAD WITH WALNUTS

If you are using raw artichokes, they must be dropped into water mixed with lemon juice as soon as the outer leaves are removed or they will blacken. The celery should, ideally, be white because green celery is very tough and strongly flavoured. If you use green celery, any strings should be removed. Serve with baked mozzarella on toast (page 68).

SERVES 6

12 red radicchio leaves

3 fennel bulbs (or 4 globe artichokes or 6 white celery stalks), trimmed and thinly sliced

6 red radishes, trimmed and thinly sliced

120 g/4 oz Parmesan cheese

salt

1 tbsp red wine vinegar

4 tbsp extra virgin olive oil

210 g/7 oz/1¾ cups coarsely chopped walnuts

Tear the lettuce into bite-size pieces and put into a salad bowl. Add the fennel and radishes.

Using a vegetable peeler, shave the Parmesan over the salad.

In a cup dissolve salt to taste in the vinegar. Pour over the salad and toss well. Sprinkle with the oil and walnuts, toss again and serve at once.

Insalata di Pomodori e Mozzarella

TOMATO AND MOZZARELLA SALAD

For variety, add slices of hard-boiled egg or use fresh marjoram instead of basil. In winter, when fresh herbs are hard to come by, sprinkle with dried oregano. This can be served with tuna and bean salad (page 137).

● **Tomato and Mozzarella Salad** ●

SERVES 6

6 medium-size ripe tomatoes

300 g / 10 oz mozzarella cheese

a handful of fresh basil leaves

salt and pepper

4 tbsp extra virgin olive oil

Cut the tomatoes and mozzarella into slices 5 mm / ¼ inch thick. Arrange the slices, alternating tomato and mozzarella, in a ring on a serving dish. Put the extra tomato slices in the middle and the basil leaves around the edge.

Season with salt and pepper. Sprinkle with the oil and serve.

Making Salad Dressing

*T*he classic Italian salad dressing is extra virgin olive oil, vinegar and salt with, perhaps, a little pepper. First the salt is dissolved in the vinegar by stirring it with a fork and it is then poured over the salad. Only then is the oil and, occasionally, pepper added. The vinegar and salt are poured on first because oil would coat the salad leaves and their flavours would not be as well absorbed. For most salads the proportions are 1 tbsp of vinegar to 4 tbsp of oil.

Dressing the Salad

*T*o avoid wilting, the salad must always be tossed with the dressing at the last minute. If you want to prepare the dressing in advance, in a cup dissolve the salt in the vinegar, then add the oil. This can also be done in the bottom of the salad bowl, in which case cover the dressing with crossed salad servers and put the salad on top so it does not come into contact with the dressing. Toss just before serving.

Insalata di Uva

Grape, Cheese and Apple Salad

*T*he fontina can be replaced by Gruyère or emmenthal cheese or other semi-hard cheeses such as scamorza or provolone. This salad can be served as an antipasto or as part of a buffet with cold tomato ring (page 73) and ham mousse (page 79).

SERVES 6

180 g / 6 oz fontina cheese

450 g / 1 lb seedless white grapes

1 Golden Delicious apple

½ bottle of dry white wine

1 tsp lemon juice

salt and pepper

4 tbsp extra virgin olive oil

1 soft-leaved lettuce (round or Boston), about 300 g / 10 oz

2 tbsp coarsely chopped walnuts

Cut the cheese into julienne strips and set aside.

Put the grapes in a bowl. Peel, core and dice the apple and add to the grapes. Pour the wine into the bowl and leave the fruit to marinate for about 2 hours.

Prepare a dressing with the lemon juice, seasoning and olive oil. Tear the lettuce into bite-size pieces and toss in half the dressing.

Drain the fruit and arrange it in the middle of a serving plate. Sprinkle with the rest of the dressing and stir. Scatter the cheese and walnuts on top. Arrange the lettuce around the fruit and serve.

Involtini di Bietola

Swiss Chard Rolls

*T*he rolls can be prepared ahead of time and refrigerated, covered, for up to 8 hours before baking. Brush with the melted butter just before putting into the oven. They could accompany the onion tart on page 80.

SERVES 6

1.2 kg / 2½ lb Swiss chard

45 g / 1½ oz / 3 tbsp unsalted butter

90 g / 3 oz / ¾ cup freshly grated Parmesan cheese

salt and pepper

Bring a large saucepan of salted water to the boil. Wash the chard and cut the leaves off the stalks. Scrape the stalks with a vegetable peeler and cut into pieces about 7.5 cm / 3 inches long. Drop the stalks into the boiling water and after about 2 minutes add the leaves. Cook for a further 1 minute. Drain and refresh in cold water so that the leaves do not lose their colour.

Dice the stalks. Spread out the leaves on a flat surface.

In a small frying pan melt 30 g / 1 oz / 2 tbsp butter over low heat. Add the chard stalks and cook until all the moisture has evaporated. Stir in the Parmesan and season with salt and pepper.

Put a little of the mixture on each chard leaf. Fold in the sides of the leaves and carefully roll up, sealing in the stuffing.

In a small saucepan melt the rest of the butter. Brush a baking dish with half the melted butter. Arrange the rolls in it and brush them lightly with the rest of the butter. Bake in a preheated 180°C/350°F/gas 4 oven until hot, about 5 minutes.

Arrange on a warm platter and serve.

LENTILS

We use small, dry, greenish-brown lentils that are about 5 mm/¼ inch long. They should be soaked in abundant water for at least 12 hours before being cooked, and any found floating on the surface should be discarded. After soaking, lentils take about 1 hour to cook. Traditionally they are served on New Year's Day with cotechino, a large sausage, because superstition has it that lentils bring money.

Lenticchie al Ginepro

JUNIPER-FLAVOURED LENTILS

In Italy lentils are the traditional New Year fare, because they are said to bring money. They are usually cooked with a little chopped onion sautéed in olive oil and white wine, but the juniper berries and tomatoes give them a nicer flavour. Lentils go well with roast leg of lamb with anchovies (page 97).

SERVES 6

3 tbsp extra virgin olive oil

60 g / 2 oz pancetta, chopped

½ medium-size onion, chopped

½ celery stalk, chopped

1 medium-size carrot, chopped

900 g / 2 lb soaked lentils (450 g / 1 lb when dry)

300 g / 10 oz ripe plum tomatoes, peeled and diced (or use canned)

1 tbsp juniper berries

salt and pepper

● **Sliced Baked Potatoes with Rosemary** ●

In a saucepan heat the olive oil. Add the pancetta, onion, celery and carrot. Sauté gently until the onion is translucent. Add the lentils, tomato and juniper berries. Season with salt and pepper.

Cover the saucepan and cook over low heat for about 1 hour or until the tomato juice has been absorbed and the lentils are tender.

Transfer to a warm platter and serve.

FRYING POTATOES

To achieve crisp fried potatoes, remove them from the oil when half cooked and drain on paper towels. Then return them to the oil at a higher temperature and fry until golden. Another method is to use two pans, each with the oil at a different temperature.

Patate al Forno

SLICED BAKED POTATOES WITH ROSEMARY

If you don't have a gadget that slices potatoes rapidly, as they are sliced they should be dropped into a bowl of cold water to prevent them turning black. Then drain and dry in a cloth before cooking. I suggest you serve these with the chicken roasted in bay leaves on page 110.

SERVES 6

6 large baking potatoes

2 tbsp extra virgin olive oil

salt

1 tbsp finely chopped fresh rosemary

Scrub the potatoes but do not peel them. Cut them lengthways into very thin slices.

Line several baking sheets with foil and brush the foil with a little oil. Arrange the sliced potatoes on the foil, in a single layer, and brush them with oil. Season with salt and sprinkle with the rosemary.

Transfer to a preheated 180°C/350°F/gas 4 oven and bake until crisp and just golden, about 15 minutes.

Arrange on a warm platter and serve at once.

BOILING POTATOES

I always boil potatoes in their skins because they absorb much less water than peeled potatoes. After draining, they should be peeled while still hot, and mashed hot too – cold potatoes tend to form lumps. I find that cooked potatoes turn sour after 12 hours even when refrigerated.

Patate al Prezzemolo

PARSLEYED POTATOES

I sometimes add a spoonful of balsamic vinegar to the dressing. Serve with the baked stuffed sardines on page 116.

SERVES 6

1.2 kg / 2½ lb boiling potatoes

salt and pepper

2 garlic cloves, finely chopped

2 tbsp chopped fresh parsley

4 tbsp extra virgin olive oil

Cook the potatoes, in their skins, in boiling salted water until tender. Drain, then peel and slice the potatoes. Arrange them in a warm serving dish.

In a small bowl combine the garlic, parsley, oil and pepper. Stir well. Pour the mixture over the potatoes and serve. Or, leave to cool before serving.

Patate al Rosmarino

POTATOES WITH ROSEMARY

These potatoes should be crisp and golden outside and tender within. I sometimes boil them in their skins until they are half cooked, then peel and dice them before transferring them to the oven to bake for about 30 minutes.

SERVES 6

1.2 kg / 2½ lb boiling potatoes

240 ml / 8 fl oz / 1 cup extra virgin olive oil

2 garlic cloves

3 sprigs of fresh rosemary

salt and pepper

Peel the potatoes and cut into cubes of about 2.5 cm / 1 inch.

In an ovenproof pan heat the olive oil on top of the stove. Add the garlic, rosemary and potatoes and stir well. Transfer the pan to a preheated 180°C/350°F/gas 4 oven and, stirring occasionally, cook until golden, about 40 minutes.

Discard the rosemary and garlic. Remove the potatoes with a slotted spoon and arrange them on a warm platter. Season with salt and pepper and serve immediately.

Patate al Tonno ed Erba Cipollina

POTATOES WITH TUNA AND CHIVES

In summer I mash the potatoes with the tuna and then stir in about 240 ml / 8 fl oz / 1 cup mayonnaise flavoured with chives. I make this into a loaf shape and serve it with the spaghetti omelette on page 70.

SERVES 6

1.2 kg / 2½ lb boiling potatoes

240 g / 8 oz canned tuna fish, drained

salt and pepper

4 tbsp extra virgin olive oil

2 tbsp finely chopped fresh chives

Cook the potatoes, in their skins, in boiling salted water until tender. Drain, then peel and dice the potatoes. Leave to cool.

Arrange the diced potatoes on a serving dish. Crumble the tuna over the potatoes. Season with salt and pepper. Sprinkle with the olive oil and toss carefully.

Just before serving sprinkle with the chives.

Pomodori Gratinati

BAKED PARMESAN TOMATOES

The Parmesan cheese can be replaced by chopped fresh herbs, leaving out the dried oregano, of course.

SERVES 6

6 medium-size ripe tomatoes

6 tbsp freshly grated Parmesan cheese

6 tbsp fine dry breadcrumbs (page 132)

2 tbsp dried oregano

1 egg, lightly beaten

3 tbsp extra virgin olive oil

salt and pepper

Cut the tomatoes crosswise in half and carefully scoop out the seeds. Sprinkle with a little salt and leave them to drain upside down on paper towels while you prepare the stuffing.

In a bowl combine the Parmesan, breadcrumbs, oregano, egg and olive oil. Season with salt and pepper and mix well. Fill the tomatoes with the mixture. Arrange them on a baking sheet and transfer to a preheated 180°C/350°F/ gas 4 oven. Bake until tender, about 30 minutes. Arrange the tomatoes on a warm platter and serve.

Pomodori alla Maionese Verde

TOMATOES WITH GREEN MAYONNAISE

The tomatoes and mayonnaise can be prepared ahead of time and refrigerated separately for up to 8 hours. The tomatoes should be filled at the last minute and served at room temperature.

SERVES 6

6 medium-size ripe tomatoes

salt

1 egg and 1 egg yolk

3 tbsp fresh flat-leaf (Italian) parsley leaves

2 tbsp fresh tarragon leaves

120 ml/4 fl oz/½ cup extra virgin olive oil

3 tbsp milk

1 tbsp lemon juice

Cut the tomatoes crosswise in half and carefully remove the seeds. Sprinkle with salt and place upside down on paper towels. Leave to drain for about 30 minutes.

In a blender combine the egg, egg yolk and herbs with a pinch of salt. Process until the herbs are puréed. With the blender running, gradually add the oil in a slow steady stream. When the mayonnaise is ready add the milk and lemon juice. Check the seasoning.

Arrange the tomatoes on a platter. Fill them with the mayonnaise and serve at room temperature.

Pomodori Ripieni

TOMATOES STUFFED WITH BEANS AND TUNA

If tender-skinned dried beans are not available, use 240 g/8 oz of the excellent Italian canned cannellini: pour the contents of the can into a colander and rinse the beans under cold running water, then drain well and add to the rest of the ingredients.

SERVES 6

120 g/4 oz/⅔ cup dried cannellini, haricot or great northern beans

6 medium-size ripe tomatoes

salt and pepper

1 small onion, sliced paper-thin

2 tbsp lemon juice

120 g/4 oz canned tuna fish, drained

2 tbsp chopped fresh basil

6 tbsp extra virgin olive oil

Soak the beans in water to cover for about 12 hours. Drain the beans and transfer them to a saucepan. Add water to cover by 2.5 cm/1 inch and bring to the boil, then cover the pan and simmer over very low heat for about 1½ hours. Drain and leave to cool completely.

Slice the tops off the tomatoes and discard. Cut out the central membrane and carefully remove seeds and pulp, leaving a thick shell. Sprinkle with a little salt and leave upside down to drain.

Soak the onion slices in cold water for about 30 minutes.

In a bowl, stir the lemon juice into the tuna. Add the beans, drained onion, basil and half the olive oil. Season with salt and pepper and mix carefully.

Spoon the mixture into the tomato shells. Transfer the tomatoes to a serving plate and pour the rest of the oil into them. Keep at room temperature until ready to serve.

Pomodori in Tortiera

BAKED MEDLEY OF VEGETABLES

This dish can be varied by substituting porcini mushrooms for the onion or sweet peppers for the potatoes and then sprinkling with capers or black olives. For a simple buffet serve with tagliatelle and ricotta omelette (page 70) and a rice ring with tarragon mayonnaise (page 26).

● **Baked Medley of Vegetables** ●

SERVES 6

6 tbsp fine dry breadcrumbs (page 132)

3 tbsp chopped fresh basil

salt and pepper

6 tbsp extra virgin olive oil

6 medium-size ripe tomatoes, sliced

3 large potatoes, peeled and sliced

1 medium-size oval aubergine (eggplant), sliced crosswise

1 large onion, sliced

In a bowl combine the breadcrumbs, basil and seasoning to taste. Blend well. Grease an ovenproof dish with a little of the oil and make a layer of tomato slices on the bottom of it. Sprinkle with a little of the basil and breadcrumb mixture. Top with a layer of potatoes, then aubergine (eggplant) and onion, seasoning each layer with the basil and breadcrumbs. It does not matter how many layers you make, but you should finish with tomatoes. Pour over the rest of the oil.

Transfer to a preheated 180°C/350°F/gas 4 oven and bake for about 50 minutes. Serve hot or cold.

Radicchio alla Pancetta

Radicchio with Pancetta

Blanched spinach and Swiss chard are also delicious sautéed in pancetta or bacon fat. Serve with the grilled marinated swordfish on page 109, or make half the quantity and add it to a risotto after the rice has been cooking for about 10 minutes. Or, use for dressing tagliatelle.

SERVES 6

1.2 kg / 2½ lb red radicchio

120 g / 4 oz pancetta, chopped

salt and pepper

Cut the radicchio into quarters. Wash, dry and set aside.

Put the pancetta in a frying pan. Stirring frequently, cook until the fat has melted and the pancetta is crisp.

Add the radicchio and cover the pan. Shaking the pan occasionally, cook for about 5 minutes.

Sprinkle with salt and pepper, transfer to a warm platter and serve.

Rotolo di Patate

Potato and Spinach Roll

This very pretty dish is a speciality of north-eastern Italy. It can be prepared in advance and refrigerated, but do this no more than 8 hours ahead because the potato tends to turn sour. It should be cooked just before serving and is the ideal accompaniment for a sole fillet with courgettes (zucchini) and tomato (page 102).

SERVES 6

900 g / 2 lb boiling potatoes

60 g / 2 oz / 4 tbsp unsalted butter

2 egg yolks, lightly beaten

salt and pepper

900 g / 2 lb spinach leaves

a pinch of grated nutmeg

60 g / 2 oz / ⅔ cup fine dry breadcrumbs (page 132)

Cook the potatoes, in their skins, in boiling salted water until tender. Drain, then peel and mash them while still hot. Add the butter and egg yolks and stir until they are completely absorbed. Season with salt and pepper and leave the mashed potato to cool completely.

Cook the spinach in a little salted water. Drain and rinse under cold running water. Squeeze out the excess water and chop the spinach very finely. Add the nutmeg and breadcrumbs, blending well.

On a sheet of foil, spread the mashed potato into a rectangle about 1 cm/½ inch thick. Spread the spinach in a layer over the potato. Roll up the potato as you would a Swiss (jelly) roll using the foil to help. Wrap the potato roll in a linen towel or table napkin and tie both ends securely.

Bring a saucepan of water to the boil. Lower the potato roll into it and simmer gently for about 40 minutes. Unwrap the roll and slice it.

Arrange the slices on a warm platter and serve at once.

Seasonal Vegetables

Always use vegetables that are in season. Besides being much more expensive, forced vegetables have very little flavour. In summer stick to tomatoes, aubergines (eggplants), sweet peppers, courgettes (zucchini), beans and so on. In autumn choose mushrooms, spinach, Swiss chard, celery and bulb fennel. In winter there are all the different types of cabbage, onions, carrots, globe artichokes and turnips, while spring brings asparagus, peas, broad or fava beans and a variety of salad leaves.

Choosing and Preparing Moulds

Vegetables are often cooked in moulds. These come in all shapes and sizes, and I find that smooth non-stick moulds are the most practical. Obviously the contents of a ring mould will take less time to cook. I find the best way to butter a mould thickly is to brush on a layer of melted or softened butter and to refrigerate it until the butter has hardened, then to add another layer of butter and to refrigerate it until needed. After buttering, moulds are sometimes coated with breadcrumbs or grated Parmesan cheese.

Rucola in Insalata con le Pere

ROCKET (ARUGULA) AND PEAR SALAD

In temperate climates, rocket (arugula) grows throughout the year. If you plant it in a small box, you'll find that the more you pick it the more it flourishes. The combination of sweet pears and sharp greens makes an unusual salad suitable for serving with meat dishes such as pork loin with mustard (page 103).

SERVES 6

3 firm dessert pears

juice of $\frac{1}{2}$ lemon

210 g / 7 oz rocket (arugula)

salt

3 tbsp extra virgin olive oil

Peel, core and slice the pears. Arrange the slices in a salad bowl and sprinkle them with the lemon juice.

Wash and dry the rocket (arugula), removing any tough stalks. Add to the salad bowl, sprinkle with salt and olive oil and toss lightly. Serve immediately.

Sformatini di Fagiolini

BAKED GREEN BEAN CUSTARDS

This recipe can also be made with peas or spinach and can be cooked in one large mould. The custards are very elegant served with the roast veal with herbs and lemon sauce on page 120.

SERVES 6

450 g / 1 lb green beans

30 g / 1 oz / 2 tbsp unsalted butter + extra for the ramekins

3 tbsp flour

240 ml / 8 fl oz / 1 cup milk

6 tbsp freshly grated Parmesan cheese

2 eggs, well beaten

salt and pepper

4 tbsp fine dry breadcrumbs (page 132)

Bring a saucepan of salted water to the boil. Add the beans and cook until just tender. Drain and refresh under cold running water. Dice the beans and set aside.

In a saucepan melt the butter over moderate heat. Add the flour and, stirring constantly, cook for a few minutes. Still stirring, gradually add the milk. Bring to the boil and cook for a few more minutes. Remove from the heat. Stir in the Parmesan, green beans and beaten eggs. Mix well and season with salt and pepper.

Butter 12 small ramekins or custard cups and coat them with the breadcrumbs. Spoon in the custard mixture. Place the ramekins or cups in a roasting pan filled with about 2.5 cm / 1 inch water. Transfer to a preheated 180°C / 350°F / gas 4 oven and cook until firm and lightly browned, about 40 minutes.

Unmould the custards on to a warm platter and serve immediately.

Spinaci con Uvetta e Pinoli

SPINACH WITH RAISINS AND PINE NUTS

I particularly enjoy fresh young spinach, either raw with a simple dressing of extra virgin olive oil and lemon juice or served in this way. Serve with the meat patties in Marsala sauce on page 104.

SERVES 6

90 g / 3 oz seedless raisins

1.2 kg / 2½ lb fresh spinach, with stalks

3 tbsp extra virgin olive oil

salt

60 g / 2 oz / ⅔ cup pine nuts

Soak the raisins in lukewarm water to cover for about 30 minutes. Drain well.

Bring a large saucepan of salted water to the boil over high heat. Add the spinach and, stirring, cook until just wilted, about 2 minutes. Drain the spinach in a colander and refresh under cold running water to keep green. When cool, squeeze out the excess liquid.

In a large frying pan heat the oil over moderate heat. Add the spinach and raisins and, stirring, cook until heated through, about 5 minutes. Season with salt.

Arrange the spinach on a warm platter, sprinkle with the pine nuts and serve.

Verdure alla Griglia

GRILLED MIXED VEGETABLES

I vary the vegetables according to the season, and in winter I often grill sliced bulb fennel, carrot and celeriac (celery root). The secret is to make sure that the heat is not too fierce or the vegetables will burn before they are cooked. You can also grill the vegetables on a barbecue or under the grill (broiler). For a vegetarian lunch serve with the potatoes with rosemary on page 141.

SERVES 6

2 medium-size courgettes (zucchini)

2 aubergines (eggplants)

1 green sweet pepper

1 red sweet pepper

1 yellow sweet pepper

3 ripe plum tomatoes

3 small heads of red radicchio

2 medium-size onions, halved

3 tbsp extra virgin olive oil

salt and pepper

● **Grilled Mixed Vegetables** ●

Cut the courgettes (zucchini) and aubergines (eggplants) lengthwise into slices about 3 mm/⅛ inch thick. Cut the peppers into quarters lengthwise and remove the ribs and seeds. Cut the tomatoes in half crosswise and the radicchio in half lengthwise.

Heat a large ridged cast-iron grill pan on top of the stove. Arrange the onions on it and brush them with very little oil. Cook on both sides for about 5 minutes or until soft.

Arrange the rest of the vegetables on the grill, brush lightly with oil and cook for about 2 minutes on each side.

Cut the grilled peppers into strips and arrange them on a warm platter with the rest of the vegetables. Season with salt and pepper, sprinkle with the rest of the oil and serve at once.

Zucchine alla Menta

FRIED COURGETTES (ZUCCHINI) IN
MINT SAUCE

This is always one of the most successful vegetable dishes during the cookery classes. The same method can be used to prepare small oval aubergines (eggplants). They go well with the sausages in pastry on page 115.

SERVES 6

3 medium-size courgettes (zucchini)
120 g / 4 oz / 1 cup flour
2 eggs, lightly beaten
salt
180 g / 6 oz / 2 cups fine dry breadcrumbs (page 132)
60 g / 2 oz / 4 tbsp unsalted butter
4 tbsp extra virgin olive oil
120 ml / 4 fl oz / ½ cup red wine vinegar
a handful of fresh mint leaves, or 1 tbsp dried mint
90 g / 3 oz / 7 tbsp sugar

Cut the courgettes (zucchini) lengthwise into slices about 3 mm / ⅛ inch thick.

In three different soup plates put the flour, the beaten egg with a pinch of salt and the breadcrumbs. Dip the courgettes (zucchini) first in flour, then in egg and lastly in breadcrumbs.

In a heavy frying pan heat the butter and oil over moderate heat. Add the

courgettes (zucchini) and fry until crisp and golden, a few minutes on each side. Remove with a slotted spoon and drain on paper towels. Arrange the fried courgettes (zucchini) on a warm platter. Sprinkle with salt and keep warm.

● Fried Courgettes (Zucchini) in Mint Sauce ●

In a small saucepan combine the vinegar, mint and sugar. Cook until syrupy. Spoon this sauce over the courgettes (zucchini) and serve at once.

Le Salse — Salate e Dolci

— SAUCES — SAVOURY AND SWEET —

*I*t is a point of pride for Italian cooks that our dishes do not require elaborate sauces to make them appealing. We prepare our food in such a way that the natural flavours of the fine ingredients remain clear and distinct to the taste. Usually our sauces are simply the juices obtained from the cooking of fish, poultry, meat, vegetables and fruit.

When I serve a sauce with roast meat, I normally skim off the fat from the cooking juices and sediments left in the pan and then dissolve, or deglaze, them with a little red or white wine. I use a good wine: cheap wine would add an undesirable acidic taste to the sauce. I would never thicken the cooking juices with flour or enrich them with butter. To my palate, a sauce made in that way not only kills the flavour of the dish but makes everything taste the same. Should I want to enhance a particular dish, I make a light, fresh vegetable sauce. In this case I might choose fresh peas, sauté them in olive oil and put them through a blender with a little water to thin the sauce. I do the same with fennel bulbs, globe artichokes and the skin of courgettes (zucchini) as well as various kinds of fruit to accompany desserts.

*T*he one sauce that could be considered an Italian culinary classic, and typical of regional cooking the entire length and breadth of the peninsula, is SALSA DI POMODORO, tomato sauce. There are two basic types with many variations. The Neapolitan or southern-style sauce is made with fresh plum tomatoes, garlic sautéed in olive oil and, maybe, a little chili pepper and fresh basil leaves added to taste. In the north we begin with a SOFFRITTO. This cooking base for many sauces consists of a little onion, celery, carrot and parsley, all finely chopped and sautéed in olive oil. When this is ready the tomatoes are added and cooked for a long time until all the water in them has evaporated. My mother used to add butter to her tomato sauce, which made it deliciously sweet. Now, even in northern Italy, everyone uses olive oil.

● **Milanese Tomato Sauce (p. 157)** ●

I use plum tomatoes, which are meaty and have comparatively few seeds. I buy crates of them in the summer (even my generous garden does not supply enough) and make enough sauce to last me through the winter — I hope. If I should run out, I do not hesitate to use Italian canned tomatoes which are excellent. They come already peeled and I leave them in their juice.

After the tomatoes have finished cooking, you can leave the little pieces of pulp in the sauce or, if you prefer, you can pass the mixture through a food mill. It should not, however, have too creamy a consistency. I usually add a herb to my tomato sauce. Basil, tarragon and parsley are the best with tomatoes, but a little bit of chive and fresh or even dried oregano can be tasty as well.

There are a couple of useful and simple variations of the basic tomato sauce. One is a kind of tomato mayonnaise. I put peeled and seeded tomatoes into a food processor and purée them with olive oil. This sauce is very versatile, and I use it with pasta, rice and meat dishes. The simplest tomato sauce of all is made by chopping or dicing peeled tomatoes, salting and letting them drain, and then adding olive oil and a few leaves of fresh basil. In a few minutes you have a perfectly fresh, healthy sauce for summer pasta.

A classic northern Italian sauce is SALSA VERDE, green sauce. I make it with finely chopped parsley (or sometimes tarragon as they do in Siena), anchovy fillet, capers, hard-boiled egg, breadcrumbs soaked in vinegar to give the sauce more body, and extra virgin olive oil. Traditionally every Thursday, restaurants in the north served this sauce with the regional speciality, BOLLITO MISTO, a mixture of boiled meats such as brisket of beef, tongue, calf's head, veal and chicken. I use the sauce with many dishes. For a light summer luncheon it is one of my favourite sauces to serve with a rice mould.

I also steal the tuna sauce that traditionally accompanies the veal dish, VITELLO TONNATO, and adapt it in much the same way. This is made by blending chunks of tuna with anchovy, capers and egg yolk and thinning the mixture with lemon juice and cream or milk. I find this sauce delicious with boiled rice and steamed vegetables.

I don't know whether the Marquis de Béchamel really invented the French BÉCHAMEL or whether he was inspired by the Italian BESCIAMELLA (once called BALSAMELLA), but this quick and easy white sauce, made with butter, flour and milk, is basic to many of my recipes. I use it for all baked pasta dishes. It keeps them soft and moist while they are cooking. I tend to make my sauce as light as possible, adjusting the amount of butter to the particular recipe and sometimes adding grated Parmesan cheese.

A special sauce that brings back memories of my childhood in Piemonte is FONDUTA. It is made from the semi-soft cow's milk cheese, fontina, creamed

with milk and egg yolk. We would eat it like a pudding, with a spoon, or spread it on bread for a snack. My parents sometimes grated white truffles over it. FONDUTA is the traditional topping for a stuffed square pasta called AGNOLOTTI.

Although I am not beyond being tempted by a rich, dark chocolate sauce, my dessert sauces are almost exclusively made from fruit. I blend whatever fresh fruit of the season I choose — apples, berries, pears — and add it to a sugar syrup. I serve these fresh fruit sauces hot on ice cream or cold on cooked fruit, puddings and fruit tarts. They are light, colourful and decorative as well as delicious.

Finally, a superb condiment that is often called a vinegar but is used more like a sauce is the unique and exquisite ACETO BALSAMICO, balsamic vinegar, from Emilia Romagna. Unlike vinegar it is not made from wine but from the must of sweet white grapes that is simmered very slowly until reduced to a dense, concentrated liquid. Genuine BALSAMICO is then aged for a minimum of 10 years in a series of barrels of various types of wood, and blended with much older vintages during this process.

The finished product has a syrupy consistency and a warm, brown colour. Because of its sweet-sour taste it complements many dishes. I do not like to mix it into green salads because it overwhelms the delicate taste of the fresh leaves, but I do use it, mixed with olive oil, as a dressing on luscious fresh tomatoes. When I deglaze the cooking juices of roast meats, I sometimes add a few drops to the pan. Try some over strawberries for dessert. For a memorable snack, sprinkle a few drops over shavings of the finest Parmesan cheese.

Ragú di Carne alla Bolognese

BOLOGNESE MEAT SAUCE

There are two golden rules for making a good meat sauce. The first is that minced (ground) meat should never be used because, as it cooks, it forms into lumps. The second is that the sauce must be simmered gently for at least 3 hours. This recipe is for a basic *ragú* to which dried mushrooms, chicken livers, or cooked ham or pork can be added. The sauce is generally served on home-made tagliatelle, lasagne and ravioli, but it also goes well with spaghetti, penne or rice. It can be kept in the refrigerator for up to 24 hours.

MAKES 600 G / 1¼ LB

300 g / 10 oz boneless stewing beef

300 g / 10 oz boneless stewing veal

60 g / 2 oz / 4 tbsp unsalted butter

2 tbsp chopped onion

60 g / 2 oz pancetta, chopped

2 tbsp chopped fresh flat-leaf (Italian) parsley

2 tbsp chopped carrot

2 tbsp chopped celery

1 bay leaf

120 ml / 4 fl oz / ½ cup red wine

300 g / 10 oz very ripe tomatoes, peeled and chopped (or use canned with their juice)

salt and pepper

Cut the meat into 2.5-cm / 1-inch cubes.

In a saucepan, combine the butter, onion and pancetta. Stirring occasionally, cook over low heat until the onion is translucent, about 3 minutes. Add the parsley, carrot, celery and bay leaf. Stir and cook for a further 2 minutes.

Add the meat, raise the heat to moderate and, stirring frequently, continue cooking until the meat starts to brown. Remove the bay leaf and pour the contents of the saucepan on to a large board.

A VARIETY OF SAUCES

Italians are not great sauce lovers. Generally speaking, they don't like sauces to change the flavour of their food. On the other hand, they really indulge their whims in a vast variety of sauces for pasta and rice. There are so many versions just of tomato sauce. It can be raw, barely cooked, well cooked or concentrated and is almost always flavoured with a herb of some kind. A few sauces are also served on vegetables and of course, on some desserts.

● **Bolognese Meat Sauce** ●

Chop it very finely and return to the saucepan.

Pour in the wine and boil to evaporate, scraping well to mix with the cooking juices. Add the tomatoes, season with salt and pepper and stir well. Cover the saucepan and simmer gently over very low heat for about 3 hours. If necessary, add a little water from time to time. When all the excess liquid has evaporated, the sauce is ready to serve.

AROMATICS AND HERBS

A great variety of herbs are used for flavouring food and sauces. One of the most often used is parsley. It must, however, be flat-leaf (Italian) parsley, because the curly kind is tough and has very little flavour. Other popular herbs are chives, thyme, wild fennel, basil (perfect on tomatoes), oregano, marjoram and, in Liguria, borage. Other much-used seasonings are threads of saffron for risotto, black and white pepper, *peperoncino* (a small, very hot chili pepper), capers (which in Italy are generally preserved in salt and must be rinsed before use) and fresh garlic.

Salsa di Arance e Cipolle

ORANGE AND ONION SAUCE

A very tasty sauce to serve with boiled or roast meat, game or grilled ham or bacon. It is essential to make this sauce with oranges that have not been sprayed with chemicals, otherwise the sauce will have a bitter flavour. If in doubt, peel the oranges, removing all the white pith, before slicing them. The sauce can be kept up to 24 hours in the refrigerator.

MAKES 480 ML / 16 FL OZ / 2 CUPS

450 g / 1 lb organically grown oranges

450 g / 1 lb onions, sliced

60 g / 2 oz / 5 tbsp sugar

4 tbsp white wine vinegar

a pinch of ground cinnamon

salt

• **Orange and Onion Sauce** •

Slice the oranges without peeling them.

In a heavy saucepan, combine the oranges, onions, sugar, vinegar, cinnamon and salt to taste. Cover and simmer over low heat, stirring frequently, for about 1 hour.

Transfer the mixture to a blender. Process until a smooth, creamy sauce is formed. Reheat before serving.

Salsa di Cipolle al Rafano

ONION AND HORSERADISH SAUCE

This sauce goes well with smoked ham and roast pork or turkey.

MAKES 240 ML / 8 FL OZ / 1 CUP

60 g / 2 oz / 4 tbsp unsalted butter

3 medium-size onions, finely chopped

1 tbsp flour

30 g / 1 oz / 2 tbsp freshly grated horseradish

salt

300 ml / ½ pint / 1¼ cups light chicken stock (page 216)

1 tbsp chopped fresh parsley

In a saucepan melt the butter over low heat. Add the onions and, stirring frequently, cook gently until translucent. Stir in the flour and horseradish and season with salt. Stirring constantly, gradually add the stock and cook until the sauce has thickened, about 20 minutes. Stir in the parsley and serve hot.

OIL IN SAUCES

I generally try to keep the flavour of a sauce as delicate as possible so it does not mask the taste of the dish it is accompanying. I nearly always use oil instead of butter because it is less fatty. Many of my sauces are based on puréed vegetables to which I add oil the way you would to a mayonnaise. I do this with tomatoes, sweet peppers, peas, raw courgettes (zucchini) and bulb fennel. I also dilute rosemary-flavoured potato purée with a little water and gradually add oil to it. These sauces I make in a blender.

Salsa di Fagioli

BEAN SAUCE

This very particular sauce is delicious with the potato ravioli on page 46 instead of the potato sauce, or on steamed prawns or shrimp. It can be kept in the refrigerator for up to 12 hours before serving.

MAKES 480 ML / 16 FL OZ / 2 CUPS

150 g / 5 oz / scant 1 cup dried cannellini, haricot or great northern beans

1 tbsp fresh thyme leaves

90 g / 3 oz sliced pancetta

1 small onion, finely chopped

6 tbsp extra virgin olive oil

salt and pepper

Soak the beans in water to cover for about 12 hours. Drain the beans and transfer them to a saucepan. Add the thyme and enough water to cover by about 2.5 cm / 1 inch. Bring slowly to the boil, then cover the saucepan and simmer gently over very low heat for about 1½ hours.

Spread the pancetta slices flat on the bottom of a frying pan and fry over low heat until the fat has melted and the pancetta is crisp, about 10 minutes. Remove the pancetta and set aside.

To the fat in the pan add the onion and sauté over very low heat until translucent. Add the beans and any remaining cooking liquid, cover the pan and simmer for a further 10 minutes.

Transfer the contents of the pan to a blender. Add the pancetta and oil and blend until you get a smooth, creamy sauce. Season with salt and pepper. Reheat just before serving.

Salsa al Gorgonzola

GORGONZOLA SAUCE

You might like to serve this with the potato gnocchi on page 32 instead of the other sauce. Pour it over polenta or spoon a little on top of fried eggs. To get a nice sauce, it is essential to use a fresh piece of mild gorgonzola. The sauce can be kept in the refrigerator for up to 24 hours and reheated gently just before serving.

MAKES 600 ML / 1 PINT / 2½ CUPS

150 g / 5 oz fresh gorgonzola cheese

450 ml / ¾ pint / scant 2 cups whipping cream

Cut the gorgonzola into small pieces. In a saucepan, combine the gorgonzola and cream. Bring to the boil, then lower the heat and, stirring occasionally, cook over low heat until all the cheese has melted.

Salsa al Limone

SAVOURY LEMON SAUCE

This sauce goes well on vegetable moulds such as the one made with peas on page 76, or with steamed vegetables such as asparagus, bulb fennel or green beans, or with boiled chicken and rice. One of my first memories of Badia a Coltibuono is a one-course luncheon of boiled chicken and rice served accompanied by this sauce. The sauce cannot be reheated or the eggs will cook and curdle.

MAKES 600 ML / 1 PINT / 2½ CUPS

2 egg yolks

2 tbsp lemon juice

30 g / 1 oz / 2 tbsp unsalted butter

3 tbsp flour

480 ml / 16 fl oz / 2 cups light chicken stock (page 216), at room temperature

salt and pepper

In a bowl beat the egg yolks and the lemon juice together.

In a small saucepan melt the butter over moderate heat. Add the flour and, stirring constantly, cook until well absorbed, about 3 minutes. Still stirring constantly, gradually add the stock. Bring to the boil and boil to make a smooth, thin sauce. Remove the saucepan from the heat.

Add the egg yolk and lemon mixture and stir well. Season with salt and pepper and serve immediately.

USING HERBS

I always use fresh parsley, basil, rosemary and sage to flavour sauces because they are now available throughout the year. Thyme, oregano, tarragon and mint keep their flavour when dried, but use only about one-quarter of the quantity you would use of fresh herbs. Parsley and basil, chopped with a little salt to help keep their colour, will freeze well, but unfortunately they quickly turn black when put on hot food.

Salsa Maionese al Pomodoro

LIGHT TOMATO AND OIL MAYONNAISE SAUCE

This very light sauce goes particularly well with the fish fillets with artichokes on page 102. It can also be served on spaghetti or with the vegetable ring on page 77 in place of the green sauce. It should not be kept in the refrigerator for more than a few hours before serving because peeled tomatoes become acidic easily.

MAKES 600 ML / 1 PINT / 2½ CUPS

450 g / 1 lb firm, very ripe plum tomatoes, peeled, seeded and chopped

salt and pepper

1 tbsp chopped fresh oregano, or 1 tsp dried oregano

120 ml / 4 fl oz / ½ cup extra virgin olive oil

Sprinkle the tomatoes with salt and leave to drain in a colander for 30 minutes.

● **Tuna Sauce with Tarragon (p. 158),** ●
Gorgonzola Sauce

In a blender combine the tomatoes, oregano, salt and pepper. Blend until creamy. With the motor running, gradually add the oil in a slow, steady stream. Process until well blended and creamy.

Pour into a sauce boat and serve.

Salsa di Peperoni

SWEET PEPPER SAUCE

This is a very useful sauce to accompany pasta or rice, as well as roast veal, or the grilled lamb on skewers (page 119). You could also reheat leftover potatoes in it or spoon it over an omelette. The sauce can be kept in the refrigerator for 12 hours.

MAKES 240 ML/8 FL OZ/1 CUP

3 red or yellow sweet peppers, halved and seeded

1 garlic head, unpeeled

1 anchovy fillet in oil, drained

6 fresh basil leaves

salt

120 ml/4 fl oz/$\frac{1}{2}$ cup extra virgin olive oil

Arrange the pepper halves, cut sides down, on a baking sheet with the head of garlic. Bake in a preheated 200°C/ 400°F/gas 6 oven until the pepper skins blister, about 30 minutes. Wrap the peppers in foil and leave them to cool for a few minutes, then peel them. Slice the peppers. Press the garlic cloves one by one into a small bowl to get rid of the skins.

In a blender, combine the garlic, peppers, anchovy and basil. Season with a little salt. Gradually pour in the oil with the motor running and process until a creamy sauce is formed. Reheat for serving or serve at room temperature.

● **Sweet Pepper Sauce** ●

Salsa alla Piemontese

PIEDMONTESE SAUCE

In Piemonte this sweet and sour sauce is served with mixed boiled meats. Because of the vinegar in the sauce, it should never be served on pasta or rice.

MAKES 600 ML / 1 PINT / 2½ CUPS

---

900 g / 2 lb ripe plum tomatoes, peeled and sliced

---

2 red or yellow sweet peppers, cored and sliced

---

1 medium-size onion, sliced

---

60 g / 2 oz / 5 tbsp sugar

---

1 dried hot chili pepper

---

240 ml / 8 fl oz / 1 cup white wine vinegar

---

1 tbsp mixed freshly ground cloves, cinnamon, nutmeg and fennel seeds

---

salt

In a saucepan, combine the tomatoes, peppers, onion, sugar and chili pepper. Cover and simmer very gently for about 2 hours, stirring occasionally.

Strain the sauce into a bowl through a

PREPARING TOMATOES

In Italy plum tomatoes are used for sauce because they have few seeds and are less watery than salad tomatoes. If you have to use round tomatoes, after peeling them cut them in half and remove the seeds, sprinkle with salt and leave them to drain in a colander for at least 1 hour. All tomatoes must be peeled before using to make a sauce. Plunge them into boiling water for 30 seconds, drain and allow to cool slightly, then make a small incision with a sharp knife and slide off the skin.

fine sieve. Add the vinegar and spices. Season with salt.

Return the sauce to the pan. Bring back to the boil, then lower the heat and simmer gently until the excess liquid has evaporated and the sauce is thick, about 50 more minutes. Serve very hot.

Salsa di Pomodoro a Crudo

RAW TOMATO SAUCE

I only prepare this sauce in summer when tomatoes are very ripe and full of flavour. I always use salad tomatoes for this because, although they are more watery than plum tomatoes, they have a much stronger flavour and enhanced by herbs, make a delicious sauce. Serve on cold spaghetti cooked *al dente*, with a spaghetti omelette (page 70), or on slices of toasted country bread. Chopped tomatoes can only be refrigerated for a few hours because they quickly turn sour.

MAKES 720 ML / 24 FL OZ / 3 CUPS

---

900 g / 2 lb ripe salad tomatoes, peeled and coarsely chopped

---

salt and pepper

---

20 fresh basil leaves, or 1 tbsp chopped fresh chives, or 1 tbsp fresh oregano leaves (or 1 tsp dried oregano), or 2 tbsp chopped fresh flat-leaf (Italian) parsley

---

6 tbsp extra virgin olive oil

---

1 garlic clove, chopped

Put the tomatoes in a colander, sprinkle with salt and leave to drain for 1 hour. Tear the basil leaves into pieces with your fingers to avoid them blackening.

In a bowl combine the tomatoes, basil (or one of the other herbs), oil and garlic. Check salt and season with pepper. Stir well and serve at room temperature.

Salsa di Pomodoro alla Milanese

MILANESE TOMATO SAUCE

Although generally used for cooking chicken, rabbit and meatloaf, this sauce also goes very well with fresh pasta because it is milder than the Neapolitan version. Try it with tagliatelle or the potato gnocchi on page 32 instead of the aubergine (eggplant) sauce.

MAKES 480 ML / 16 FL OZ / 2 CUPS

---

1 tbsp chopped onion

---

1 tbsp chopped carrot

---

1 tbsp chopped celery

---

1 tbsp chopped fresh flat-leaf (Italian) parsley

---

2 tbsp extra virgin olive oil

---

30 g / 1 oz / 2 tbsp unsalted butter

---

900 g / 2 lb ripe plum tomatoes, peeled and quartered lengthways (or use canned with their juice)

---

salt and pepper

In a saucepan combine the onion, carrot, celery, parsley, oil and half the butter. Fry gently over low heat until the vegetables are translucent, being careful not to let them brown.

Add the tomatoes, stir and half-cover the saucepan so that the steam can escape. Cook over moderate heat until the excess liquid has evaporated and the sauce is thick, about 50 minutes. Season with salt and pepper.

Push the sauce through a food mill or roughly purée in a blender. Add the rest of the butter and stir until it has melted. The sauce is now ready to reheat and serve.

Salsa di Pomodoro alla Napoletana

NEAPOLITAN TOMATO SAUCE

The small fried pizzas on page 74 are always a great success at the Villa Table. They are served with this tomato sauce which also goes perfectly on *al dente* spaghetti. In summer I sometimes season the sauce with fresh basil, and in winter with a little dried oregano or a few capers.

MAKES 480 ML / 16 FL OZ / 2 CUPS

3 garlic cloves

1 small dried hot chili pepper

6 tbsp extra virgin olive oil

900 g / 2 lb ripe plum tomatoes, peeled and sliced (or use canned with their juice)

1½ tsp sugar

salt

Chop the garlic with the chili pepper. In a saucepan combine with the oil and sauté over low heat until the garlic is just translucent.

Add the tomatoes and sugar. Half-cover the saucepan so the steam can escape and cook over low heat until all the excess liquid has evaporated and a thick sauce has formed, about 50 minutes, stirring occasionally.

Season with salt and serve.

Salsa di Pomodori Verdi

GREEN TOMATO SAUCE

This is a typical old Tuscan recipe, best served with the pork chops in mustard sauce on page 100.

MAKES ABOUT 720 ML / 24 FL OZ / 3 CUPS

1 small onion, thinly sliced

2 tbsp extra virgin olive oil

1.2 kg / 2½ lb green tomatoes, unseeded, peeled and chopped

salt and pepper

1 tbsp cumin seeds

Fry the onion in the olive oil until translucent, for about 3 minutes. Add the chopped tomatoes, salt and pepper and 120 ml / 4 fl oz / ½ cup water. Cook the mixture on a low heat for about 1 hour until it reaches the consistency of a jam. Mix in the cumin seeds at the end of the cooking, and serve hot or cold.

FREEZING TOMATOES

As plum tomatoes are very easy to freeze, it is a good idea to buy a large quantity at the end of the summer when they have ripened well in natural sunlight, are full of flavour and cost less. Wash and dry them well and seal them in bags before freezing. To use frozen tomatoes, first soak them in very hot tap water for a couple of minutes. As soon as the water is sufficiently cool, gently rub them in your hands and the skins will peel off immediately. Still frozen, place them in a covered pan over moderate heat where they will release their juices while gradually thawing.

Salsa di Spinaci alla Noce Moscata

SPINACH AND NUTMEG SAUCE

This is delicious on savoury rice and leek pie (page 82), or in place of the aubergine (eggplant) sauce on the potato gnocchi on page 32. The sauce can be kept in the refrigerator for up to 12 hours.

MAKES 480 ML / 16 FL OZ / 2 CUPS

600 g / 1¼ lb fresh spinach leaves

30 g / 1 oz / 2 tbsp unsalted butter

1 tsp grated nutmeg

240 ml / 8 fl oz / 1 cup whipping cream

salt and pepper

Bring a saucepan of salted water to the boil. Add the spinach and blanch for 2 minutes until just wilted. Drain the spinach and squeeze out the water.

In the pan melt the butter over low heat. Add the spinach, cover the pan and simmer gently for about 5 minutes, stirring occasionally.

Transfer the spinach to a blender. Add the nutmeg and process until puréed. Pour in the cream and process just enough to blend the ingredients.

Season with salt and pepper and reheat before serving.

Salsa Tonnata al Dragoncello

TUNA SAUCE WITH TARRAGON

A very famous Italian dish, vitello tonnato, consists of thin slices of boiled veal covered with this sauce. You can also serve it to cover hard-boiled eggs. During the summer I sometimes use the sauce around a cold rice mould, which makes a very elegant dish for a buffet. If you cannot get fresh tarragon, flat-leaf (Italian) parsley can be used instead. The sauce can be kept in the refrigerator for up to 24 hours.

MAKES 600 ML / 1 PINT / 2½ CUPS

1 egg and 2 egg yolks

2 tbsp chopped fresh tarragon

salt

210 ml / 7 fl oz / ⅞ cup extra virgin olive oil

300 g / 10 oz canned tuna fish in oil, drained

2 anchovy fillets in oil, drained

1 tbsp capers in vinegar, drained

juice of 1 lemon

6 tbsp milk

In a blender combine the egg, egg yolks, tarragon and a pinch of salt. Process for 2 seconds. With the motor running, add the oil in a slow steady stream.

Add the tuna, anchovy fillets and capers and process until creamy. Add the lemon juice and milk and process until a smooth sauce is formed. Refrigerate until just before serving.

● **Green Tomato Sauce** ●

USING A SIEVE

*A*lthough I use a blender for the vegetable and oil sauces, I never use one in preparing sauces of cooked vegetables for braised and roast meats. I prefer to push them through a sieve or food mill because the resulting consistency isn't so creamy. In the kitchen I frequently use an old-fashioned round metal sieve with wooden sides; these can still be found in street markets and in a few household stores. I find they give the best results and are easy to keep clean.

Salsa di Zucchine

COURGETTE (ZUCCHINI) SAUCE

During the summer there are so many vegetables growing in the garden that courgettes (zucchini) are sometimes left to grow until they are too big to be eaten as a vegetable. So I use them to make this sauce. Very quick, it is perfect served on very *al dente* spaghetti, on vegetable moulds, or as a complement to the spinach and veal roll on page 92.

MAKES 600 ML / 1 PINT / 2½ CUPS

900 g / 2 lb large courgettes (zucchini)

120 ml / 4 fl oz / ½ cup extra virgin olive oil

20 fresh basil leaves

6 tbsp freshly grated Parmesan cheese

120 ml / 4 fl oz / ½ cup whipping cream

salt and pepper

Remove the skins from the courgettes (zucchini) with about 2 mm / ¹⁄₁₆ inch of the pulp. Save the rest of the pulp for making a soup. Cut the skin into pieces.

In a frying pan combine 3 tbsp of the oil and the pieces of skin. Cook over low heat, stirring occasionally, until tender, about 5 minutes.

Transfer the contents of the pan to a blender. Add the basil, Parmesan and the rest of the oil. Process until creamy. Add the cream and season with salt and pepper. Process just until blended.

Reheat for a few minutes before serving or serve at room temperature.

Salsa Verde

GREEN SAUCE

This sauce can be stored for about 3 days in the refrigerator.

SERVES 6

1 tbsp stale crumbs from country-style bread

4 tbsp red wine vinegar

4 tbsp chopped flat-leaf (Italian) parsley

1 hard-boiled egg, chopped

● Sweet Orange Sauce ●

1 tbsp capers, chopped

salt and pepper

120 ml / 4 fl oz / ½ cup olive oil

Soak the breadcrumbs in the vinegar for about 10 minutes. Drain and squeeze out excess liquid.

Combine the breadcrumbs, parsley, chopped egg, capers and salt and pepper to taste. Add the oil, mix well and pour into a sauceboat.

Salsa all'Arancia

SWEET ORANGE SAUCE

Use this simple sauce to fill a baked sweet short pastry case (page 218). Or serve with biscuits (cookies).

MAKES 360 ML / 12 FL OZ / 1½ CUPS

2 oranges

2 egg yolks

4 tbsp sugar

240 ml / 8 fl oz / 1 cup whipping cream

Grate the zest from the oranges. Squeeze the fruits and strain the juice through a fine sieve. Set aside.

In the top of a double boiler, or a heatproof bowl set over a pan of hot water, combine the egg yolks and sugar. Whisk until foamy and light. Add the orange zest and juice and stir until the custard sauce starts to thicken. Remove from the heat and leave to cool.

In a bowl whip the cream until soft peaks form. Carefully fold the cream into the orange sauce and serve.

● **Date and Nut Sauce (p. 162)** ●

Salsa di Ciliege

CHERRY SAUCE

The crushed cherry stones add a wonderful perfume to this sauce. Although it is generally served with game birds or with meat such as the grilled lamb on skewers on page 119, the sauce is also excellent with a dessert, particularly on chocolate ice cream. You can also serve it cold, in which case omit the potato flour.

MAKES 600 ML / 1 PINT / 2½ CUPS

450 g / 1 lb ripe dark cherries

1 whole clove

180 g / 6 oz / ⁷/₈ cup sugar

grated zest of ½ orange

240 ml / 8 fl oz / 1 cup red wine

1 tbsp potato flour or arrowroot, dissolved in 2 tbsp water

Stone the cherries, reserving about 15 stones. Crush the reserved stones and tie them in a piece of muslin or cheesecloth with the clove.

In a saucepan combine the cherries, sugar, orange zest, red wine and the muslin bag. Bring to the boil, then lower the heat and simmer until the cooking juices become syrupy and coat a spoon, about 15 minutes.

Remove the muslin bag and transfer the cherries and syrup to a blender. Add the potato flour and purée until creamy.

Return the sauce to the pan and heat gently, stirring, for a couple of minutes without boiling. Serve hot.

Salsa di Datteri e Noci

DATE AND NUT SAUCE

I usually serve this sauce warm on vanilla ice cream or stewed peaches, but it is perfect cold to fill a baked short pastry case (page 218) or served with the peach meringues on page 188. When warm the sauce is very runny but it thickens as it cools. It can be kept in the refrigerator for a few days.

MAKES 480 ML / 16 FL OZ / 2 CUPS

60 g / 2 oz walnut kernels

450 g / 1 lb dates, stoned (pitted)

90 g / 3 oz / ¼ cup honey

Bring a small saucepan of water to the boil and blanch the walnuts for 30 seconds. Drain and remove the skins.

In a blender, combine the dates, walnuts and honey. Process until thoroughly blended. Keep refrigerated and heat just before serving.

Salsa di Fragole

STRAWBERRY SAUCE

Redcurrants, raspberries, pears and peaches can be substituted for strawberries here. These fruit sauces can be served with many desserts such as sliced raw fruit, cooked fruits and the raspberries in wine jelly on page 186.

MAKES 480 ML / 16 FL OZ / 2 CUPS

120 g / 4 oz / 9½ tbsp sugar

1 tbsp lemon juice

450 g / 1 lb strawberries

1 tbsp kirsch or other fruit liqueur

In a saucepan combine the sugar, lemon juice and 6 tbsp water. Bring to the boil over low heat and cook until the syrup coats the spoon, about 5 minutes.

In a blender combine the strawberries, syrup and kirsch. Blend until a creamy sauce is formed. Allow to cool before serving.

Salsa di Pere

PEAR SAUCE

I usually serve this sauce with pigeons on the spit (page 108), but obviously it is suitable for all roast game. Without the mustard, it can be served with cooked fruit, lemon sorbet or the lemon tart on page 192. It can be kept in the refrigerator for about 12 hours.

MAKES 360 ML / 12 FL OZ / 1½ CUPS

450 g / 1 lb pears, peeled, cored and thinly sliced

30 g / 1 oz / 2 tbsp unsalted butter

a piece of cinnamon stick, about 2.5 cm / 1 inch long

1 whole clove

1 tsp powdered mustard

2 tbsp sugar

In a saucepan, combine the sliced pears, butter, cinnamon, clove, mustard and sugar. Cover the saucepan and cook over very low heat, stirring occasionally, until the pears are very soft, about 20 minutes.

Push the mixture through a sieve. Reheat before serving.

● **Strawberry Sauce** ●

I Formaggi

CHEESE

*D*uring my week of cooking classes I usually serve a selection of Italian cheese at a special lunch, combining different types with several breads. This is merely an introductory course, as it were, because it has been estimated that there are over 400 Italian cheeses. Every region of Italy has milk-producing animals — cows in the north, sheep in the central and southern parts of the peninsula, as well as goats and even water buffalo in certain areas of the south — and each region makes cheese from the milk. Some of these cheeses are internationally known while others are available only locally and sometimes differ from each other solely in shape and name.

It would be impossible to categorize them all. For my luncheon platter I select a sampling of cheeses of different consistencies and try to include two of each type.

*F*irst, there are the fresh, unripened cheeses, creamy in texture and delicate in taste. These should be eaten within a few days of their making. One of the most famous of these is mascarpone, a cow's milk cheese from Lombardy made with fresh cream. It is usually eaten as a dessert cheese with fruit and, because it combines so well with other flavours, it is also used in cooking. Perhaps the most popular dish made with mascarpone is TIRAMISU in which it is combined with sponge cake, liqueur, coffee and chocolate. A little dessert wine or Cognac stirred into mascarpone is also delicious.

Crescenza and Stracchino are two names for what is essentially the same fresh cheese, made from cow's milk while it is still warm from the udder. It has a rich, buttery taste and is sold in small, rectangular forms. Crescenza spread on a piece of grilled bread accompanied by a glass of red wine makes a tasty light lunch. Caprino, a goat's milk cheese, also belongs to this category of fresh cheeses. It is usually slightly piquant.

*T*hen there is the broad classification of semi-soft to semi-hard cheese. These need to be ripened before they are ready to eat, a process that develops their distinctive flavour and texture. From this category I include on my platter taleggio, a cow's milk cheese

● Goat's Cheese in Extra Virgin Olive Oil (p. 168) ●

from the Val Taleggio in Lombardy. It needs 2 or 3 months in order to develop its rich, mildly piquant flavour and soft, fatty texture. It is delicious with salad and fruit.

Fontina is a semi-soft cheese made from a particular breed of cow from the Valle d'Aosta in Piemonte. It has a slightly sweet, nutty flavour, with small eyes in its paste, and comes in rounds. Fontina is used for several Piemontese regional dishes, particularly the sauce called FONDUTA, made with the addition of eggs and milk.

The celebrated, blue-veined gorgonzola also belongs to this category. Fine gorgonzola should be smooth and moist in texture and savoury in flavour. It is another cow's milk cheese that originates in a town near Milan. Although it is often used in cooking, a fine piece of gorgonzola merits appreciation on its own.

Tuscany's regional cheese, pecorino toscano, a sheep's milk cheese, can be eaten when it is young, about a week to several months old and semi-soft, and also aged, up to 9 months and semihard. When I first came to live at Coltibuono, the women who worked on the estate were still making pecorino by hand. I often watched, and sometimes joined in. They first added a rennet to the sheep's milk, which curdles it. Then they extracted the curds from the whey and pressed them into little terracotta bowls in order to force out the remaining whey. When the curds became compact and the cheese was formed, they rubbed it with salt. The fresh cheeses were stored in their own special room until ready to be eaten. It is part of my cooking class agenda to take the students to a nearby farm where they can watch pecorino being made in that same traditional way.

Sheep's milk ricotta is a by-product of making pecorino. The whey is heated and ricotta is formed from the fat content contained in the liquid that rises to the top. Ricotta is also made from cow's milk, but sheep's milk ricotta is the most flavourful. Its creamy, delicate taste is lovely on its own or used in several regional specialities, such as ravioli stuffed with spinach and ricotta.

The most famous of all Italian cheeses, parmigiano reggiano, better known in English as Parmesan, belongs to a category called GRANA or 'grained' cheeses. These are made by cooking the milk, compressing the curds and aging for lengthy periods. Grana padano and pecorino romano, a salty and piquant hard sheep's milk cheese from Lazio, are also of this type. They have a crumbly texture and pronounced flavour — perfect for grating over other foods. Parmigiano reggiano is the finest of the grained cheeses. It can always be identified by the words 'PARMIGIANO REGGIANO' moulded into the rind.

Another Italian cheese known world-wide, mozzarella, is in a class apart called PASTA FILATA or 'spun paste' cheese. To make such cheese, the curd is covered with hot whey and worked in such a way that it is spun into long threads and then shaped into a ball-

like form. Provolone and caciocavallo, both specialities from the south of Italy, also belong to this category. Mozzarella made from buffalo's milk is the rarest and richest of these cheeses. It is produced in only two or three areas of Campania, around Naples. Today mozzarella is mostly manufactured commercially from cow's milk.

I think it should be pointed out that all Italian cheeses are table cheeses. Some are also grating and cooking cheeses. I am always surprised how many of my students have never tasted Parmesan except grated over pasta, nor mozzarella except melted on a pizza. A golden nugget of genuine parmigiano reggiano accompanied by a juicy bunch of grapes is a superb finish to a meal. It would be almost sinful to do anything to fresh buffalo mozzarella except enjoy it with an equally fresh tomato. A wedge of pecorino toscano and a handful of freshly shelled broad or fava beans, washed down with a class of young white wine, is a spring speciality.

We usually eat cheese with salad and fruit at the mid-day meal, never in the evening. When I prepare a platter of cheeses, I provide a separate knife to slice each cheese so as not to mix the tastes. I provide my guests with individual knives and plates for their portions of cheese and serve bread but never butter.

The most extravagant way to serve cheese, and something you might consider for a very special occasion, is the following: buy an entire wheel of parmigiano reggiano, scrape out the inside leaving about 2.5 cm / 1 inch of cheese around the walls of the wheel, and fill with ravioli dressed simply with cream and grated Parmesan. Although this impressive banquet and grand buffet dish requires a considerable initial investment, it does not mean that you have thrown your money away. You can refrigerate the cheese you took from the inside of the wheel; well wrapped, it will keep for months.

Bomboline al Mascarpone

MASCARPONE CROQUETTES

This delicately flavoured dessert should be served piping hot. For an easier version, mix the mascarpone and ground amaretti with a little sugar, roll into small balls, chill and serve.

SERVES 6

180 g / 6 oz amaretti biscuits (cookies)

420 g / 15 oz mascarpone

3 eggs

60 g / 2 oz / 5 tbsp sugar

90 g / 3 oz / 1 cup fine dry breadcrumbs (page 132)

90 g / 3 oz / 6 tbsp unsalted butter

6 tbsp extra virgin olive oil

In a blender or food processor finely grind the amaretti. Add the mascarpone, 1 egg and the sugar. Process until smooth and well blended.

In a soup plate beat the 2 remaining eggs. Pour the breadcrumbs into another soup plate.

Roll the mascarpone mixture into walnut-size balls. Dip them in the egg and roll in the breadcrumbs.

In a heavy frying pan heat the butter and oil over moderate heat. Add the balls a few at a time and fry, turning carefully,

COOKING WITH CHEESE

Cheese plays a very important role in the Italian kitchen. It is frequently used as a basic ingredient and to add flavour. As most cheeses contain salt, check before adding salt to any cheese dish.

until golden all over, about 6 minutes.

Drain on paper towels. Arrange on a warm platter and serve immediately.

WHEN TO SERVE CHEESE

In Italy cheese often replaces a dessert. As in France, when both are served, cheese is eaten before the dessert. Unless a special cheese, such as the log on page 175, is served, at least three cheeses are always offered. Generally speaking, there is a soft, a blue and a hard cheese on the board and it is often passed with the salad.

Burro di Gorgonzola

GORGONZOLA BUTTER

I generally prepare a fairly large quantity of this butter, because it is useful to have on hand for pasta or grilled steaks. You can also serve it on small rounds of toast or as a dip for carrot and celery sticks, with a glass of white wine.

MAKES 600 G / 1¼ LB / 5 STICKS

300 g / 10 oz / 2½ sticks unsalted butter, at room temperature

300 g / 10 oz gorgonzola cheese, at room temperature

2 tbsp lemon juice

2 tbsp Cognac

2 tbsp chopped fresh parsley

In a bowl, combine all the ingredients and mash with a fork until well amalgamated and smooth. Or, combine in a food processor and process until smooth and well blended.

Pile the mixture in a bowl, cover tightly and refrigerate until needed.

Caprini all'Olio

GOAT'S CHEESE IN EXTRA VIRGIN OLIVE OIL

After marinating for a few days the cheese is much more tasty and piquant. I always keep a small supply of this in the refrigerator because it is excellent crumbled on spaghetti.

MAKES 600 G / 1¼ LB / 4 CUPS

2 tbsp salted capers

600 g / 1¼ lb fresh soft-textured goat's cheese

¼ tsp freshly ground black pepper

240 ml / 8 fl oz / 1 cup extra virgin olive oil

In a sieve, rinse the capers under cold running water.

Cut the cheese into 3-cm / 1¼-inch dice and put in a bowl. Sprinkle with the pepper and capers. Cover with the olive oil and leave to marinate in the refrigerator for at least 8 days before serving at room temperature.

The cheese will keep for up to 14 days.

STORING CHEESE

Ideally cheese should be kept in a cool larder, but well-wrapped semi-hard and hard cheeses can be stored at the bottom of the refrigerator. Remember that, like vegetables, cheese soon loses its flavour when chilled. Fresh cheeses should not be kept at all even for a short time, in the refrigerator. All cheese should be left at room temperature for at least 1 hour before going to the table.

Costolette di Formaggio

BREADED CHEESE SLICES

Served with the salad with herbs on page 136, these make an excellent luncheon dish. For a buffet, fry meat, fish, bulb fennel, globe artichokes and Swiss chard stalks in the same way and serve them with the Milanese tomato sauce on page 157.

SERVES 6

600 g / 1¼ lb provolone, caciocavallo or fontina cheese

2 eggs

salt and pepper

60 g / 2 oz / ½ cup flour

120 g / 4 oz / 1⅓ cups fine dry breadcrumbs (page 132)

6 tbsp extra virgin olive oil

90 g / 3 oz / 6 tbsp unsalted butter

Remove the rind from the cheese and cut it into slices about 5 mm / ¼ inch thick.

Beat the eggs in a soup plate and season with salt and pepper. Pour the flour and breadcrumbs into separate soup plates. Dredge the cheese slices in the flour, then dip them in the egg and coat with breadcrumbs.

In a large, heavy frying pan, heat the oil and butter. Fry the breaded cheese slices, a few at a time, over moderate heat for about 3 minutes on each side. Drain on paper towels.

Arrange the breaded slices on a warm platter and serve piping hot.

Crocchette di Formaggio

CHEESE CROQUETTES

These croquettes can be served with the tomato and mozzarella salad on page 138 or as a first course with the Milanese tomato sauce on page 157. Or serve them with a glass of white wine as an aperitif.

SERVES 6

270 g / 9 oz / 3 cups fine dry breadcrumbs (page 132)

5 eggs

180 g / 6 oz / 1½ cups freshly grated Parmesan cheese

60 g / 2 oz / ½ cup flour

4 tbsp milk

a pinch of grated nutmeg

extra virgin olive oil for deep-frying

In a bowl combine 150 g / 5 oz / 1⅔ cups breadcrumbs with 3 of the eggs, the cheese, flour, milk and nutmeg. Beat with a fork until well mixed and fairly stiff.

With a spoon lift out portions of the mixture about the size of a walnut. Roll them into balls between the palms of your hands.

In a soup plate beat the 2 remaining eggs. Pour the rest of the breadcrumbs into another soup plate. Dip the balls into the egg and roll them in the breadcrumbs.

In a deep heavy pan, heat the oil to 180°C/350°F. Fry the balls, a few at a time, until golden, about 3 minutes. Remove with a slotted spoon and drain on paper towels.

Serve piping hot.

Crostoni di Formaggio

TOASTED CHEESE

Starting the menu with the onion and almond soup on page 28, these would make a delightful light supper. Or serve with cauliflower salad with olives (page 131).

SERVES 6

300 g / 10 oz Gruyère or emmenthal cheese, grated

3 eggs, separated

4 tbsp milk

2 tbsp grappa (optional)

salt and pepper

12 slices of white bread

3 tbsp extra virgin olive oil

In a bowl combine the grated cheese, egg yolks and milk and stir until thick and creamy. Stir in the grappa, if using. Season with salt and pepper. Whisk the egg whites until stiff and fold them carefully into the cheese mixture.

Brush the sliced bread with oil and arrange on a lightly oiled baking sheet. Spread the cheese mixture on the slices of bread, covering them completely. Transfer to a preheated 180°C/350°F/gas 4 oven and bake until the cheese is slightly golden and the toast crisp, about 10 minutes.

Arrange on a warm platter and serve immediately.

Formaggio al Comino

CHEESE WITH CARAWAY SEEDS

For a light supper I occasionally serve this dish with the winter salad with walnuts on page 138. You can use Gruyère, emmenthal or Edam cheese instead of fontina, and replace the caraway with fennel seeds and the mascarpone with ricotta cheese.

SERVES 6

---

300 g / 10 oz mascarpone

---

300 g / 10 oz fontina cheese, grated

---

3 tbsp caraway seeds

In a bowl, combine the mascarpone, fontina and 1 tbsp caraway seeds. Mix until throughly blended.

On a serving plate, arrange the mixture in a dome. Smooth the surface with a spatula and sprinkle it with the remaining caraway seeds, pressing them in lightly so that they do not fall off. Chill until ready to serve.

Formaggio alle Noci

CHEESE AND WALNUT MOULD

Served in this way, gorgonzola is even more tasty than usual. Offer it with the wholewheat bread on page 201, or the sesame breadsticks on page 200, and a glass of red wine. The cheese can be refrigerated for up to 1 week. If you like, use Camembert instead of taleggio.

SERVES 6

---

extra virgin olive oil for the mould

---

300 g / 10 oz gorgonzola cheese

---

300 g / 10 oz taleggio cheese

---

300 g / 10 oz / 2½ cups walnuts

Brush a 20- × 6-cm/8- × 4½-inch rectangular mould with oil.

Cut the cheeses into very thin slices. Divide the walnuts in half lengthwise. Line the mould with a layer of gorgonzola, cover that with a layer of taleggio, then make a layer of walnuts.

● **Cheese with Caraway Seeds** ●

Continue until all the ingredients are used, finishing with a layer of cheese.

Chill the mould for at least 3 hours. Turn it out on to a serving plate and serve at room temperature.

PARMESAN

*P*armigiano reggiano and grana padano are never matured for less than 1 year, and stravecchio, the best variety, is matured for 3 years. Parmesan should be finely grated just before serving and, if well wrapped, keeps for several weeks. Avoid buying already grated Parmesan. The best quality is parmigiano reggiano, and these two words are stamped on the crust. It is worth remembering that 100 g / 3½ oz of Parmesan cheese contains more protein than 240 g / 8 oz of meat.

Gelato di Parmigiano

PARMESAN ICE CREAM

*P*armesan cheese makes a very tasty ice cream. You can, however, vary the flavour by using Swiss or Dutch cheese or fontina. Occasionally, I add 1 tbsp of very finely chopped fresh thyme, rosemary or sage.

SERVES 6

300 g / 10 oz / 2½ cups freshly grated Parmesan cheese

300 ml / ½ pint / 1¼ cups whipping cream

1 tsp sweet paprika

In a saucepan combine the cheese and cream. Stirring constantly over low heat, melt the cheese in the cream without allowing it to boil. This will take about 5 minutes. Leave the mixture to cool.

Pour the cold cream into an ice cream maker and freeze, following the manufacturer's instructions. Or pour it into a bowl and freeze for about 3 hours, whisking the mixture at least three times during this period.

Spoon the ice cream on to a cold serving plate in separate little heaps. Sprinkle with paprika and serve immediately.

Gorgonzola al Limone

LEMON GORGONZOLA

*T*he oil and lemon give the gorgonzola a special flavour. Served with thin slices of bulb fennel and carrot and white celery sticks and followed by the fruit soufflé omelette on page 186, you have a delightful light luncheon. Chilled, this keeps for 12 hours.

SERVES 6

600 g / 1¼ lb gorgonzola cheese

3 tbsp lemon juice

6 tbsp extra virgin olive oil

In a bowl combine the gorgonzola, lemon juice and olive oil. Mash with a spoon until a soft, smooth cream is formed.

Arrange in a mound on a serving plate. Refrigerate until just before serving.

Insalata di Formaggio

CHEESE SALAD

*F*ollowed by the sweet flatbread with grapes on page 188, this salad can be served as a main course. I don't put in too many ingredients, because cheese should

be the dominating flavour. Obviously you can replace the fennel with lettuce, curly endive, finely sliced artichokes or mushroom caps.

SERVES 6

450 g / 1 lb fontina, Gruyère, emmenthal, Edam or Gouda cheese

300 g / 10 oz fennel bulbs

salt and pepper

juice of ½ lemon

6 tbsp extra virgin olive oil

90 g / 3 oz / ¾ cup coarsely chopped walnuts

Remove the rind and cut the cheese into julienne strips. Remove the hard outer leaves from the fennel and slice into julienne strips. In a salad bowl, combine the fennel and cheese. Mix well.

In a cup, dissolve a pinch of salt in the lemon juice. Add the oil, season with pepper and stir well.

Pour the dressing over the salad and toss well. Sprinkle with the walnuts and serve at room temperature.

BUFFALO MOZZARELLA

*B*uffalo milk mozzarella has almost disappeared and most mozzarella is now made with cow's milk. There are now only two areas where buffalo mozzarella is produced: Battipaglia, near Salerno, and another going towards the coast from Caserta. Fresh buffalo mozzarella deteriorates very rapidly and turns rubbery. It is flown to a few select shops in Milan and Rome and is easily recognized when cut because the layers tend to open. It is also much less smooth than mozzarella made from cow's milk. A little milk also seeps out of it.

Mozzarella alla Griglia

GRILLED MOZZARELLA

This dish must be prepared at the last minute and served immediately. Pecorino, provolone and fontina cheese also grill well.

SERVES 6

---

600 g / 1¼ lb mozzarella cheese

---

3 tbsp extra virgin olive oil

---

salt and pepper

---

1 tbsp dried oregano

Heat a cast-iron grill pan well.

Cut the mozzarella into 1-cm/½-inch slices and, if they are too damp, pat dry with paper towels.

Pour the oil into a soup plate and season it with salt and pepper to taste.

Dip the sliced mozzarella in the oil. Grill for 1 minute on each side. Arrange on a warm platter, sprinkle with the oregano and serve at once.

USING MOZZARELLA

Often cheese dishes such as Crostoni di Mozzarella (toasted cheese) or Spiedini di Mozzarella (cheese skewers) are served as a main course or a single-course meal. Also substantial is the celebrated Mozzarella in Carrozza, mozzarella in a carriage, a Neapolitan speciality that consists of a mozzarella sandwich dipped in egg and breadcrumbs before being deep-fried. Onions, courgettes (zucchini) and sweet peppers are also stuffed with mozzarella.

● **Cheese Salad (p. 171)** ●

Pomodori al Formaggio di Capra

CHEESE-STUFFED TOMATOES

As this is a cold dish, I usually serve it with a vegetable, such as parsleyed potatoes, at room temperature (page 141), or with the tagliatelle and ricotta omelette on page 70, left to cool to room temperature.

SERVES 6

6 medium-size ripe tomatoes

salt

600 g / 1¼ lb fresh goat's milk cheese

2 tbsp chopped fresh flat-leaf (Italian) parsley

4 tbsp extra virgin olive oil

1 tbsp balsamic vinegar

Cut a slice off the top of each tomato. Remove the seeds with a teaspoon and sprinkle the inside of the tomato shells with salt. Turn the shells upside down and leave them to drain.

In a bowl, combine the cheese, parsley, oil and balsamic vinegar. Mash with a fork until smooth and well blended.

Fill the tomatoes with the mixture. Arrange on a platter and serve.

Provolone in Tegame

FRIED PROVOLONE

This dish should be made with a strong cheese like provolone or caciocavallo, although fontina will do. With the sliced baked roast potatoes with rosemary on page 140, it can be served as a main course.

● Grilled Mozzarella, Mozzarella ●
Skewer (p. 174)

SERVES 6

600 g / 1¼ lb provolone cheese

3 tbsp extra virgin olive oil

2 garlic cloves

3 tbsp white wine vinegar

1 tbsp dried oregano

Remove the rind from the cheese and cut it into slices about 3 mm / ⅛ inch thick.

In a large frying pan or two pans if necessary because the cheese slices should not overlap, heat the oil over moderate heat. Add the garlic and cook until translucent, about 2 minutes.

Remove the garlic and arrange the cheese slices in the pan. Cook until they start to melt without changing colour. Sprinkle with the vinegar and leave it to evaporate.

Arrange the cheese on a warm platter, sprinkle with the oregano and serve at once.

Ricotta al Miele

HONEYED RICOTTA

The sweet and savoury combination of cheese and honey is delicious, and it is particularly good prepared with chestnut blossom honey. I often serve this dish as a dessert with rice and amaretti fritters (page 186).

SERVES 6

600 g / 1¼ lb / 2½ cups fresh ricotta cheese

6 tbsp chestnut blossom or other honey

In a bowl, whisk the ricotta to get rid of any lumps. Gradually whisk in the honey and continue until well blended.

Pile into a bowl and serve at room temperature.

KEEPING MOZZARELLA

If a cheese such as mozzarella has to be kept for more than a couple of hours, it should be wrapped in a damp cloth and put in a cool place without refrigerating.

Ricotta al Peperoncino

RICOTTA WITH RADISHES AND PAPRIKA

This dish has a number of possibilities. It can be served for brunch, as a first course for luncheon followed by the grape, cheese and apple salad on page 139, or just followed by the peach and amaretti tart on page 185. You can also serve it with thin slices of bulb fennel or white celery.

SERVES 6

600 g / 1¼ lb / 2½ cups ricotta cheese

a pinch of hot paprika

6 tbsp extra virgin olive oil

salt

18 radishes, trimmed and thinly sliced

In a bowl combine the ricotta, paprika and olive oil. Add salt to taste. Mix well to blend. Stir in two-thirds of the sliced radishes.

On a serving plate, pile the mixture in a dome. Cover with the rest of the radish slices. Serve chilled.

Spiedino di Mozzarella

MOZZARELLA SKEWER

This makes an excellent supper dish accompanied by broccoli with pancetta and garlic (page 128). You can substitute provolone, Gruyère, emmenthal or fontina cheese for the mozzarella.

SERVES 6

12 slices of white bread

1 tbsp anchovy paste

240 ml / 8 fl oz / 1 cup milk

450 g / 1 lb mozzarella cheese

unsalted butter for the dish

Thinly spread the slices of bread with anchovy paste. Dip them briefly in the milk. Cut the mozzarella into 10 slices about 1 cm / ½ inch thick.

Starting and ending with a slice of bread, thread alternating bread and mozzarella on to a skewer and place it in a buttered baking dish. Alternatively, hold the bread and mozzarella together by sticking a wooden cocktail stick in either end.

Transfer the baking dish to a preheated 180°C / 350°F / gas 4 oven and bake until crisp and golden, about 30 minutes. Serve immediately.

● **Honeyed Ricotta (p. 173)** ●

Spuma di Gorgonzola allo Sherry

GORGONZOLA AND SHERRY MOUSSE

This is a good starter for an elegant luncheon, particularly in autumn when I sometimes shave fresh white truffle over it. It can also be served with the radicchio with pancetta on page 144 as a main course. For a lighter dish, use ricotta instead of mascarpone.

SERVES 6

210 g / 7 oz gorgonzola cheese, diced

180 ml / 6 fl oz / ¾ cup dry sherry

210 g / 7 oz mascarpone

240 ml / 8 fl oz / 1 cup whipping cream

extra virgin olive oil for the mould

6 tbsp freshly grated Parmesan cheese

Put the gorgonzola in a bowl. Add the sherry. Stir and leave to marinate for about 12 hours, stirring occasionally.

Drain the gorgonzola. In a bowl combine the mascarpone and gorgonzola and beat until well blended. Whip the cream until stiff peaks form. Gently fold the whipped cream into the cheese mixture.

Brush a 23-cm/9-inch ring mould with olive oil and coat it well with the grated Parmesan cheese. Spoon the cheese mixture into the mould. Refrigerate until firm, at least 3 hours.

Turn out on to a platter to serve.

Tronco di Formaggio alle Nocciole

HAZELNUT CHEESE LOG

At summer buffets I often serve cheese in this elegant way, with tomato and mozzarella salad (page 138) and a basket of wholewheat bread (see page 201), accompanied by red wine. I usually finish with a great tray of fruit.

SERVES 6

120 g / 4 oz / 1 cup shelled hazelnuts

300 g / 10 oz fontina or emmenthal cheese, grated

300 g / 10 oz fresh soft-textured goat's cheese

3 tbsp extra virgin olive oil

Arrange the hazelnuts in a single layer in a baking tray and toast lightly in a preheated 180°C/350°F/gas 4 oven for

about 5 minutes, shaking the tray once. Rub the nuts in a coarse kitchen towel to remove the skins, then chop them coarsely.

In a bowl combine the grated cheese, goat's cheese and olive oil. Mash with a fork until smooth and well blended. Shape the mixture into a log with a diameter of about 5 cm/2 inches. Roll the log in the chopped nuts to cover it all over.

Refrigerate until just before serving. This will keep for up to 12 hours.

Tronco di Formaggio al Prezzemolo

PARSLEYED CHEESE LOG

This is another elegant way of serving cheeses that go well together. It may be prepared well ahead of time as it keeps for up to 12 hours in the refrigerator. Present it in slightly overlapping slices.

SERVES 6

120 g / 4 oz / 1 cup freshly grated Parmesan cheese

120 g / 4 oz / ½ cup mascarpone or ricotta cheese

120 g / 4 oz fontina or emmenthal cheese, grated

240 g / 8 oz gorgonzola cheese

3 tbsp finely chopped fresh flat-leaf (Italian) parsley

Either in a bowl or a food processor blend the four cheeses together thoroughly. Chill the mixture for about 2 hours to harden it.

Shape the cheese mixture into a log with a diameter of about 5 cm/2 inches. Roll it in the chopped parsley. Keep

● **Parsleyed Cheese Log** ●

I Dolci

DESSERTS

We normally conclude our family meals with cheese or fresh fruit. But when I have guests, I always serve a dessert. I choose one that is suitable for the finish of a meal that would have included three other courses. Therefore, it will be something light: I want to give my guests a sense of sweet satisfaction without stuffing them. Although they are delicious, many of the rich pastries for which Italy is famous are really too filling to be served at the end of a meal today. Perhaps they are best enjoyed on their own, in the late afternoon with tea or with a glass of dessert wine. Personally I do not enjoy creamy pastries at any time of the day.

These elaborate desserts are almost always made by a professional pastry cook and bought by restaurants and by families from pastry shops. Traditional home-made Italian desserts are much more simple, both in substance and in style. Many of our finest restaurants today are creating their own desserts with these lighter, cleaner tastes. On more than one occasion I have returned home and tried to duplicate the results in my kitchen.

Because we eat with our eyes, I think it is particularly important that a dessert be elegant and attractive. Your guests should leave the table with a pleasant visual memory of a happy ending to what was, one hopes, a delicious experience from beginning to end. I try to achieve this more by the combination of the colours of the ingredients and their shapes than by the addition of any fussy decoration. I serve them as simply as possible – a tart on a plain white or silver platter covered with a linen cloth, white always, never on a doily. I must confess that I do not even own a doily.

The types of dessert I have included here are all (or almost all – I could not leave out chocolate) appropriate for ending a meal on a light note. Many are fruit-based. Nothing is so refreshing and cleansing to the palate as the taste of fresh fruit, even when it is cooked, baked in a tart or puréed as a sauce. Here I let the season be my guide. The only type of dessert I give with a pastry base is a CROSTATA, a tart with a thin case made of butter, eggs, flour and sugar, filled with fruit.

● Vin Santo Sorbet (p. 192) ●

*R*icotta cheese is another of my favourite ingredients for desserts. Because it is made from the whey that has been separated from the curd, it is lighter than cream. Sheep's milk ricotta is especially flavourful and is excellent eaten as is. Cow's milk ricotta is creamier. They both combine well with various sweet ingredients to make tasty puddings.

Moulded desserts, whether fruit-, cream- or ricotta-based, are one of my preferred ways to end a meal, probably because they are so lovely to serve. They are a favourite of my students too. In class we make little individual moulds of colourful pieces of various fruits encased in a sweet jelly (gelatine), surrounded on their plates with a fruit sauce. With the help of a piping bag, I decorate the sauce with a spider web design from a thin thread of cream. All my students design their own decorations, giving full freedom to their artistic fantasy, often with humorous results.

Banane all'Arancia

FRIED BANANAS IN ORANGE SAUCE

I sometimes serve this simple dessert with sponge finger biscuits (ladyfingers).

SERVES 6

6 bananas

30 g / 1 oz / 2 tbsp unsalted butter

120 ml / 4 fl oz / ½ cup orange juice

3 tbsp orange marmalade

6 tbsp sugar

2 tbsp grated orange zest

6 tbsp finely chopped almonds

Peel the bananas, remove the threads and cut in half lengthwise.

In a large frying pan melt the butter over moderate heat. Add the bananas and cook for 5 minutes. Add the orange juice, marmalade and half the sugar. Carefully turn the bananas over and cook for a further 5 minutes.

Arrange the bananas side by side in an ovenproof dish. Spoon over the cooking juices and sprinkle with the rest of the sugar, the orange zest and almonds. Place under the grill (broiler) and, basting twice, cook until the sugar caramelizes slightly, about 5 minutes.

Serve at once.

Biscotti con Ricotta al Caffé

COFFEE RICOTTA WITH HONEY FINGERS

This simple dessert is ideal for lunch. The ricotta can also be flavoured with cocoa powder and a drop of brandy or a pinch of ground cinnamon. Flavoured ricotta is a good tart filling: follow the recipe for the baked sweet short pastry case on page 218 and fill with this ricotta mixture.

SERVES 6

600 g / 1¼ lb / 2½ cups ricotta cheese

1 tbsp instant coffee powder or granules

90 g / 3 oz / 7 tbsp granulated sugar

For the honey fingers

60 g / 2 oz / 4 tbsp unsalted butter

75 g / 2½ oz / 10 tbsp icing (confectioners') sugar

75 g / 2½ oz / 10 tbsp flour

60 g / 2 oz / 3 tbsp honey, warmed

1 egg white

First make the honey fingers. Line a baking sheet with siliconized baking parchment (non-stick silicone paper). In a bowl cream the butter until very soft. Gradually add the icing (confectioners') sugar and flour, beating constantly. Blend in the warm honey and then the egg white. Fill a piping bag fitted with a large ribbon nozzle with the mixture.

Pipe strips about 7.5 cm / 3 inches long, 2.5 cm / 1 inch apart, on the baking sheet. Bake in a preheated 180°C / 350°F / gas 4 oven until golden, just a few minutes.

Remove the baking sheet from the oven and leave to cool for about 30 seconds. Using a spatula, remove the biscuits (cookies) to a wire rack and leave to cool completely.

In a bowl combine the ricotta, instant coffee and granulated sugar. Mix very well and invert the bowl on to a platter. Remove the bowl and arrange the honey fingers around the ricotta just before serving.

COATING A MOULD WITH CARAMEL

To coat a mould with caramel successfully, the mould should be hot, so that the caramel does not stick and harden too quickly. Wear oven gloves to do this because the caramel reaches a very high temperature. While the mould is in the refrigerator, the caramel will melt naturally and the dessert will be easy to turn out. For a more elastic caramel, add a little lemon juice.

Budino di Albicocche al Caramello

APRICOT CARAMEL CUSTARD

Try this recipe with a purée of stewed pears, peaches, cherries or plums. It can be served with the strawberry sauce on page 162 and decorated with whipped cream rosettes. It will keep in the refrigerator for up to 24 hours.

SERVES 6

1.2 kg / 2½ lb ripe apricots

300 g / 10 oz / 1½ cups sugar

4 tbsp Vin Santo or another dessert wine

3 eggs and 3 yolks

Cut the apricots in half and remove the stones. In a saucepan combine the apricots with half the sugar and all the wine. Cook over low heat until the apricots are tender, about 10 minutes. Transfer the contents of the saucepan to a blender and purée. Return the purée to the saucepan and, stirring frequently, cook until the excess liquid has evaporated, about 5 minutes. Leave to cool completely.

Heat a 20-cm / 8-inch ring mould in a

preheated 180° C / 350° F / gas 4 oven for 5 minutes.

In a bowl, whisk the whole eggs and egg yolks together. Stir into the apricot purée.

Pour the rest of the sugar into a small heavy saucepan. Place over moderate heat and melt until the sugar starts to darken around the sides of the pan. Then, stirring with a wooden spoon, cook to a caramel. Pour it into the hot ring mould and use a brush to spread the caramel evenly.

Pour the apricot custard into the mould. Set in a large shallow pan containing about 2.5 cm / 1 inch water and bake in the oven until the custard is set but not dry, about 50 minutes. Remove from the oven and allow to cool for 5 minutes.

Turn out the custard on to a serving plate and leave to cool completely before serving.

AMARETTI

When I am preparing desserts I often find myself using a special kind of biscuit (cookie) called amaretti. They have their own unique flavour, which blends well with many others. In Italy they are very popular and not particularly expensive. The best are called Amaretti di Saronno, after a small city north of Milan where they originated. For cooking, I often buy other brands. Finely crumbled, they make an excellent crumb crust.

Budino di Amaretti

AMARETTI PUDDING

This is a very useful pudding because it is easy to make and always turns out well. Also, it can be kept in the refrigerator for some time, or frozen. It can be enriched by serving it with the cherry sauce on page 162 or by decorating it with whipped cream rosettes topped with whole amaretti or toasted, chopped almonds or hazelnuts.

SERVES 6

4 egg yolks

90 g / 3 oz / 7 tbsp caster (US granulated) sugar

240 g / 8 oz amaretti biscuits (cookies), crumbled

60 g / 2 oz bittersweet chocolate, finely grated

480 ml / 16 fl oz / 2 cups whipping cream

sweet almond oil for the mould

In a bowl, whisk the egg yolks with the sugar until foamy, about 5 minutes. Beat in the amaretti and chocolate. Whip the cream until it forms stiff peaks and fold it carefully into the amaretti mixture.

Brush a 20-cm / 8-inch round mould with almond oil. Pour in the amaretti mixture and smooth the surface. Refrigerate for at least 3 hours.

Turn out the pudding on to a platter. Decorate and serve.

Budino di Miele

MOULDED HONEY PUDDING

The pudding can be kept in the refrigerator for up to 12 hours. Before serving, I usually decorate it with slices of candied orange. To make these, dissolve sugar in very little water over moderate heat and cook the syrup until it starts to colour; remove from the heat. Dip thin slices of unpeeled orange into the syrup and leave them to cool on a wire rack.

SERVES 6

90 g / 3 oz / 7 tbsp sugar

4 egg yolks

90 g / 3 oz / 1/4 cup honey

2 tbsp grated orange zest

480 ml / 16 fl oz / 2 cups whipping cream

sweet almond oil for the mould

In a saucepan combine the sugar and 6 tbsp water. Simmer over low heat until the sugar dissolves and the syrup will coat a spoon, about 5 minutes.

In a bowl whisk the egg yolks until foamy, about 5 minutes. Beat in the hot syrup, honey and orange zest. Leave to cool completely.

Whip the cream until it forms stiff peaks and fold it carefully into the mixture.

Brush a 20- × 6-cm / 8- × 2½-inch rectangular mould with almond oil and pour in the mixture. Chill for about 3 hours. Turn out on to a platter to serve.

Budino alla Nocciola in Salsa di Miele

HAZELNUT PUDDING WITH HONEY SAUCE

This pudding can be served straight from the oven like a soufflé, in which case the sauce is served separately. Almonds can be used instead of hazelnuts. The pudding is also excellent served with the cherry sauce on page 162.

SERVES 6

For the pudding

90 g / 3 oz / 6 tbsp unsalted butter, in small pieces + extra for the mould

120 g / 4 oz bittersweet chocolate

3 eggs, separated

90 g / 3 oz / 7 tbsp caster (US granulated) sugar

120 g / 4 oz sponge finger biscuits (ladyfingers), crumbled

120 g / 4 oz / 1 cup peeled hazelnuts, chopped

30 g / 1 oz / ¼ cup icing (confectioners') sugar

For the sauce

3 egg yolks

90 g / 3 oz / ¼ cup honey

240 ml / 8 fl oz / 1 cup milk

In the top part of a double boiler or a bowl set over a pan of gently simmering water, heat the butter and the chocolate until melted and smooth, stirring occasionally. Leave to cool slightly.

In a bowl whisk the egg yolks with 60 g / 2 oz / 5 tbsp of the caster (US granulated) sugar until light and creamy. Whisk in the melted chocolate mixture, crumbled biscuits (cookies) and hazelnuts.

In a bowl whisk the egg whites with the icing (confectioners') sugar until stiff. Gently fold into the chocolate mixture.

Generously butter a 23-cm/9-inch ring mould and coat with the rest of the sugar. Fill with the mixture and set the mould in a shallow pan containing about 2.5 cm/1 inch of water. Bake in a preheated 180°C/350°F/gas 4 oven for about 50 minutes. Remove from the oven and leave to cool for about 20 minutes.

Meanwhile, make the sauce. In the top of a double boiler or a bowl set over a pan of gently simmering water, whisk the egg yolks, honey and milk, without boiling, until fairly thick about 5 minutes.

Turn out the pudding on to a serving platter. Pour the sauce in the centre and around it and serve warm.

Budino di Riso alle Pesche

RICE PUDDING WITH PEACH SAUCE

I usually serve this dessert for lunch or brunch. If you would prefer a richer dish, flavour whipped cream with chocolate and mint and pipe into the peach halves.

SERVES 6

For the pudding

480 ml / 16 fl oz / 2 cups milk

180 g / 6 oz / ¾ cup arborio rice

grated zest of 1 lemon

90 g / 3 oz / 6 tbsp unsalted butter + extra for the mould

90 g / 3 oz / 7 tbsp sugar

3 eggs, separated

For the sauce

6 peaches

180 g / 6 oz / 14 tbsp sugar

4 tbsp Vin Santo or another sweet dessert wine

In a saucepan bring the milk to the boil. Add the rice and lemon zest and, stirring constantly, cook over moderate heat until the rice has absorbed all the milk, about 20 minutes. Remove the saucepan from the heat and stir in the butter and sugar. Leave the mixture to cool. (At this point the rice can be refrigerated for several hours.)

In separate bowls beat the egg yolks lightly and the whites until stiff. Stir the yolks into the rice mixture and carefully fold in the beaten egg whites.

Butter a 23-cm/9-inch ring mould and spoon the rice mixture into it. Set the mould in a shallow pan containing 2.5 cm/1 inch of water and bake in a preheated 180°C/350°F/gas 4 oven for 45 minutes. Transfer the mould from the bain-marie (water bath) to the oven shelf and bake for a further 10 minutes. The pudding is ready when a knife blade inserted in the centre comes out clean.

Meanwhile, blanch and peel the peaches. Cut them in half and remove the stones. In a wide saucepan combine the sugar and 240 ml/8 fl oz/1 cup water. Bring to a slow boil over low heat. Add the peaches and poach until soft, about 10 minutes.

With a slotted spoon remove 6 peach halves and set aside. Continue cooking the rest of the peaches until the liquid is syrupy, about 10 minutes.

Transfer the contents of the saucepan to a food processor and add the Vin Santo. Purée the mixture (or put it through a food mill).

Turn the rice mould on to a platter. Surround with the reserved peach halves, pour on the sauce and serve warm.

Coppe di Ciliege al Mascarpone

POACHED CHERRIES WITH MASCARPONE CREAM

I vary the fruit for this cream according to the season, using 180 g/6 oz each of raspberries, blackberries and strawberries, or segments of 3 oranges and 3 tangerines sprinkled with a little Grand Marnier. While the cherries need poaching, the other fruit can be left uncooked.

SERVES 6

600 g/1¼ lb cherries, stalks and stones removed

300 ml/½ pint/1¼ cups dry red wine

300 g/10 oz/1½ cups caster (US granulated) sugar

2 eggs, separated, and 2 yolks

120 ml/4 fl oz/½ cup Vin Santo or another dessert wine

150 g/5 oz/⅔ cup ricotta cheese

150 g/5 oz/⅔ cup mascarpone

In a saucepan combine the cherries, red wine and 120 g/4 oz/10 tbsp sugar. Poach, covered, over low heat for about 10 minutes. Remove the cherries with a slotted spoon and set aside.

Reduce the syrup until it will coat a spoon, about 5 minutes. Leave to cool.

In a heatproof bowl combine the 4 egg yolks and half the remaining sugar. Whisk until light and creamy, then stir in the Vin Santo. Set the bowl over a pan of gently simmering water or use a double boiler. Cook the mixture, whisking constantly, until it has doubled in volume and will coat a spoon. Do not let it boil. Remove the bowl from the heat and, stirring occasionally, leave the zabaione custard to cool completely.

Beat the 2 egg whites until stiff and peaky. In another bowl combine the ricotta and mascarpone with the rest of the sugar. Beat until soft and light. Using a spatula, fold in the custard and then, very gently, the beaten egg whites.

Divide the cream among 6 dessert glasses. Pour over the wine syrup, arrange the cherries on top and serve.

MASCARPONE AND RICOTTA

In Milan fresh mascarpone is sold in cheesecloth bags and is superbly light: the long-life variety in plastic boxes is much less so. When that is the only mascarpone available, I prefer to use ricotta cheese. Ricotta is light and delicate and can be transformed in a thousand ways. A typical mascarpone dessert is tiramisù which certainly can't be called light, as it includes zabaione and chocolate or coffee. It is the perfect example of something that should never be served at the end of a meal.

● **Rice Pudding with Peach Sauce (p. 181)** ●

MAKING CARAMEL

*I*n order to caramelize sugar without a thermometer, pour a 3-mm/⅛-inch layer of sugar into a heavy-bottomed saucepan. Place the saucepan over moderate heat and cook the sugar until it begins to melt around the sides of the pan and to turn golden. Start stirring with a wooden spoon and keep on stirring until the sugar is a rich golden colour and the surface is covered in small bubbles. Remove from the heat before the caramel gets too dark.

Crema agli Amaretti

AMARETTI CREAM

The cream can be prepared in advance as it keeps well in the refrigerator for up to 24 hours. If you unmould it much before time, sprinkle with amaretti crumbs only at the last minute to prevent them becoming soggy. For a richer dessert, serve with sponge finger biscuits (ladyfingers).

SERVES 6

8 g / ¼ oz / 1 tbsp powdered unflavoured gelatine

90 g / 3 oz / 7 tbsp sugar

480 ml / 16 fl oz / 2 cups whipping cream

4 tbsp Amaretto liqueur

90 g / 3 oz amaretti biscuits (cookies)

Sprinkle the gelatine over 4 tbsp luke-warm water, stir and leave to soften.

In a heavy saucepan melt the sugar over low heat, starting to stir only when it starts to bubble around the edge of the pan. When the caramel is dark brown, remove the pan from the heat.

Meanwhile, in another saucepan warm half the cream over low heat.

Gradually stir the hot cream into the caramel. Still stirring, add the Amaretto liqueur and softened gelatine. Leave to cool to room temperature.

Whip the rest of the cream until stiff and gently fold into the caramel mixture. Spoon the cream into 6 ramekins, individual soufflé dishes or custard cups with a diameter 6 cm / 2½ inches. Refrigerate for about 3 hours or until set.

Crumble the amaretti biscuits (cookies) in a blender. Turn out the creams on to individual dishes, sprinkle with the crumbled amaretti and serve.

Crema al Mascarpone

MASCARPONE AND COFFEE DESSERT

It is better if you make this dessert a day ahead and keep it in the refrigerator, to give the flavours time to blend. You can vary it by adding a little melted chocolate instead of coffee and decorating it with chocolate flakes, or raspberries when in season.

SERVES 6

3 egg yolks

90 g / 3 oz / 7 tbsp caster (US granulated) sugar

120 ml / 4 fl oz / ½ cup dry Marsala wine

1 tbsp instant coffee powder or granules

300 g / 10 oz / 1¼ cups mascarpone

180 g / 6 oz sponge finger biscuits (ladyfingers)

60 g / 2 oz candied coffee beans

In a heatproof bowl combine the egg yolks and sugar. Whisk until light in colour, about 2 minutes. Add 6 tbsp Marsala and whisk well. Set the bowl over a pan of gently simmering water or use a double boiler. Whisking constantly, gently heat the mixture until it is creamy and double in volume, about 4 minutes. Make sure it never boils.

Remove the bowl from the heat. Stir in the coffee and mascarpone. Mix until well blended. Set aside.

Line the sides and bottom of an 18-cm / 7-inch springform pan with grease-proof or parchment paper. Lightly brush both sides of the biscuits (ladyfingers) with the rest of the Marsala. Arrange them, smooth side up, in a daisy petal pattern on the bottom of the pan, being careful not to leave any empty spaces. Cut the rest of the biscuits (ladyfingers) in half crosswise and stand them, cut side down and smooth side in, all around the inside of the pan to line it completely.

Spoon in the cool mascarpone cream. Cover tightly and chill until set, about 8 hours but preferably for 1 day.

Before serving trim the tops of the biscuits (ladyfingers) flush with the filling. Remove the sides of the pan, then invert the dessert on to a platter. Remove the pan bottom and lining paper. Decorate with the coffee beans and serve.

Crosta di Pere allo Zabaione

PEAR AND ZABAIONE TART

This elegant tart can, of course, be made with apples, peaches or apricots, as well as berries. Everything can be prepared ahead of time, but the tart should be served as soon as it is filled or the pastry will get soft.

SERVES 6

unsalted butter for the pan

1 recipe quantity short pastry dough (page 218)

1 egg, separated, and 3 yolks

180 g / 6 oz / 14 tbsp caster (US granulated) sugar

180 ml / 6 fl oz / ¾ cup Vin Santo, dry Marsala or another dessert wine

3 firm dessert pears

Butter a 23-cm/9-inch flan or tart pan with a removable bottom. Roll out the dough and use to line the pan. Prick the pastry case all over with a fork and bake in a preheated 180°C/350°F/gas 4 oven until the pastry starts to colour, about 30 minutes. Should the pastry rise during baking, push it down firmly with the palm of your hand. Transfer the pastry case to a serving plate and leave to cool.

In a saucepan, combine the 4 egg yolks and half the sugar. Whisk until the mixture is light and foamy, about 5 minutes. Set the pan in a larger pan of water. Cook over low heat, whisking constantly and gradually adding 6 tbsp of the wine, until the zabaione custard coats a spoon. Do not let the custard boil. Remove from the heat and leave to cool, stirring occasionally to room temperature. Whisk the egg white until stiff and fold it into the zabaione.

Peel, core and halve the pears. In a saucepan combine the pears with the rest of the wine and sugar. Cover the pan and cook over moderate heat until the pears are tender, about 10 minutes. Remove the pears with a slotted spoon and set aside. Continue cooking the wine syrup until it will coat a spoon. Leave to cool.

Just before serving, cover the bottom of the tart shell with the pears. Glaze with the wine syrup and spoon over the zabaione.

Crostata di Mele

APPLE TART

This is one of the most successful desserts of my cooking classes. It's nice to look at and very tasty. Other fruits – peaches, pears and apricots – can be used instead of apples.

SERVES 6

For the pastry

240 g / 8 oz / 2 cups flour

120 g / 4 oz / 1 stick unsalted butter in small pieces + extra for the pan

a pinch of salt

3 tbsp caster (US granulated) sugar

2 tbsp milk

1 egg yolk

For the filling

2 egg yolks

120 g / 4 oz / 10 tbsp caster (US granulated) sugar

1 tbsp flour

240 ml / 8 fl oz / 1 cup milk

grated zest of 1 lemon

4 Golden Delicious apples

60 g / 2 oz / 4 tbsp unsalted butter

½ tsp ground cinnamon

First make the pastry. Heap the flour on a board. Make a well in the centre and place in it the butter, salt and the sugar. Using the tips of your fingers, rub the ingredients together until they are the consistency of large crumbs. Add the milk and egg yolk and knead quickly with the palms of your hands until smooth. Roll the dough into a ball, wrap tightly and refrigerate for 2 hours. (The uncooked dough can be kept in the refrigerator for a week.)

To make the filling, in a bowl combine the egg yolks and half the sugar. Whisk until pale in colour, about 2 minutes. Add the flour and whisk until well blended and free of lumps. Gradually whisk in the milk and lemon zest. Set the bowl over a pan of simmering water (or use a double boiler). Slowly bring to the boil, whisking constantly. Remove from the heat immediately and leave to cool completely. (At this point the custard can be refrigerated for several hours.)

Peel and core the apples and cut into 1-cm/½-inch dice. In a frying pan melt the butter over moderate heat. Add the apples and, stirring occasionally, cook until tender, about 10 minutes. Add the rest of the sugar, cook for a further 2 minutes and leave to cool. (They can be cooked several hours in advance.)

Butter a 23-cm/9-inch flan or tart pan with a removable bottom. Roll out the dough and use to line the pan. Prick the bottom of the pastry case all over with a fork. Bake in a preheated 180°C/350°F/gas 4 oven for 30 minutes. If the pastry pops up in places, press it down with the palm of your hand. Remove the pastry case when it is slightly golden and leave it to cool completely.

PASTRY

I have included a few recipes for tarts, as they are often served in Italy and there is such a variety of them. They can be filled with fruit or jam and made with or without a lattice decoration. Whenever I make pastry, I prepare at least a double amount and freeze part of it. This means I always have the basis for preparing a dessert for unexpected guests, because there is also always a lot of fruit in the house.

Remove the pastry case from the pan and put it on a platter. Pour in the custard and spread it evenly. Arrange the diced apples on top, sprinkle with the cinnamon and serve.

Crostata di Pesche e Amaretti

PEACH AND AMARETTI TART

The flavours of the peaches and amaretti are enhanced by the chocolate, while the crumbled biscuits (cookies) absorb the peach juice during cooking. In winter canned peaches or apricots are a good substitute.

SERVES 6

3 large ripe but firm peaches

90 g / 3 oz amaretti biscuits (cookies), crushed

For the pastry

180 g / 6 oz / 1½ cups flour

90 g / 3 oz / 6 tbsp unsalted butter, in small pieces + extra for the pan

90 g / 3 oz / 7 tbsp caster (US granulated) sugar

1 egg

For the filling

60 g / 2 oz / 4 tbsp unsalted butter

120 g / 4 oz bittersweet chocolate

2 eggs, separated

90 g / 3 oz / 7 tbsp caster (US granulated) sugar

First make the pastry. Heap the flour on a board. Make a well in the centre and place in it the butter and sugar. Using the tips of your fingers, rub the ingredients together until they are the consistency of large crumbs. Add the egg and knead quickly with the palms of your hands until smooth. (Or make the pastry in a food processor.) Roll the dough in a ball, wrap tightly and chill for 2 hours.

Butter a 23-cm / 9-inch flan or tart pan with a removable bottom. Roll out the pastry dough and use to line the pan.

To make the filling, in a bowl set over a pan of simmering water, melt the butter and chocolate, stirring occasionally. Leave to cool.

In another bowl combine the egg yolks and sugar. Whisk until thick and pale. Stir in the cooled chocolate mixture, blending well. Beat the egg whites until stiff. Carefully fold into the chocolate mixture.

Blanch the peaches in boiling water for 30 seconds, then drain and peel. Cut them into quarters.

Sprinkle the crushed amaretti over the bottom of the pastry case. Arrange the peaches in the pastry case and spread the chocolate filling over them. Bake in a preheated 180°C / 350°F / gas 4 oven until the pastry is crisp, about 45 minutes. Leave to cool on a wire rack before removing the tart from the pan.

A SIMPLE ENDING

I am not particularly fond of desserts because I think that they just make meals unnecessarily rich. I find the ideal way to end a meal is with a fruit salad, perhaps laced with a little liqueur, or a fruit sorbet with a delicate sauce. However, I think it would be impossible to write a recipe book without a chapter on desserts. At the same time I would never serve a bought dessert or ice cream because you can tell the difference immediately. If I don't have time to make a dessert, I serve a large basket of fruit instead.

Dolce al Cioccolato

CHOCOLATE AND PRUNE PUDDING

This pudding can be kept in the refrigerator for up to 12 hours. Decorate it with whipped cream or, using a vegetable peeler, with chocolate shavings. It is also very good served with the cherry sauce on page 162.

SERVES 6

90 g / 3 oz pitted prunes

4 tbsp Vin Santo or another dessert wine

180 g / 6 oz bittersweet chocolate

60 g / 2 oz / 4 tbsp unsalted butter

3 eggs, separated

60 g / 2 oz / 5 tbsp caster (US granulated) sugar

sweet almond oil for the mould

Soak the prunes in the Vin Santo for about 2 hours. Drain the prunes and chop them finely or purée in a blender.

In a bowl set over a pan of simmering water melt the chocolate and butter, stirring occasionally. Leave to cool until lukewarm.

In a bowl whisk the egg yolks with the sugar until light and foamy, about 5 minutes. In another bowl, beat the egg whites until stiff. Add the yolks to the chocolate mixture and stir well. Add the prune purée and stir carefully. Fold in the egg whites.

Brush a 20- × 6-cm / 8 × 2½-inch rectangular mould with the almond oil and pour in the mixture. Chill for 6 hours.

Dip the mould into hot water for a few seconds, then turn out the pudding on to a serving plate.

Frittata di Mele

FRUIT SOUFFLE OMELETTE

A luncheon or brunch dessert, this can be very successfully flambéed on more elegant occasions. The apples can be replaced by firm peaches or pears. Served the omelette with the strawberry sauce on page 162 or with whipped cream.

SERVES 6

3 tbsp seedless raisins

4 tbsp Cognac

6 Golden Delicious apples

60 g / 2 oz / 4 tbsp unsalted butter

1 tsp ground cinnamon

6 eggs, separated

120 g / 4 oz / 10 tbsp caster (US granulated sugar)

Soak the raisins in the Cognac for about 2 hours; drain.

Peel and core the apples. Cut the apples into quarters and cut each quarter into three slices. In a frying pan melt half the butter over moderate heat. Add the apples and, carefully turning once, cook for 10 minutes. Sprinkle with the cinnamon and cook for a further 2 minutes.

In a bowl, whisk the egg yolks and sugar together to mix. Beat the egg whites until stiff and carefully fold into the yolks.

In a 23-cm/9-inch round non-stick pan melt the rest of the butter. Remove from the heat and add the egg mixture. Arrange the sliced apples in overlapping rings on top of the eggs. Sprinkle with the raisins. Transfer the pan to a pre-heated 180°C/350°F/gas 4 oven and bake until the omelette has almost doubled in size, it is set and the top is golden, about 20 minutes.

Slide on to a platter and serve at once.

Frittelle di Riso agli Amaretti

RICE AND AMARETTI FRITTERS

Traditionally these little fritters are made during Carnival. As they are too rich for a dessert, I generally serve them in the afternoon with a glass of Vin Santo. They must be fried at the last minute because, like all fried foods, they should be served very crispy.

SERVES 6

480 ml / 16 fl oz / 2 cups milk

150 g / 5 oz / 2/3 cup arborio rice

grated zest of 1 lemon

salt

80 g / 2½ oz / 6½ tbsp granulated sugar

30 g / 1 oz / 2 tbsp unsalted butter

90 g / 3 oz amaretti biscuits (cookies), powdered in a blender

3 eggs, separated

extra virgin olive oil for deep-frying

1 tbsp icing (confectioners') sugar

In a saucepan bring the milk to the boil. Add the rice, lemon zest and a pinch of salt. Stirring frequently, simmer over moderate heat until the rice has absorbed all the milk, about 20 minutes.

Remove the saucepan from the heat and stir in the granulated sugar, butter and crushed amaretti. Pour the mixture on to a large platter and spread it out. Leave to cool completely. (At this point, covered tightly, the mixture can be refrigerated for several hours.)

Whisk the egg yolks in a bowl. Add the cold rice mixture and stir well.

In a deep pan heat the oil to 180° C/350° F. While the oil is heating,

beat the egg whites until stiff and fold them delicately into the rice mixture. A few at a time, drop spoonfuls of the rice mixture into the hot oil. Fry for a couple of minutes, then turn over with a slotted spoon and fry the other side until golden.

Remove the fritters with the slotted spoon and drain on paper towels. Sprinkle with sifted icing (confectioners') sugar and serve piping hot.

Lamponi in Gelatina

RASPBERRIES IN WINE JELLY

This light and elegant jelly is perfect for dinner. If you cannot find raspberries, substitute diced pears, kiwi fruit, pineapple or bananas or a mixture of them. To make it even prettier, I often use a fancy mould and serve it with the cherry sauce on page 162. Either in the mould or turned out, it can be kept in the refrigerator for up to 24 hours.

SERVES 6

11 g / 1/3 oz / 1½ tbsp powdered unflavoured gelatine

60 g / 2 oz / 5 tbsp sugar

6-cm / 2½-inch cinnamon stick

300 ml / ½ pint / 1¼ cups dry white wine

450 g / 1 lb raspberries

Soften the gelatine in 4 tbsp water for about 10 minutes.

In a saucepan combine the sugar, cinnamon stick, and 300 ml / ½ pint / 1¼ cups water. Bring to the boil over moderate heat. Remove the saucepan from the heat, add the gelatine and stir until it dissolves. Strain the mixture into a bowl. Pour in the wine, stir well and leave to cool to room temperature.

Rinse an 18-cm/7-inch round mould with cold water. Pour a very thin layer of jelly, about 3 mm/⅛ inch, on the bottom of the wet mould. Leave it to set in the refrigerator for about 1 hour.

Remove the mould from the refrigerator and fill it with the raspberries. Pour in the rest of the jelly and refrigerate for at least 6 hours.

Dip the mould up to its rim in very hot water for about 10 seconds. Place a serving platter, inverted, over the mould and turn them over together so the jelly drops out. Decorate and serve.

Meringa di Prugne

PRUNE MERINGUE TART

The meringue and prunes can be prepared well ahead of time, but once assembled, the tart should be served immediately. Prunes can be replaced by dried apricots or figs.

SERVES 6

For the filling

300 g/10 oz pitted prunes

120 ml/4 fl oz/½ cup Vin Santo or another dessert wine

1 tsp ground cinnamon

juice of 1 lemon

120 ml/4 fl oz/½ cup whipping cream

For the meringue

3 egg whites

60 g/2 oz/5 tbsp caster (superfine) sugar

60 g/2 oz/½ cup icing (confectioners') sugar

unsalted butter and flour for the baking sheet

In a saucepan combine the prunes, wine, cinnamon and lemon juice. Cover and,

stirring occasionally, simmer over low heat until the prunes are soft, about 10 minutes. Remove the saucepan from the heat and leave the prunes to cool in the wine, then drain well.

In a large bowl beat the egg whites with the caster (superfine) sugar until stiff. Using a spatula gently fold in the icing (confectioners') sugar.

Butter a baking sheet and sprinkle it lightly with flour. Spread half the meringue in a 23-cm/9-inch round, 1 cm/½ inch thick, on the baking sheet. Put the rest of the meringue into a piping bag fitted with a star nozzle and pipe rosettes, 5 cm/2 inches apart, on another part of the baking sheet.

Transfer the baking sheet to a preheated 90°C/195°F oven and leave to dry until the meringue is crisp and easy to lift from the baking sheet, about 1½ hours. Leave to cool completely.

Whip the cream and transfer it to a piping bag. Place the meringue shell on a serving plate. Cover it with piped whipped cream. Arrange the prunes on top, decorate with the meringue rosettes and serve.

Pere con Crema in Forma alla Cannella

PEARS IN WINE WITH CINNAMON CREAM

Although cinnamon adds a wonderful flavour to pears, I sometimes prepare this mould with cocoa instead, tripling the quantity to darken the cream. As wine syrup is delicious on ice cream and sorbets and keeps very well for weeks in the refrigerator, when cooking pears I usually make extra syrup.

SERVES 6

8 g/¼ oz/1 tbsp powdered unflavoured gelatine

3 firm dessert pears

180 g/6 oz/14 tbsp sugar

240 ml/8 fl oz/1 cup red wine

1 tbsp ground cinnamon

480 ml/16 fl oz/2 cups whipping cream

Soften the gelatine in 3 tbsp cold water for about 10 minutes.

Peel and core the pears and cut them in half lengthwise. Arrange the pears in a saucepan with 120 g/4 oz/10 tbsp of the sugar and all the wine. Simmer over low heat until the pears are tender, about 30 minutes.

Remove the pears with a slotted spoon and set aside. Reduce the wine syrup until it will coat a spoon. Leave to cool completely.

Put the cinnamon into a saucepan and gradually add half the cream, stirring constantly to avoid the formation of lumps. Stir in the rest of the sugar. Heat the mixture over moderate heat. Remove the saucepan from the heat and add the gelatine, stirring until completely dissolved. Leave to cool.

Whip the rest of the cream until stiff. Fold it gently into the cooled cinnamon cream. Rinse an 18-cm/7-inch mould. Pour the cinnamon cream into the wet mould and refrigerate for at least 4 hours or until set.

Turn out on to a serving dish. Arrange the pears around the cinnamon cream, spoon the wine sauce over them and serve.

Pesche alla Menta

POACHED PEACHES WITH MINT CREAM

The peaches are very attractive served in a deep dish surrounded by the sauce, decorated with fresh mint leaves. I sometimes make the sauce into ice cream and serve the peaches with it instead.

SERVES 6

6 firm peaches

180 g / 6 oz / 14 tbsp caster (US granulated) sugar

4 tbsp medium dry white wine

1 egg, separated, and 3 yolks

450 ml / ¾ pint / scant 2 cups milk

4 tbsp mint syrup

Bring a saucepan of water to the boil. Add the peaches and blanch for 30 seconds, then drain and peel them.

In a saucepan, combine the whole peaches, half the sugar and all the wine. Cover and cook over low heat until the peaches are tender, about 10 minutes.

Remove the peaches with a slotted spoon, drain and set aside. Continue boiling the syrup until it will coat the spoon, about 10 minutes. Set aside.

In a bowl, combine the 4 egg yolks and remaining sugar. Whisk until foamy. Gradually beat in the milk and mint syrup. Set the bowl over a pan of simmering water (or use a double boiler). Cook, stirring frequently, until the custard thickens without ever boiling. Remove the bowl from the heat and leave to cool.

Beat the egg white until stiff and fold it into the mint custard cream. Pour into a deep dish, arrange the peaches on top and spoon the wine syrup over the peaches. Chill before serving.

UNMOULDING DESSERTS

You will find it easier to turn out a cold dessert if you dampen the inside of the mould with cold water or brush it with sweet almond oil. Never use butter to grease a mould for a cold dessert because it makes a thick coating. Sweet almond oil is perfect, it is completely flavourless. To turn out a stubborn mould, insert a sharp knife around the edge to let in air, then dip the mould in hot water, up to the rim, for 10 seconds, cover the top with an inverted serving plate, and turn the whole thing over.

Pesche Meringate

PEACH MERINGUES

Try to find freestone peaches for this recipe: they are easier to halve and stone. They can be served either hot or cold, and can be accompanied by strawberry sauce (page 162) or cherry sauce (page 162).

SERVES 6

6 fairly large peaches

90 g / 3 oz / 7 tbsp granulated sugar

4 tbsp Cognac

6 amaretti biscuits (cookies)

60 g / 2 oz / ½ cup blanched almonds

1 egg, separated, and 1 egg white

1 tbsp cocoa powder

unsalted butter for the dish

90 g / 3 oz / ¾ cup icing (confectioners') sugar

Blanch the peaches in boiling water for 30 seconds, then drain and peel. Cut the peaches in half lengthwise and remove the stones. Arrange the peach halves in a shallow baking pan, cut sides up. Sprinkle with the granulated sugar and Cognac and transfer to a preheated 180°C/350°F/gas 4 oven. Bake for about 10 minutes. Remove the pan from the oven.

In a blender, powder the amaretti and almonds. Add the egg yolk and cocoa powder and blend. Fill the hollows in the peaches with the mixture and arrange them in a buttered ovenproof dish.

In a bowl beat the 2 egg whites until stiff and peaky. Add the icing (confectioners') sugar, beating. Spoon or pipe the meringue over the peaches to cover each one completely.

Put the dish in the oven and bake for about 10 minutes or until the meringue is slightly golden.

Leave to cool slightly before serving.

Schiacciata con l'Uva

SWEET FLATBREAD WITH GRAPES

In Chianti this dessert is made in all the farmhouse kitchens, with as many different recipes as there are farmhouses. Black grapes are generally used. The great specialists of this dessert are the Bianchi family, who are bakers in Gaiole in Chianti, and who gave me their very special recipe, which makes quite a 'high' flatbread.

SERVES 6

30 g / 1 oz fresh (compressed) yeast or 2 tbsp dried yeast

450 g / 1 lb / 4 cups flour + extra for the bowl and board

120 g / 4 oz / 10 tbsp caster (US granulated) sugar

a pinch of salt

extra virgin olive oil for the pan

150 g / 5 oz shelled walnuts, coarsely chopped

600 g / 1¼ lb black or purple seedless grapes

Combine the yeast and 240 ml / 8 fl oz / 1 cup lukewarm water and leave to dissolve and start to foam, about 10 minutes.

Heap the flour on a board. Make a well in the centre and gradually pour in the yeast mixture. Mix with a fork until all the water is absorbed by the flour. Add one-third of the sugar and the salt and knead with the palms of your hands until you have a smooth, elastic dough. Roll the dough into a ball and put it in a lightly floured bowl. Cover and leave to rise in a warm place until double in size, about 2 hours. (At this point the dough can be refrigerated for up to 12 hours.)

Brush a 23-cm / 9-inch springform pan with oil.

Punch the dough on a lightly floured board to knock out the air. Divide the dough in half and roll out both pieces to fit the pan.

Place one round of dough in the bottom of the pan and arrange half the nuts and grapes on it. Sprinkle with half the remaining sugar and cover with the second round of dough. Arrange the rest of the nuts and grapes on top and sprinkle with the rest of the sugar. Leave to rise for about 30 minutes.

Bake in a preheated 200°C/400°F/ gas 6 oven until just golden, about 40 minutes. Remove the flatbread from the pan and allow to cool before serving.

● **Pears in Wine** ●
with Cinnamon Cream (p. 187)

Sformatini di Cioccolata

CHOCOLATE CUSTARDS

Serve these on individual plates, surrounded by the cherry sauce on page 162, either warm or at room temperature, but never straight from the refrigerator. At room temperature they will flatten a little but will still be very light.

SERVES 6

180 g / 6 oz bittersweet chocolate

120 g / 4 oz / 1 stick unsalted butter + extra for the moulds

6 eggs, separated

210 g / 7 oz / 1 cup caster (US granulated) sugar

grated zest of 1 orange

3 tbsp Grand Marnier

3 tbsp flour

In a bowl set over a pan of simmering water, or in a double boiler, combine the chocolate and butter cut in pieces. Melt over simmering water, stirring frequently. Leave to cool completely.

Lightly beat the egg yolks with the sugar and mix them with the melted chocolate and butter. Stir in the orange zest and Grand Marnier. Beat the egg whites until stiff and fold into the mixture.

Butter six 6-cm/2½-inch-diameter ramekins, individual soufflé dishes or custard cups and coat them with the flour. Fill them with the chocolate mixture and transfer to a preheated 180°C/350°F/gas 4 oven. Bake for about 20 minutes.

Remove from the oven and turn out on to individual dessert plates. Serve immediately or cool to room temperature before serving.

Sformato di Ricotta alla Cioccolata

RICOTTA MOULD WITH CHOCOLATE SAUCE

Delicious hot or cold. You can prepare the pudding and sauce ahead of time and refrigerate until just before serving. For a richer dessert, use mascarpone instead of ricotta.

SERVES 6

For the mould

360 g / 12 oz / 1½ cups ricotta cheese

120 g / 4 oz / 10 tbsp sugar

3 eggs, separated

1 tbsp grated orange zest

2 tbsp Grand Marnier

sweet almond oil for the mould

For the sauce

120 ml / 4 fl oz / ½ cup whipping cream

60 g / 2 oz / 5 tbsp sugar

120 g / 4 oz bittersweet chocolate

In a bowl combine the ricotta, sugar, egg yolks, orange zest and Grand Marnier. Whisk until smooth and creamy. Beat the egg whites until stiff and fold into the mixture.

Brush a 23-cm/9-inch ring mould with almond oil and pour in the mixture. Smooth the top lightly with a spatula. Set the mould in a baking pan containing 2.5 cm/1 inch water. Transfer to a preheated 180°C/350°F/gas 4 oven and bake for about 50 minutes.

Meanwhile, in a bowl set over simmering water or in a double boiler, combine the cream, sugar, chocolate and 2 tbsp water. Cook gently until the chocolate has completely melted, stirring occasionally.

FRUIT SORBETS

I consider my ice cream machine an extremely useful piece of kitchen equipment. It enables one to make fruit sorbets very easily, with raw puréed fruit and a little sugar. I find these the perfect way to finish a meal. On more elegant occasions I serve them with a fruit sauce or home-made biscuits (cookies).

Remove the mould from the oven and leave it to rest for 5 minutes, then turn out on to a warm platter. Pour the sauce around and serve at once. Or, leave the mould to cool completely and refrigerate it, and the sauce, to serve cold.

Sorbetto di Mele

APPLE SORBET

As they keep well in the freezer and require very little extra work, I usually make double the quantity of ice creams and sorbets. Use this recipe also for pear, peach and apricot sorbet.

SERVES 6

1.2 kg / 2½ lb Granny Smith apples

juice of 2 limes

grated zest of 1 lemon

120 g / 4 oz / 10 tbsp sugar

4 tbsp dry white wine

Peel, core and slice the apples. In a saucepan combine the apples, lime juice, lemon zest, sugar and wine. Bring to the boil over low heat and, stirring occasionally, cook until the apple is soft, about 10 minutes.

Transfer the contents of the pan to a blender and purée. Leave to cool. Pour the mixture into an ice cream maker and freeze, following the manufacturer's instructions. Or, place it in a bowl in the freezer and freeze for at least 3 hours, whisking it at 30-minute intervals, until the sorbet is formed.

Spoon into dessert glasses to serve.

● **Sweet Flatbread with Grapes (p. 188)** ●

Sorbetto al Vin Santo

VIN SANTO SORBET

This very delicate sorbet can be made with other dessert wines or with champagne. I generally serve it in dessert glasses surrounded by diced peaches, pears, apples or apricots at luncheon or with berries for an elegant dinner dessert.

SERVES 6

150 g / 5 oz / ¾ cup sugar

600 ml / 1 pint / 2½ cups Vin Santo

1 egg white, lightly beaten

In a saucepan, combine the sugar and 300 ml / ½ pint / 1¼ cups water. Simmer over low heat until the sugar is completely dissolved. Remove from the heat and stir in the wine. Leave to cool completely.

Pour the mixture into an ice cream machine and freeze, following the manufacturer's instructions, adding the egg white halfway through the freezing time.

Or, pour the mixture into a bowl and freeze for 3 hours, whisking the mixture every 30 minutes. After about 2 hours, whisk the egg white into the mixture.

Serve in individual dessert glasses.

RING MOULDS

I prefer to set desserts in ring moulds because they cook evenly and quickly and are easy to unmould. They are also simple to decorate by pouring sauce in the middle or piping whipped cream rosettes around the sides. Obviously the smoother the mould, the easier it is to use. I particularly like non-stick moulds.

Spuma di Limone con Fragola

LEMON MOULD WITH STRAWBERRIES

If you decide to use individual moulds, instead of decorating with the strawberries, make a sauce by puréeing them in a blender with a couple of tablespoons of sugar. Turn out the moulds on to individual dishes and pour this sauce around.

SERVES 6

15 g / ½ oz / 2 tbsp powdered unflavoured gelatine

4 eggs, separated

120 g / 4 oz / 10 tbsp caster (US granulated) sugar

120 ml / 4 fl oz / ½ cup lemon juice

grated zest of 1 lemon

240 g / 8 oz / 1 cup ricotta cheese

180 g / 6 oz / 1 cup strawberries

Soften the gelatine in 5 tbsp cold water for 10 minutes.

In a bowl combine the egg yolks and sugar and whisk until light and frothy. Whisk in the lemon juice and zest. Set the bowl over a pan of gently simmering water or use a double boiler and whisk the mixture, without ever letting it boil, until thick.

Remove from the heat. Stir in the gelatine until dissolved, then leave the custard to cool.

Push the ricotta cheese through a sieve on to the cooled custard and whisk until well blended. Beat the egg whites until stiff and gently fold them into the mixture. Pour it into an 18-cm/7-inch ring mould and refrigerate for at least 5 hours.

Turn out the mould on to a platter, decorate with the strawberries and serve.

Torta di Limone

LEMON TART

This very light dessert can be prepared ahead of time by baking the tart shell blind and making the filling; assemble just before serving. Naturally, orange juice can be used instead of lemon.

SERVES 6

For the pastry

240 g / 8 oz / 2 cups flour

120 g / 4 oz / 1 stick unsalted butter, in small pieces, + extra for the pan

a pinch of salt

60 g / 2 oz / 5 tbsp caster (US granulated) sugar

3 tbsp milk

1 egg yolk

For the filling

2 eggs, separated

60 g / 2 oz / 5 tbsp caster (US granulated) sugar

4 tbsp lemon juice

grated zest of 2 lemons

finely pared zest of 1 orange

4 tbsp whipping cream

Heap the flour on a board. Make a well in the centre and place in it the butter, salt and sugar. Using the tips of your fingers, rub the ingredients together until they are the consistency of large crumbs. Add the milk and egg yolk and

knead quickly with the palms of your hands until smooth. (Or make the dough in a food processor.) Roll the dough into a ball, wrap and refrigerate for 2 hours. (The uncooked dough can be kept in the refrigerator for a week.)

Butter a 23-cm/9-inch flan or tart pan with a removable bottom. Roll out the dough and use to line the pan. Using a fork, prick the bottom of the pastry case all over. Bake in a preheated 180°C/350°F/gas 4 oven until golden, about 30 minutes. If the pastry pops up in places, flatten it by gently pressing with the palm of your hand. Remove the tart case from the oven. Cool, then remove the tart case from the pan.

In a bowl beat the egg yolks and sugar.

● Coffee Ricotta with Honey ●
Fingers (p. 179)

Add the lemon juice and grated zest and mix well. Set the bowl over a pan of simmering water (or use a double boiler). Stirring constantly, cook until slightly thick, about 3 minutes. Leave to cool.

Cut the orange zest into julienne strips and blanch them in a small saucepan of boiling water for 1 minute. Drain and pat dry.

In separate bowls beat the egg whites and whip the cream until stiff. Gently fold the beaten egg whites and cream into the cooled lemon custard.

Fill the tart case with the lemon cream and sprinkle the top with the orange zest. Serve at room temperature.

Torta di Nocciole

HAZELNUT CAKE

This very light cake is a speciality of Stefano Borghino, pastry chef at Altopalato, a Milanese cooking school. I decorate it either with whipped cream rosettes or with a sugared leaf silhouette: put a fresh grape vine leaf in the middle, dredge it with sifted icing (confectioners') sugar and carefully remove the leaf.

SERVES 6

120 g / 4 oz / 1 stick unsalted butter, melted, + extra for the pan

90 g / 3 oz / ³/₄ cup shelled and peeled hazelnuts, coarsely chopped

2 eggs and 3 egg yolks

150 g / 5 oz / ³/₄ cup caster (US granulated) sugar

1 tbsp honey

60 g / 2 oz / ½ cup flour

60 g / 2 oz / ½ cup potato flour or cornflour (cornstarch)

Butter a 23-cm/9-inch springform pan and coat the bottom and sides with the chopped nuts.

In a bowl combine the eggs, egg yolks, sugar and honey. Using an electric beater, beat the mixture until it is almost as soft and light as whipped cream, about 10 minutes.

Combine the flours and sift them on top of the egg mixture. Fold in gently with a rubber spatula until blended. Stir in the hot melted butter and blend well.

Pour the mixture into the springform pan and transfer to a preheated 180° C/350° F/gas 4 oven. Bake for about 45 minutes or until a wooden skewer inserted in the middle comes out clean.

Remove the cake from the oven and leave it to stand for about 10 minutes. Turn it on to a platter, remove the pan side and bottom, and cool completely before decorating.

SEMOLINA

Semolina is durum wheat and comes in fine or large granules. It is the main ingredient of the very popular Gnocchi alla Romana, but semolina is also used in puddings and cakes. When boiled in water, stock or milk, it takes about 10 minutes to cook. Available everywhere in Italy, it is now easier to find in other countries, in Italian markets and health food stores. The metric proportions to use when cooking semolina are 1 to 4: 400 grams of semolina to 1200 millilitres of liquid. For dessert it is better to use a finely ground semolina.

Zabaione gratinato alla Frutta

GRILLED ZABAIONE WITH FRUIT

In the summer substitute fresh peaches for pears, if in a hurry, use canned.

SERVES 6

3 firm dessert pears

450 ml / ³/₄ pint / scant 2 cups dry white wine

300 g / 10 oz / 1½ cups caster (US granulated) sugar

2 eggs, separated, and 2 yolks

180 g / 6 oz / 1 cup fresh strawberries, halved lengthwise

Peel and core the pears and cut them in half. In a saucepan combine them with 200 ml/7 fl oz/⁷/₈ cup of the wine and 200 g/7 oz/1 cup of the sugar. Simmer over low heat until soft, about 20 minutes. Remove the pears with a slotted spoon and set aside. Turn up the heat and cook the wine until syrupy. Leave to cool completely.

In a bowl whisk the 4 egg yolks with the rest of the sugar until light and creamy. Add the rest of the wine and set the bowl over a pan of gently simmering water (or use a double boiler). Continue whisking, without ever allowing it to boil, until it coats a spoon, about 5 minutes. Leave to cool completely.

Beat the 2 egg whites until stiff and gently fold them into the cooled zabaione. Pour the zabaione into a flameproof dish and arrange the pears, flat side down, on it. Decorate with the strawberries and place the dish under a preheated grill (broiler) until the top starts to turn golden, about 5 minutes.

Pour the wine syrup over and serve immediately from the flameproof dish.

● **Peach and Amaretti Tart (p. 185),** ●
Lemon Tart (p. 192)

Il Pane

BREAD

I cannot imagine eating without a piece of bread at hand and a basket on the table with more, because one piece would never be enough to last me through my meal. There is an old Italian term, COMPANATICO, that refers to what one eats with bread, which is practically everything. Bread even holds a place of honour in the setting of the table — sometimes it is placed on a small, separate plate, but more usually it is right on the cloth itself, to the left of the dinner plate, never on the plate with other foods. Nor do we feel our bread needs butter. We prefer to taste it unadulterated.

In Italy we bake and consume an enormous quantity of bread. There must be tens of thousands of bakers turning out thousands of delicious and different kinds of bread daily from their ovens. This may be why Italians, especially in cities, don't make bread at home. None of the old or new recipe books in my large collection give instructions on how to make it. When recipes are given for special flatbreads or enriched loaves for feast days, they assume you start with dough bought from the local bakery. In many rural sections of the country it was the custom to bake bread once a week, usually on Friday. I can remember horse-drawn carts full of city-baked bread arriving in the tiny towns of Tuscany. Now everyone buys loaves and rolls at the local bread shop, the PANETTERIA.

*T*o an Italian there is even something sacred about bread. It is a symbol of the gift of life itself and that which sustains it. It would be easier for me to throw out a piece of meat than a piece of bread. That is why we have so many recipes for using left-over bread. There are hearty soups such as RIBOLLITA, made with dried bread, beans and vegetables, especially CAVOLO NERO, dark cabbage: PAPPA AL POMODORO, a bread and tomato soup; bread salads such as PANZANELLA, made with slightly stale bread moistened with water and mixed with tomatoes, onions, herbs and olive oil; and bread puddings like MIASCIA, made with thin slices of stale, coarse-textured bread and fruit, seasoned with herbs. We even make good use of breadcrumbs to bind together basic dishes such as POLPETTE, meatballs, and POLPETTONE, meatloaf (see I SECONDI).

● Miscellaneous Breads ●

*A*nother way in which we enjoy our excellent bread are PANINI. These have now become as popular in Italy as the sandwich in North America. Today every town has a PANINOTECA, or sandwich shop, where you can buy PANINI already prepared or have them made to your specifications. The Italian versions, usually made with rolls, feature the bread rather than what is inside it. We fill them with a great variety of good ingredients — meat, cheeses, vegetables — but never more than one or a combination of two at a time so that you can still taste the bread. I always have at least one PANINI for lunch when I am on the go in the city; even the bars along our highways have a tasty selection.

Had it not been for the requests of my students I would probably not have begun to bake bread myself. It is not easy to find good-quality bread (Italy and Germany have the best in Europe) and they quite rightly want to reproduce at home the tasty breads they have eaten here. Now I always include bread recipes during my cooking class weeks. Sometimes I devote an entire morning session to baking, and we enjoy the breads with a green salad and several regional cheeses at lunch. At other times I include one special bread with each day's menu. Just as I do when I entertain, I select a bread that goes particularly well with the courses of that meal.

To make the antipasto of CROSTINI, little toasts with various toppings, PANE FRANCESE, the northern Italian version of French bread, is best. Tuscan saltless bread is perfect for any recipes that involve combining bread with food. Because of its coarse, dry texture it does not become mushy when you douse it with olive oil for a BRUSCHETTA or when you ladle a thick soup over a toasted slice for ZUPPA.

When I am preparing an elegant luncheon, I bake small rolls made with milk instead of water in the dough. GRISSINI, home-made breadsticks that can be flavoured with herbs such as rosemary and sage or sesame seeds, are especially nice for party occasions.

Italian flatbreads such as FOCACCIA from Genoa and the thinner, more crunchy Tuscan SCHIACCIATA, served with a salad, make a meal in themselves.

Biscotti Salati

SALTED CRACKERS

These are excellent served with white wine as an aperitif and, as they keep well in a tin, I usually make a double batch for unexpected guests.

MAKES ABOUT 60

30 g / 1 oz fresh (compressed) yeast

360 g / 12 oz / 3 cups strong plain flour or US bread flour + 6 tbsp for working

1 tsp salt + extra for sprinkling

6 tbsp extra virgin olive oil + extra for the bowl and baking sheet

In a small bowl, combine the yeast and 210 ml/7 fl oz/⅞ cup lukewarm water and leave to dissolve and start to foam, about 10 minutes.

In a large bowl, combine the flour and salt. Heap the flour into a mound with a well in the centre. Pour 4 tbsp of oil into the well, then gradually add the yeast mixture, using a fork to stir in the flour until a dough is formed.

Lightly flour a work surface. Put the dough on it and knead until smooth and elastic, about 10 minutes. Roll the dough into a ball. Lightly oil a large bowl. Put

YEAST

I prefer fresh (compressed) yeast to dried yeast for breadmaking. It is smooth and compact and I find it more reliable. It dissolves easily in lukewarm water, and at a room temperature of about 20°C/68°F it is ready to use in 10 minutes. If using dried granular yeast, substitute 15 g/½ oz/2 tbsp for each 30 g/1 oz of fresh yeast. Make sure the liquid used for dissolving yeast is not too warm because heat stops the yeast from expanding.

RISING TIMES

Rising time varies according to room temperature, humidity and other factors, but the first rising generally takes about 2 hours. As soon as the dough is fully risen it must be punched or knocked down, or the bread will taste yeasty and will have a bad texture.

the dough in it, cover tightly and leave to rise until doubled in size, about 2 hours.

Lightly flour the work surface. Put the dough on it and punch out the air. Roll out the dough into a rectangle about 2 mm/¹⁄₁₆ inch thick.

Brush a baking sheet with olive oil. Transfer the dough to it and, with the back of a knife, mark the dough into 3-cm/1¼-inch squares. Brush the top with the rest of the olive oil and sprinkle with a little salt.

Transfer to a preheated 200°C/400°F/gas 6 oven and bake for 10 minutes. Cut the squares all the way through, separate them slightly and bake for a further 5 minutes or until crisp.

Remove from the oven and leave to cool completely before serving.

Bretzeln

BOILED AND BAKED ROLLS (PRETZELS)

Funnily enough these are often offered in Naples as a summertime snack with a glass of chilled beer. They are particularly suitable for a luncheon or buffet.

MAKES 18

30 g / 1 oz fresh (compressed) yeast

360 g / 12 oz / 3 cups strong plain (all-purpose) flour + 2 tbsp for working

extra virgin olive oil for the bowl

1 egg yolk

1 tbsp milk

1 tbsp coarse salt

In a small bowl, combine the yeast and 210 ml/7 fl oz/⅞ cup lukewarm water and leave to dissolve and start to foam, about 10 minutes.

In a large bowl, heap the flour into a mound with a well in the centre. Gradually pour the yeast mixture into the well, using a fork to stir in the flour with a circular motion, until a dough is formed.

Lightly flour a work surface. Put the dough on it and knead with the palms of your hands until smooth and elastic, about 10 minutes. Roll the dough into a ball. Lightly oil a large bowl. Put the dough in it, cover tightly and leave to rise until doubled in size, about 2 hours.

Lightly flour a work surface and put the dough on it. Punch the dough to remove the air and divide it into 18 equal pieces. Using your hand roll each piece into a stick, about 1.5 cm/¾ inch wide, with pointed ends. Twist the two ends together.

Bring a very large pot of salted water to the boil. Add the rolls, a few at a time,

MIXING THE DOUGH

If in doubt, make a sticky dough rather than a dry one because it is easier to correct. If the dough is too sticky you can just add a little flour, but a dry dough is practically impossible to correct. Although dough can be started in a machine, to have a good result it must be kneaded by hand for at least 10 minutes.

and cook until they rise to the surface, about 3 minutes. Remove with a slotted spoon and drain on a cloth.

Lightly flour a baking sheet. Arrange the rolls on it. In a cup, mix the egg yolk with the milk. Brush the rolls with the egg glaze and sprinkle with the coarse salt. Transfer to a preheated 200°C/400°F/gas 6 oven. Bake until golden, about 20 minutes. Allow the rolls to cool completely before serving.

Ciaccino al Rosmarino

VERY FLAT ROSEMARY BREAD

Ciaccino is rolled very thin and is only left to rise once. Serve with a glass of white wine as an aperitif. You can also substitute sage, thyme, a pinch of chili powder or chopped garlic for the rosemary.

SERVES 6

---

30 g / 1 oz fresh (compressed) yeast

360 g / 12 oz / 3 cups strong plain flour or US bread flour + 2 tbsp for working

---

1 tbsp salt

---

6 tbsp extra virgin olive oil + extra for the bowl and baking sheet

---

2 tbsp finely chopped fresh rosemary

In a small bowl, combine the yeast and 210 ml / 7 fl oz / $\frac{7}{8}$ cup lukewarm water and leave to dissolve and start to foam, about 10 minutes.

In a large bowl, combine the flour and salt. Heap the flour into a mound with a well in the centre. Pour the oil into the well and gradually add the yeast mixture, using a fork to stir in the flour with a circular motion, until a dough is formed.

Lightly flour a work surface. Put the dough on it, sprinkle with half the rosemary and knead with the palms of your hands until the dough is smooth and elastic, about 10 minutes. Lightly oil a large bowl. Roll the dough into a ball, put it in the bowl and cover tightly. Leave to rise until double in size, about 2 hours.

● **Sesame Breadsticks** ●

On a lightly floured surface, punch the dough to knock out air. Roll out the dough until it is paper-thin. Lightly oil a baking sheet. Arrange the dough on it, prick with a fork and sprinkle with the remaining rosemary. Immediately transfer to a preheated 200°C/400°F/gas 6 oven and bake for about 10 minutes or until golden.

Leave to cool, then break the bread into pieces for serving.

Grissini al Sesamo

SESAME BREADSTICKS

Breadsticks are usually served at table with bread. However, they make delicious appetizers with prosciutto wrapped around the top. They will keep fresh in an airtight container for several days. Before baking, you can also roll the breadsticks in chopped fresh rosemary or poppy seeds.

MAKES 16

---

30 g / 1 oz fresh (compressed) yeast

---

120 g / 4 oz / 1 cup strong plain flour (or US bread flour)

---

180 g / 6 oz / 1½ cups wholewheat flour

---

60 g / 2 oz / 6½ tbsp coarse semolina

---

1 tbsp salt

---

2 tbsp extra virgin olive oil + extra for the bowl

---

60 g / 2 oz / 6½ tbsp sesame seeds

In a small bowl, combine the yeast and 210 ml/7 fl oz/⅞ cup lukewarm water and leave to dissolve and start to foam, about 10 minutes.

In a large bowl, combine the flours with three-quarters of the semolina and the salt. Heap the flour into a mound with a well in the centre. Pour the oil into the well and gradually add the yeast mixture, using a fork to stir in the flour with a circular motion, until a dough forms.

Lightly sprinkle a work surface with semolina. Transfer the dough to it and knead with the palms of your hands until the dough is smooth and elastic, about 10 minutes.

Lightly oil a large bowl. Roll the dough into a ball and place it in the oiled bowl. Cover tightly and leave to rise until double in size, about 2 hours.

Sprinkle the work surface with the rest of the semolina and half the sesame seeds. Transfer the dough to it and punch it to knock out air. Roll the dough into a rectangle about 15 × 20 cm/6 × 8 inches. Cut the dough into 1-cm/½-inch strips and gently roll the strips into sticks.

Sprinkle a baking sheet with the rest of the sesame seeds and arrange the breadsticks on it, about 2.5 cm/1 inch apart. Cover with a towel and leave to rise for 20 minutes.

Bake in the middle of a preheated 200°C/400°F/gas 6 oven until lightly golden and crisp, about 20 minutes. Cool slightly on a wire rack before serving.

Freezing Bread

When baking bread I generally make quite a large quantity. I divide the extra bread into serving portions and freeze them in bags. When needed, I reheat the bread in a preheated 180°C/350°F/gas 4 oven for about 10 minutes. It emerges crisp and just like freshly baked bread.

Pane Integrale

Wholewheat Bread

To make the coarse-textured bread called for in some of these recipes, substitute strong plain flour *or US bread flour* for wholewheat flour. You can also replace part of the flour with soya flour, buckwheat flour or yellow cornmeal.

MAKES 2 LOAVES

30 g / 1 oz fresh (compressed) yeast

360 g / 12 oz / 3 cups strong plain wholemeal (wholewheat bread) flour + 60 g / 2 oz / ½ cup for working

½ tsp salt

extra virgin olive oil for the bowl

In a small bowl, combine the yeast and 210 ml/7 fl oz/⅞ cup lukewarm water and leave to dissolve and start to foam, about 10 minutes.

In a large bowl, combine the flour and salt. Heap the flour into a mound with a well in the centre. Gradually add the yeast mixture, using a fork to stir in the flour with a circular motion, until a dough forms.

Lightly sprinkle a work surface with flour. Transfer the dough to it and knead with the palms of your hands until the dough is smooth and elastic, about 10 minutes. Lightly oil a large bowl. Roll the dough into a ball and place it in the bowl. Cover tightly and leave to rise until double in size, about 2 hours.

On a lightly floured surface punch the dough to knock out air. Divide the dough in half and shape each piece into an oval loaf about 20 cm/8 inches long. Transfer the loaves to a lightly floured baking sheet and leave to rise for 30 minutes.

Bake in a preheated 200°C/400°F/ gas 6 oven until the loaves sound hollow when tapped, about 30 minutes. Cool before slicing.

Pane alla Pancetta

Pancetta Bread

This bread has a fairly fine texture and goes very well with cheese. You could make it with bacon rather than pancetta, although bacon contains much more fat than pancetta. Discard some of the fat if you like.

MAKES 1 LOAF

1 tbsp extra virgin olive oil + extra for the bowl and baking sheet

120 g / 4 oz pancetta, chopped

30 g / 1 oz fresh (compressed) yeast

360 g / 12 oz / 3 cups strong plain flour or US bread flour + 2 tbsp for working

1 tsp salt

In a small frying pan heat the olive oil, add the pancetta and fry over moderate heat until crisp, about 5 minutes. Drain the pancetta on paper towels and set aside. Leave the melted cooking fat in the pan to cool almost completely.

In a small bowl, combine the yeast and 210 ml/7 fl oz/⅞ cup lukewarm water and leave to dissolve and start to foam, about 10 minutes.

Sift the flour into a large bowl. Sprinkle with salt and heap the flour into a mound with a well in the centre. Pour the melted fat into the well and gradually add the yeast mixture, using a fork to stir in the flour with a circular motion, until a dough forms.

Lightly sprinkle a work surface with flour. Transfer the dough to it, sprinkle with the pancetta and knead until the dough is smooth and elastic, about 10 minutes.

Brush a large bowl with olive oil. Roll the dough into a ball and place it in the oiled bowl. Cover tightly and leave to rise until double in size, about 2 hours.

Punch the dough to knock out air and shape it into an oval loaf about

BREADCRUMBS

*N*ever throw away bread. Dry it thoroughly in a warm oven and process it in a blender or food processor until fine breadcrumbs are formed. Store the breadcrumbs in airtight jars where they will keep indefinitely.

25 cm/10 inches long. Oil a baking sheet. Place the loaf on the baking sheet, cover with a cloth and leave to rise for about 20 minutes.

Transfer to a preheated 200°C/400°F/gas 6 oven and bake until the loaf sounds hollow when tapped, about 30 minutes. Cool completely before slicing.

Pane all' Uvetta e Noci

RAISIN AND WALNUT BREAD

*T*his bread is excellent served with strong cheeses such as gorgonzola, fontina, provolone or Camembert.

MAKES 2 LOAVES

---

60 g / 2 oz / 6½ tbsp raisins

---

30 g / 1 oz fresh (compressed) yeast

---

90 g / 3 oz / ¾ cup chopped walnuts

---

5 tbsp extra virgin olive oil + extra for the bowl

---

360 g / 12 oz / 3 cups strong plain wholemeal (wholewheat bread) flour + 60 g / 2 oz / ½ cup for working

---

1 tbsp sugar

---

1 tsp salt

In a small bowl, soak the raisins in water to cover for 30 minutes; drain. In another small bowl, combine the yeast and 210 ml/7 fl oz/⅞ cup lukewarm water and leave to dissolve and start to foam, about 10 minutes.

Fry the walnuts in the olive oil for about 2 minutes. Set aside.

In a large bowl, combine the flour, sugar and salt. Heap the flour into a mound with a well in the centre. Gradually add the yeast mixture, using a fork to stir in the flour with a circular motion, until a dough is formed.

Lightly sprinkle a work surface with flour. Transfer the dough to it and knead with the palms of your hands until the dough is smooth and elastic, about 10 minutes. Lightly oil a large bowl. Roll the dough into a ball and place it in the bowl. Cover tightly and leave to rise until double in size, about 2 hours.

On a lightly floured surface punch the dough to knock out air. Add the walnuts with their oil and the raisins and work until well blended. Divide the dough in half and shape each piece into a loaf 20 cm/8 inches long. Lightly flour a baking sheet and place the loaves on it. Cover and leave to rise until double in size.

Transfer the baking sheet to a preheated 200°C/400°F/gas 6 oven and bake until the loaves sound hollow when tapped, about 30 minutes. Cool before slicing.

CRUST FINISHES

*T*o achieve a crisp crust, spray the bread with water while it is baking. If, however, you want a smooth, shiny crust, brush it with egg yolk mixed with a little milk or water. Be careful not to make the mixture too runny or it will spill on to the pan and stick.

Panini al Latte

MILK ROLLS

*T*hese rolls are suitable for an elegant luncheon or dinner. After rolling into strips, the dough can be twisted, plaited (braided) or rolled up.

MAKES ABOUT 18

---

30 g / 1 oz fresh (compressed) yeast

---

210 ml / 7 fl oz / ⅞ cup lukewarm milk

---

360 g / 12 oz / 3 cups strong plain (all-purpose) flour + 60 g / 2 oz / ½ cup for working

---

1 tbsp sugar

---

1 tsp salt

---

60 g / 2 oz / 4 tbsp unsalted butter, melted

---

extra virgin olive oil for the bowl

---

1 egg yolk

In a small bowl, combine the yeast and milk and leave to dissolve and start to foam, about 10 minutes.

In a large bowl, combine the flour, sugar and salt. Heap the flour into a mound with a well in the centre. Pour in the melted butter and gradually add the yeast mixture, using a fork to stir in the flour with a circular motion, until a dough is formed.

Lightly sprinkle a work surface with flour. Put the dough on it and knead with your hands until the dough is smooth and elastic, about 10 minutes. Lightly oil a large bowl. Roll the dough into a ball and place it in the bowl. Cover tightly and leave to rise until double in size, about 2 hours.

On a lightly floured surface, punch the dough to knock out air. Divide it into about 12 pieces and, using your hands, roll each into a strip about 1 cm/½ inch

● **Milk Rolls** ●

thick and 12 cm/5 inches long. Twist them and arrange on a floured baking sheet. Cover and leave to rise until double in size.

In a cup, stir ½ tsp water into the egg yolk. Brush the rolls with the egg yolk glaze and transfer the baking sheet to a preheated 200°C/400°F/gas 6 oven. Bake until golden, about 20 minutes.

Piadina Romagnola
FLAT GRIDDLE CAKES

These are delicious topped with pro-sciutto, cheese or mortadella. Occasionally we have very informal *Piadina* parties, with the hot griddle cakes in the middle of the table sur-rounded by broccoli sautéed with oil and garlic, prosciutto, ricotta cheese and salami.

MAKES 18

15 g / ½ oz fresh (compressed) yeast

360 g / 12 oz / 3 cups strong plain flour or US bread flour + 60 g / 2 oz / ½ cup for working

1 tsp salt

3 tbsp extra virgin olive oil + extra for the bowl

In a small bowl, combine the yeast and 210 ml/7 fl oz/⅞ cup lukewarm water and leave to dissolve and start to foam, about 10 minutes.

In a large bowl, combine the flour and salt. Heap the flour into a mound with a well in the centre. Pour the oil into the well and gradually add the yeast mixture, using a fork to stir in the flour with a circular motion, until a dough is formed.

Lightly flour a work surface. Put the dough on it and knead until smooth and elastic, about 10 minutes. Roll the dough into a ball. Lightly oil a large bowl. Put the dough in it, cover tightly and leave to rise until doubled in size, about 2 hours.

On a lightly floured work surface punch the dough to knock out air. Divide it into 18 equal pieces and roll into balls. With a rolling pin, roll each ball into a disc about 2 mm/1/16 inch thick.

Heat a cast-iron griddle or frying pan over high heat. Cook the discs, a few at a time, until golden with a few darker marks, about 3 minutes on each side. As they are cooked, wrap the griddle cakes in a table napkin. Serve hot on a warm platter.

Schiacciata
TUSCAN FLATBREAD

This flatbread can be flavoured by sprinkling it with fresh rosemary or chopped sage, with thinly sliced onion, with grated cheese or with crumbled sausage just before baking.

MAKES 1, TO SERVE 6

30 g / 1 oz fresh (compressed) yeast

360 g / 12 oz / 3 cups strong plain (all-purpose) flour + 60 g / 2 oz / ½ cup for working

2 tbsp extra virgin olive oil + extra for the bowl and pan

½ tbsp coarse salt

In a small bowl, combine the yeast and 210 ml/7 fl oz/⅞ cup lukewarm water and leave to dissolve and start to foam, about 10 minutes. In a large bowl, heap the flour into a mound with a well in the centre. Gradually add the yeast mixture, using a fork to stir in the flour with a circular motion, until a dough is formed.

Lightly flour a work surface. Put the dough on it and knead with the palms of your hands until the dough is smooth and elastic, about 10 minutes. Lightly oil a large bowl. Roll the dough into a ball and place it in the bowl. Cover tightly and leave to rise until double in size, about 2 hours.

Brush a 28-cm/11-inch tart pan with oil. On a lightly floured surface, punch the dough to knock out air and roll it out until it is about 5 mm/¼ inch thick. Transfer the dough to the pan, cover and leave to rise until double in thickness.

Using the tips of your fingers, make dents all over the surface of the dough. Brush with the oil and sprinkle with the coarse salt. Transfer to a preheated 200°C/400°F/gas 6 oven and bake until golden, about 30 minutes.

● **Tuscan Flatbread** ●

La Dispensa

THE STORE CUPBOARD

*F*reezers, supermarkets that practically never close, and the limited spaces of city living have diminished the place of the larder or pantry in the modern household. In our Milan apartment I make do with a converted wardrobe (closet). At Coltibuono, most of the large old DISPENSA was incorporated into working space for my cooking classes when I remodelled the kitchen.

Nevertheless, some kind of larder or pantry, however modest it may be, I still consider indispensable for several reasons. The large kitchen garden at Coltibuono produces, and seemingly all at once, much more than we could ever consume fresh, so I preserve a portion of its fruit and vegetables. Also, contrary to popular belief, we have serious winters here in Tuscany, not to mention in Milan, and I like to relieve the dreariness of the weather with a taste of summer that I have conserved in a bottle. Lastly, and perhaps most usefully, I do a lot of impromptu entertaining and I want always to have on hand a supply of essentials in order to be able to put together a tasty pasta dish or risotto.

*T*he first item that goes on to my larder shelves is tomatoes. Romola, my cook, and I usually spend the last days of August, before the autumn cooking classes begin, preserving tomatoes both whole and in sauce. As I have already mentioned, I now freeze most of my tomatoes, which is easier than bottling them. I find it handy, however, to have a few jars of tomatoes in my larder.

I have a special machine for processing tomatoes to make sauce. You pour the ripe tomatoes into the top and it separates the skins and seeds from the pulp, which comes out the bottom. Then we wrap the pulp in a linen cloth and pound it with a wooden pestle in order to release the remaining liquid. I add a few leaves of basil, and it is ready to be sealed in sterilized jars, where it will keep for 2 or 3 years.

If the August weather is very hot while we are preserving tomatoes, Romola cooks some of the sauce and spreads it out on tables set up in Coltibuono's large stone courtyard, which captures the heat of the sun. She lets it dry there for 2 or 3 days, bringing it in at

● Herb Vinegars (p. 209) and Flavoured Oil (p. 213) ●

night, until it becomes thick and turns almost brown. A portion of this paste I refrigerate, enough to last me for a couple of months, and the rest I conserve in jars.

From my garden I also preserve green beans, red and yellow sweet peppers, artichoke hearts and, this year for the first time, CETRIOLINI, tiny pickling cucumbers. Because these vegetables are low in natural acidity, in order to arrest fermentation, I blanch them in water and vinegar before bottling them in either fresh vinegar or extra virgin olive oil.

Another annual item on my larder shelves is a speciality of Coltibuono, fig and lemon jam. We have about 20 potted lemon trees and several purple fig trees in the garden.

It is nice to be able to warm a cold winter's night with a glass of herbal liqueur. Years ago a friend taught me a simple way to make it. She dilutes 90 proof distilled alcohol which can be bought in Italy from the local pharmacy, with distilled water. In my recipe I substitute grappa. You put a herb from the garden — mint, sage and bay work well — in 750 ml / 1¼ pints / 3 cups of grappa, cork the bottle and shake well. I store the bottles for about a month, and try to remember to give them a shake a couple of times a day. Then I strain the liquid through a paper filter into a clean bottle and it is ready to drink.

In every Italian larder you will also find bottles of dried fruits preserved in grappa. I prepare mine in two different ways. The first is a recipe for enjoying the fruit. The second provides an elegant and different way to serve grappa after a meal. You put raisins, dried apricots and prunes or a mixture of all three in enough grappa to cover them. Every day add enough grappa to keep them completely covered. Seal, and in a month they will be ready to serve.

Aceto Aromatico

HERB VINEGAR

Vinegar flavoured with thyme, basil, mint, raspberries and so on can be prepared in exactly the same way. Vinegar absorbs the flavour of basil more quickly, so it will be ready in about 2 weeks. Use a paper coffee filter to strain the vinegar. As the vinegar keeps indefinitely, always choose a good quality one for this purpose.

MAKES 750 ML / 1¼ PINTS / 3 CUPS

120 g / 4 oz fresh tarragon

750 ml / 1¼ pints / 3 cups red or white wine vinegar

Strip the tarragon leaves from the stalks and pack them into a jar. Cover with the vinegar and seal well.

In summer stand the jar outside in the sun for about 40 days. In winter put it by a sunny window.

Strain through a paper filter and transfer the vinegar to a clean bottle with a screw top or good cork.

Aceto di Erbe Miste

MIXED HERB VINEGAR

The vinegar acquires a very strong flavour so use just a few drops to flavour a sauce or deglaze the pan after you have roasted meat. If the vinegar is very sour, sweeten it with 1 tbsp of honey added with the herbs. It will keep indefinitely.

MAKES 750 ML / 1¼ PINTS / 3 CUPS

120 g / 4 oz mixed fresh herbs, such as bay leaves, sage, rosemary, tarragon, thyme, mint, coriander (cilantro), parsley, basil, chives, oregano or marjoram, or peppercorns or caraway seed

750 ml / 1¼ pints / 3 cups red or white wine vinegar

Remove the herb leaves from the stalks and pack them into a jar, or pack in the peppercorns or caraway seed. Cover with the vinegar and seal well.

In summer stand the jar outside in the sun for about 40 days. In winter put it by a sunny window.

Strain through a paper filter and transfer the vinegar to a clear bottle with a screw top or good cork.

Concentrato di Pomodoro

SUN-DRIED TOMATO CONCENTRATE

I always try to make quite a lot of this because it adds a great deal of flavour to a tomato sauce made with fresh or canned tomatoes. It is enough to add just 1 tbsp to 900 g / 2 lb peeled tomatoes.

MAKES ABOUT 250 ML / 8 FL OZ / 1 CUP

1.2 kg / 2½ lb very ripe plum tomatoes, peeled (or use canned)

1 tsp salt

Put the peeled tomatoes through a food mill or sieve to get rid of the seeds. Transfer the pulp to a heavy saucepan and sprinkle with the salt. Simmer over low heat, stirring occasionally, until most of the juice has evaporated and the sauce is fairly thick, about 50 minutes.

Spread the sauce into a layer about 2 cm / ¾ inch thick on a large wooden board. Put it in the sun to dry, covering with a net. Take it in at night, mix well and keep in a bowl, refrigerated. Next day spread again on the cleaned board and dry in the sun. Do this for 3 days.

When the tomato is dark and dry, transfer it to a sterilized jar. It will keep in the refrigerator for about 3 months.

Gelatina di Uva

GRAPE JELLY

This is very useful for glazing tarts and is wonderful as a sauce for sorbet: melt the jelly with a little white wine over low heat and pour over the sorbet at the last minute. Raspberries, strawberries or blackberries can be a nice substitution.

MAKES ABOUT 900 G / 2 LB

3 kg / 6½ lb purple, black, green or white grapes

600 g / 1¼ lb / 3 cups sugar

In a bowl, squeeze the grapes with your fingers to break the skins. Transfer the grapes to a jelly bag and leave the juice to drip into a bowl.

In a saucepan combine 1.2 litres / 2 pints / 5 cups grape juice with the sugar and bring to the boil over low heat. Cook over low heat for about 30 minutes or until the liquid becomes syrupy and a drop poured on a cold saucer will stay round.

Pour the jelly into sterilized jars and screw on the lids while still hot. Keeps for 1 year.

MAKING JELLY

Jellies are rather more difficult to make than jams because the syrup must be cooked to exactly the right temperature and the fruit must contain more pectin. I generally make jelly from peaches, apples, quinces, raspberries and redcurrants. If using other fruit, add commercial pectin. You will find the proportions indicated on the packet.

Grappa alle Spezie

SPICED GRAPPA

I occasionally flavour grappa with spices, or with basil, lemon verbena or mint to obtain other aromas.

MAKES 750 ML / 1¼ PINTS / 3 CUPS

750 ml / 1¼ pints / 3 cups grappa or vodka

1 tbsp juniper berries

5 whole cloves

1-cm / ½-inch piece of cinnamon stick

6 fresh sage leaves

5 fresh mint leaves

a pinch of grated nutmeg

1 tbsp aniseed

pared zest of 1 lemon

Combine all the ingredients in a screw-top jar. Seal and leave to macerate for about 1 month.

Strain through a paper filter and pour the liqueur into a clean bottle. It is now ready to be served.

● Spiced Grappa, Lemon Liqueur ●

Kirsch

HOME-MADE KIRSCH

To sweeten our grappa, I sometimes make this home-made brew that is vaguely Kirsch-flavoured. It is not very strong but its aroma makes it a good after-dinner drink; try it poured over apple sorbet (page 190).

MAKES 750 ML / 1¼ PINTS / 3 CUPS

300 g / 10 oz cherry stones

6 apricot stones

750 ml / 1¼ pints / 3 cups grappa

Crush the fruit stones and put them in a bottle. Add the grappa and leave to macerate for about 2 months.

Strain the liqueur through a paper filter and pour it into a clean bottle. Serve chilled.

Limoncino

LEMON LIQUEUR

This liqueur is famous on the island of Capri, where wonderful lemons are grown. In Italy it is made with pure alcohol, but you can use grappa or vodka which is easier to find outside Italy.

MAKES 750 ML / 1¼ PINTS / 3 CUPS

4 lemons

90 g / 3 oz / 7 tbsp sugar

750 ml / 1½ pints / 3 cups grappa or vodka

Pare the zest thinly off the lemons, making sure it is free of bitter white pith. Put the lemon zest in a screw-top jar, add the sugar and grappa or vodka and seal the jar well. Leave to macerate for about 3 months.

Strain the liqueur through a paper filter and pour it into a clean bottle. Serve chilled.

Liquore di Lamponi

RASPBERRY LIQUEUR

I save the raspberries after making this liqueur because they are superb on vanilla ice cream. The liqueur is bright red and an exquisite after-dinner drink. Strawberries and redcurrants are good substitutes for the raspberries.

MAKES ABOUT 750 ML / 1¼ PINTS / 3 CUPS

360 g / 12 oz / 1½ pints ripe raspberries

1-cm / ½-inch piece of cinnamon stick

2 whole cloves

150 g / 5 oz / ¾ cup sugar

pared zest of 2 lemons

2 bay leaves

750 ml / 1¼ pints / 3 cups grappa or vodka

In a large screw-top jar combine the raspberries, spices, 90 g / 3 oz / 7 tbsp sugar, lemon zest and bay leaves. Cover with the grappa or vodka, seal and leave to macerate for 6 months.

Pour the rest of the sugar into a smaller jar. Remove the raspberries from the big jar with a slotted spoon and add them to the sugar. Seal the jar well.

Strain the liqueur through a paper filter and pour it into a clean bottle. Cork hermetically. Serve chilled.

MAKING JAM

To make good jam you need fresh, naturally ripened fruit. It should be well washed and rubbed with a dry cloth. Jam should be made in a large heavy pan, either stainless steel or copper with tin lining. The fruit should be stirred frequently while cooking and skimmed to ensure clarity. Jams have a better flavour if the fruit is cooked for a short time, just until soft, then removed and the syrup cooked much longer.

Marmellata di Albicocche

APRICOT JAM

Because of its wonderful scent, apricot jam is one of my favourites and, when we have a good crop, I make masses of it. It is delicious on toast for breakfast and for making tarts. Use the same method for making peach, pear and plum jam.

MAKES ABOUT 1.5 KG / 3½ LB

1.5 kg / 3½ lb apricots

900 g / 2 lb / 4½ cups sugar

grated zest of 1 lemon

4 tbsp Vin Santo or another sweet dessert wine

Blanch the apricots in boiling water for 30 seconds, then drain and peel. Cut the apricots in half and remove the stones.

In a heavy saucepan, combine the apricots, sugar and lemon zest. Cover and leave to stand in a cool place for 24 hours.

Stirring occasionally, cook the apricot mixture over low heat for 10 minutes. Take the saucepan off the heat and remove the apricots with a slotted spoon. Put the apricots through a food mill or process for a few seconds in a food processor.

Return the saucepan to the heat and continue cooking the juice until a thick syrup is formed. Return the apricot purée to the saucepan, add the wine and return to the boil.

Stir well, and fill sterilized jars.

Marmellata di Fichi e Limoni

FIG AND LEMON JAM

Maria Luisa, whose husband managed the farm at Coltibuono for 35 years, used to make this jam for us, and when she retired she gave me the recipe. The figs must be ripe and the lemons untreated or they will make the jam bitter. This jam must be well cooked.

MAKES ABOUT 1.5 KG/3½ LB

1.2 kg/2½ lb ripe figs

6 lemons

900 g/2 lb/4½ cups sugar

3 whole cloves

Cut the unpeeled figs in half. Slice the lemons paper-thin, skin and all. On the bottom of a heavy saucepan make a layer of figs. Cover it with slices of lemon and cover the lemon with sugar. Continue making layers until all the ingredients are used, finishing with a layer of sugar. Add the cloves. Cover the saucepan and leave it to stand in a cool place for 24 hours.

Stirring occasionally, cook the fruit over low heat until the lemon peel is soft and the syrup thick, about 40 minutes.

Remove the cloves and ladle the jam into sterilized jars.

TESTING FOR SETTING POINT

If you are not using a thermometer, you can test the fruit syrup by putting a drop on a cold surface. If it jells and does not spread, the syrup has reached the right point. You cannot put *cold* jam in a jar. If you leave it to cool you must reheat it to fill the jar.

PROCESSING JARS OF JAM

Pour the hot jam into dry, sterilized jars and seal them immediately. They should be left to cool, then wrapped in newspaper and boiled in water to cover for about 20 minutes. Leave to cool in the water. Jam treated this way will keep much longer, particularly if it is not made with a lot of sugar.

Marmellata di Pomodori Verdi

GREEN TOMATO JAM

This is a very good way to use unripe tomatoes at the end of the summer.

MAKES ABOUT 1.5 KG/3½ LB

2 Golden Delicious apples

1.2 kg/2½ lb green tomatoes

900 g/2 lb/4½ cups sugar

Core and thinly slice the apples. Cut the tomatoes into thin slices. In a heavy saucepan combine the apples and tomatoes. Stirring frequently, cook over low heat until the tomatoes have disintegrated and most of the liquid has evaporated, about 30 minutes.

Add the sugar and cook until the syrup is thick, about 20 more minutes.

Ladle the jam into sterilized jars.

Marmellata di Susine

PLUM PASTE

This takes a long time to prepare, but it is well worth doing on a rainy weekend because it is sugarless and thus very healthy. Cut into 2-cm/¾-inch squares, it can be served instead of after-dinner mints. Use the same method for apples, pears, peaches, and so on.

MAKES ABOUT 450 G/1 LB

1.5 kg/3½ lb ripe plums

sweet almond oil for the pan

Bring a saucepan of water to the boil and blanch the plums for 30 seconds. Drain, then peel and stone the plums.

Put the plums in a heavy saucepan and bring to the boil over low heat. Reduce the heat as much as possible and, stirring from time to time, simmer for about 12 hours. When the plums have completely disintegrated and cooked to a thick paste, pour into a rectangular pan brushed with almond oil. Smooth the surface and leave to cool.

Cut into 2-cm/¾-inch squares when completely cold. Keeps for 1 year.

STORING JAM

Use several small jars rather than one large one because home-made jam tends to go mouldy if it is made with a small amount of sugar, and, once opened, it can ferment. Keep open jars of jam in the refrigerator. Should jam go mouldy or ferment, it can be saved by removing the mould and reboiling the jam. Fermented jam can also be boiled again.

Mostarda di Frutta

FRUIT MUSTARD

The most famous fruit mustard in Italy is made in Cremona. It is prepared with whole candied fruits, but it is too complicated to make at home, so I have evolved something similar that is delicious with boiled or roast meat. For centuries boiled capon has always been served in Tuscany at Christmas, so I always prepare this mustard then. Refrigerated, it keeps for up to 14 days.

MAKES ABOUT 1.5 KG / 3½ LB

1.5 kg / 3½ lb mixed fruit, such as pears, peaches, cherries, apricots, and so on

---

900 g / 2 lb / 4½ cups sugar

---

6 tbsp white wine vinegar

---

60 g / 2 oz / ½ cup powdered mustard

Peel, core and quarter pears. Peel, stone and quarter peaches. Stone cherries. Halve and stone apricots.

In a heavy saucepan combine 120 ml / 4 fl oz / ½ cup water and 600 g / 1¼ lb / 3 cups sugar. Skimming at least twice, boil until syrupy. Add the fruit and simmer for a further 20 minutes. Pour the fruit and syrup into a jar and leave it to cool completely.

FRUIT MUSTARD

Fruit mustard is very popular in Italy and should be served with roast or boiled meats. It is made in several regions, but the most famous is Mostarda di Cremona. It is superior to the one produced in Veneto. A little is added to the celebrated pumpkin tortelli. Home-made fruit mustard does not keep for more than 2 weeks in the refrigerator.

In a small saucepan combine the rest of the sugar and the wine vinegar. Cook over low heat for 15 minutes. Allow to cool completely, then stir in the mustard.

Pour the mustard mixture into the jar and stir the fruit carefully. Screw on the lid and refrigerate.

Olio Aromatico

FLAVOURED OLIVE OIL

As olive oil obviously contains far less acid than vinegar, it does not conserve herbs for very long. It is advisable to make small quantities at a time, and to use only herbs such as bay leaves, thyme and rosemary or seeds such as coriander that contain very little moisture.

MAKES 300 ML / ½ PINT / 1¼ CUPS

---

300 ml / ½ pint / 1¼ cups extra virgin olive oil

---

60 g / 2 oz fresh thyme, bay leaves, rosemary or sage, or fennel or coriander seeds

Remove the herb leaves from the stalks and pack them in a jar or place seeds in the jar. Cover with the oil, seal and leave to stand in a cool place for about 1 week.

Strain the oil through a paper filter and transfer it to a clean bottle with a screw top or good cork.

● **Apricot Jam (p. 211), Fig and Lemon Jam,** ●
Plum Paste

Pomodori in Conserva

BOTTLED WHOLE TOMATOES

At the end of the summer, when we have an abundance of ripe tomatoes, I bottle them with a few basil leaves for use in the winter. When the sauce is half-cooked I strain it through a sieve, to get rid of the skins which are always unpleasant.

MAKES 1.2 KG / 2½ LB

1.2 kg / 2½ lb ripe and unblemished plum tomatoes

a handful of fresh basil leaves

salt

Wash the tomatoes and dry them well. In a large jar or jars, arrange the tomatoes as close together as possible. Add basil leaves and sprinkle with salt. Seal the jars, wrap them in newspaper and put them in a large pan with water to cover. Boil for 25 minutes, then leave to cool in the water.

Passato di Pomodoro

BOTTLED TOMATO PULP

This is a very good way to keep tomatoes, as the pulp is fairly concentrated and does not require much cooking. In Italy we have special machines for peeling and seeding tomatoes, but they are not really necessary unless you intend bottling a large quantity. The tomato pulp will keep for over a year.

MAKES ABOUT 750 ML / 1¼ PINTS / 3 CUPS

1.2 kg / 2½ lb ripe plum tomatoes

1 tsp salt

a handful of fresh basil leaves

Bring a large pot of water to the boil. Add the tomatoes and blanch for 30 seconds, then drain and leave to cool slightly. Pierce the tomato skins with a sharp knife and slide them off; discard them, put the peeled tomatoes through a food mill or push them through a sieve.

Transfer the tomato pulp to a large sieve. Add the salt and, stirring occasionally, leave for at least 2 hours so the excess juice will drain away.

Spoon the tomato pulp into sterilized jars and add a few basil leaves to each. Seal the jars, wrap them in newspaper and put them in a large pan with water to cover. Boil for 25 minutes. Leave to cool in the water.

Uva Sotto Grappa

GRAPES IN GRAPPA

Because we have a large wine farm, I obviously find many different ways to conserve grapes. In Italy pure alcohol, 90 degrees proof, is available for conserving fruit, but as it is not easy to find elsewhere, use grappa, vodka or Cognac. These grapes and their juice are served as an after-dinner drink.

MAKES ABOUT 1.5 LITRES / 2½ PINTS / 1⅓ QUARTS

1.2 kg / 2½ lb firm green or white grapes

300 g / 10 oz / 1½ cups sugar

1.2 litres / 2 pints / 5 cups grappa

3 whole cloves

Wash the grapes and discard any damaged ones. Cut the grapes off the main stalk without removing the small individual stalk on each grape. Prick the grapes with a thin, sterilized needle and pack them in a sterilized jar.

In a bowl, dissolve the sugar in the grappa and add the cloves. Pour the liquid over the grapes to cover well. Screw on the lid.

Uvetta in Grappa

RAISINS IN GRAPPA

Fruit in grappa ages well, so I usually prepare several jars of this at a time. Dried apricots and prunes can be treated in the same way, but make sure they are well covered with grappa. The dried fruit gradually absorbs the grappa and after a minimum of 1 month, it is ready to serve. Excellent served in small glasses with after-dinner coffee. Vodka or Cognac can be substituted for grappa.

MAKES ABOUT 450 G / 1 LB

300 g / 10 oz / 2 cups raisins

300 ml / ½ pint / 1¼ cups good grappa

1 whole clove

Pour the raisins into a glass jar and cover them with the grappa. Add the clove, screw on the lid and store at room temperature for at least 2 weeks before serving.

Remove the clove. Spoon the raisins and any grappa that may be left in the jar into small glasses and serve with a coffee spoon.

• Bottled Whole Tomatoes, •
Bottled Tomato Pulp

Ricette Base

BASIC RECIPES

Besciamella

WHITE SAUCE

In recipe books one is often told to add boiling milk to the butter and flour all at once. But I find my method easier, and the thickness of the sauce can be better controlled. The sauce is smooth, free of lumps and quick to make.

MAKES 300 ML / ½ PINT / 1¼ CUPS MEDIUM-THICK SAUCE

30 g / 1 oz / 2 tbsp unsalted butter

30 g / 1 oz / ¼ cup flour

300 ml / ½ pint / 1¼ cups milk

salt and white pepper

In a saucepan melt the butter over moderate heat. Add the flour and stir with a wooden spoon, not a whisk, until the flour is well absorbed, about 1 minute; the flour should not brown. Gradually add the milk, about 4 tbsp at a time, stirring until well blended before adding more milk. The milk can be cold, at room temperature or hot.

The quantity of milk can vary according to use: when making a soufflé, I stop adding milk when the sauce is still thick (about 240 ml / 8 fl oz / 1 cup milk); when I am using the sauce for baked pasta or vegetables, I add 480 ml / 16 fl oz / 2 cups milk.

Bring to the boil, stirring constantly, and boil for a couple of minutes. Season to taste.

Brodo di Carne o Pollo

LIGHT MEAT OR CHICKEN STOCK

Very different from French stock, this is light in flavour and will not overwhelm other flavours in soups and sauces. It can be refrigerated for up to 3 days, or frozen.

MAKES ABOUT 2 LITRES / 3¼ PINTS / 2 QUARTS

1.8 kg / 4 lb beef chuck or brisket, or 1 large boiling chicken, legs and wings discarded

1 medium-size onion, sliced

2 leeks, white part only, sliced

1 carrot, sliced

2 celery stalks, sliced

a handful of fresh flat-leaf (Italian) parsley

1 tsp black peppercorns

2 whole cloves

2 bay leaves

2 sprigs of fresh thyme

2 tsp salt

In a deep pan combine all the ingredients. Add 2.4 litres / 4 pints / 2½ quarts cold water and slowly bring to the boil. Lower the heat, partially cover the pan with a lid and simmer gently for about 1 hour, skimming frequently.

Remove the meat from the stock and set aside for use in some other dish. Strain the stock into a large bowl through a fine sieve. Leave to cool, then transfer to the refrigerator. When the fat has congealed on top of the stock, lift it off and discard.

Keep the stock refrigerated until needed.

Brodo di Pesce

FISH STOCK

I never use fish heads or bones when preparing stock as they spoil its delicate flavour. This stock can be refrigerated for up to 3 days, or frozen.

MAKES 1.5 LITRES / 2½ PINTS / 1½ QUARTS

1.5 kg / 3½ lb white fish, heads removed, filleted (boned) and skinned

1 medium-size onion, sliced

2 leeks, white part only, sliced

1 celery stalk, coarsely chopped

240 ml / 8 fl oz / 1 cup dry white wine

1 tbsp lemon juice

a handful of fresh flat-leaf (Italian) parsley

1 sprig of fresh thyme

2 bay leaves

2 tsp salt

1 tsp black peppercorns

In a deep pan combine all the ingredients. Add 1.8 litres / 3 pints / 7½ cups water and slowly bring to the boil.

Reduce the heat, partially cover the pan with a lid and simmer gently for 30 minutes, skimming frequently.

Strain the stock into a large bowl through a fine sieve. Leave to cool, and refrigerate until required.

Maionese

MAYONNAISE

Mayonnaise should be fairly thick because then, if required, it can be diluted with a little milk, lemon or orange juice.

MAKES ABOUT 180 G / 6 OZ / 1 CUP

---

1 egg and 1 egg yolk

---

1 tsp white wine vinegar

---

salt

---

120 ml / 4 fl oz / ½ cup extra virgin olive oil

If you are making mayonnaise by hand, put the egg and yolk in a small bowl, add the vinegar and season with salt. Whisk to mix the ingredients, then start adding the oil in a thin steady stream, whisking constantly. If you notice a little oil around the sides, stop adding oil until the excess is well amalgamated. It is a good rule to start by adding just a drop of oil at a time until the mayonnaise starts to thicken and then to add it in a slow steady stream.

If using a blender, briefly blend the egg, yolk, vinegar and salt, then add the oil gradually with the motor running.

Pasta all' Uovo

BASIC HOME-MADE PASTA

Making good pasta is a simple skill that I think you will not only enjoy learning but will find well worth the trouble once you have mastered it. The method here is the one I use with my students at the cookery courses. However, if you have metric scales, you can't go wrong if you use 100 grams of flour for each size 3 (US large) egg. When American measuring cups are used for measuring flour the total weight can vary as much as 60 or 70 grams, according to how it was poured into the cup. Even equivalent weights are never absolutely accurate when conversions are made from grams to ounces: there are approximately 28 grams in an ounce but the conversion used is 30 grams, the nearest convenient measurement. In Italy eggs are sold according to freshness, not size.

I think you will soon learn the right consistency of the dough and I know my students enjoy this method. Pasta dough

● **Pasta Shapes** ●

should be fairly firm but neither soft nor hard, and moist without being damp. To test it, stick a finger into the middle of the dough. It should emerge slightly sticky but not damp. Keep in mind that it is much easier to add flour than it is to moisten dry dough.

To make pasta, heap about 4 times the quantity of flour required on a work surface, that is 1.2 kg (roughly 2½ lb) flour for 3 eggs. The unused flour can be sifted and put back on the shelf.

Make a well in the centre of the

EGG PASTA

The yolks of eggs laid by free-range hens tend to be quite orangey while the yolks laid by battery hens are pale yellow. They are now being fed with dye in their food to make the yolks the darker colour. However, the trick is soon revealed when you make fresh pasta. When uncooked the pasta is dark yellow, but as soon as it goes into the water it fades to ivory, whereas pasta made with free-range eggs keeps its colour.

mound and break the eggs into it. Beat them lightly with a fork. With a circular movement, gradually start adding flour from around the sides. Blend well with your finger-tips and the palm of your hand, until you have a well-amalgamated dough.

Scrape the board and sift the unused flour.

Using the palm of your hand, knead the dough as you would bread, pushing the dough against the board and turning it constantly until it is smooth, elastic and not too soft, for at least 5 minutes.

To roll the pasta, use a pasta machine or do it by hand: dust a clean board with flour. Flatten the ball of dough with the palm of your hand, then roll it out evenly until it is about 1 mm/$\frac{1}{32}$inch thick (a knife blade thickness) for tagliatelle, lasagne and taglierini, or half that thickness (a sheet of paper) for filled pasta.

Home-made fresh pasta can be cooked straightaway, or it can be dried and kept in the refrigerator for 1 month, or frozen.

Pasta Frolla Dolce

SWEET SHORT PASTRY

This recipe makes enough pastry dough to line a 23-cm/9-inch flan or tart pan. If baking unfilled, there is no need to weigh down the pastry with beans as long as you prick the bottom all over with a fork. Should the pastry puff up while baking, push it down with the palm of your hand; it will stay flat for the rest of the baking time.

240 g / 8 oz / 2 cups flour

2 egg yolks, size 5 (US medium)

60 g / 2 oz / 5 tbsp caster (US granulated) sugar

a pinch of salt

150 g / 5 oz / 10 tbsp unsalted butter

grated zest of 1 lemon

Mound the flour on a work surface and make a hollow in the centre. Drop in the egg yolks, sugar, salt, butter and lemon zest. Using a fork, gradually stir in the flour with a circular movement. Mix until well amalgamated. Lightly roll into a ball, wrap and refrigerate for about 1 hour.

Pasta Frolla Neutra

SHORT PASTRY

This recipe makes enough pastry dough to line a 23-cm/9-inch flan or tart pan. When baking a pastry case unfilled there is no need to weigh down the pastry with beans as long as you prick the bottom all over with a fork. Should the pastry puff up, push it down with the palm of your hand; it will stay flat for the rest of the baking time.

240 g / 8 oz / 2 cups flour

a pinch of salt

1 tsp caster (US granulated) sugar

120 g / 4 oz / 1 stick unsalted butter, in small pieces

1 egg yolk, size 5 (US medium)

3 tbsp cold milk

Mound the flour on a work surface and sprinkle with the salt, sugar and pieces of butter. Using the tips of your fingers work together until the mixture has the consistency of fine crumbs. Add the egg yolk and milk. Knead quickly until well amalgamated. Roll the dough into a ball, wrap and refrigerate for about 1 hour.

Pasta per Pizza

BASIC PIZZA DOUGH

Here is a reliable basic dough for pizzas. Once risen, it can be kept for about 6 hours in the refrigerator before kneading again, adding a topping and baking.

MAKES 1 PIZZA

30 g / 1 oz fresh (compressed) yeast or 15 g / $\frac{1}{2}$ oz / 2 tbsp dried yeast

360 g / 12 oz / 3 cups strong plain (all-purpose) flour

In a small bowl combine the yeast and 210 ml / 7 fl oz / $\frac{7}{8}$ cups lukewarm water and leave to dissolve and start to foam, about 10 minutes.

On a work surface heap the flour into a mound. Make a well in the centre and pour in the yeast mixture. Gradually draw in all the flour and, working with your hands, form a dough. Knead vigorously, pushing the dough away from you and pulling it back. When the dough is elastic, roll it into a ball and leave it to rise in a lightly floured bowl until double in size.

Punch the dough to knock out air and knead for a further few minutes. Roll out the dough into a round about 5 mm / $\frac{1}{4}$ inch thick. Transfer it to a lightly floured pizza pan. Add the chosen topping and bake in a preheated 220°C/425°F/gas 7 oven for 15 minutes.

Pasta Sfoglia

PUFF PASTRY

As its name implies, this pastry puffs up when baked. It is light and flaky and, because it is made with equal weights of butter and flour, very rich. Although it takes quite a long time to make, the only complication is that the dough and butter should have the same consistency and be at the same temperature or the butter will tear the dough when you roll it out.

I have suggested a water quantity, but this is only an approximate amount because it depends entirely on how much water your flour absorbs. With practice you will find the perfect combination.

MAKES 600 G / 1 ¼ LB

300 g / 10 oz / 2 ½ cups flour

a pinch of salt

300 g / 10 oz / 2 ½ sticks unsalted butter

Before making the dough, set aside one-fifth of the flour for the butter block. Heap the rest of the flour on a work surface in a mound. Make a well in the centre and pour in 5 tbsp cold water and the salt. Using the tips of your fingers, work until the mixture resembles coarse crumbs. Add another 5 tbsp cold water and knead the dough until it is smooth and very elastic. Roll the dough into a ball, wrap and refrigerate for 30 minutes.

Soften the butter and, using your fingers, work in the reserved flour, blending until it has the same consistency as the dough. Shape the butter into a square.

Using a rolling pin, roll out the dough into a square about 1 cm / ½ inch thick. Place the square of butter in the centre and fold the corners of the dough over the butter, enclosing it in an envelope of dough without allowing the edges to overlap. Press down gently with your fingers to seal. Wrap and refrigerate for 20 minutes.

Unwrap the dough and place it on a floured surface. Roll out the dough into a rectangle about 5 mm / ¼ inch thick. Fold the rectangle into thirds and flatten lightly with the rolling pin. Wrap the dough and refrigerate again for 20 minutes. This completes the first turn.

Repeat this step 5 more times for a total of 6 turns. At the sixth turn, after folding the rectangle into thirds, roll out the pastry dough to the required size for baking.

Polenta

Polenta is one of Italy's most popular dishes and is ideal for a buffet. I like to serve it accompanied with cheeses, sautéed mushrooms, braised beef, bolognese sauce, various prosciutti, ham or salami. Polenta should be served quite soft and not too dry.

SERVES 6

1.5 litres / 2 ½ pints / 6 cups water

270 g / 9 oz / 2 cups coarse cornmeal

1 tbsp salt

In a large heavy pan, bring the water to the boil. Add the salt and pour in the cornmeal in a steady stream, whisking constantly.

Change the whisk to a wooden spoon and continue cooking over low heat for about 40 minutes, stirring once in a while. The polenta is done when it pulls away easily from the sides of the pan.

Pour the polenta on to a platter and serve immediately. Or, if you have to slice the polenta, pour it on to a wet table or other work surface. With a wet spatula or rolling pin, spread to 1 cm (½ inch) thick. Leave to cool then slice or cut into rounds. (Or you can set the polenta in a roasting tray or dish.)

I Vini

When you are married to a man who owns one of the most ancient and prestigious wine estates in Tuscany and also have a son who is the wine-maker, the decision about what wine to select for supper is somewhat simplified. At Coltibuono I serve our own wines exclusively. Not only do I think they are excellent, I know that if I were a guest at a winery I would most want to taste the estate wines.

I am fortunate that we make wines to accompany every course and category of food. I like to greet my guests with a glass of Trappoline, a white wine named after one of our vineyards. It is a blend of Pinot Bianco, Trebbiano and Malvasia grapes from Chianti. I think its fruity character makes Trappoline perfect as an aperitif. With two to three years of ageing in the bottle, I also serve it with first courses, white meat and fish.

During the late-morning cooking class break we usually get through several bottles of Corale while we taste whatever *antipasto* the class has prepared for that day's meal. This white wine is a blend of equal parts Chardonnay, Trebbiano and Malvasia. It has a light straw colour, an aroma with flowery overtones and a very fresh, delicate taste. I favour it for lunch with light pasta dishes and salads.

Cancelli, our youngest red wine, is a blend of Sangioveto with small percentages of Canaiolo and Cabernet Sauvignon. It has an intense and brilliant garnet colour and a nose with lots of berries – I pick up a hint of sweet pepper. Cancelli is so velvety smooth and drinkable that it makes a pleasant match for a wide variety of foods, in particular richer first courses like polenta and baked pastas.

Chianti Cetamura, a blend of 85 percent Sangiovese and 15 percent Canaiolo, is a dry wine but round and soft. I serve it with my lighter red meat dishes, meat patties and meatloaf, and with young cheeses.

Badia a Coltibuono Chianti Classico is perhaps the most traditional red wine of our estate. Produced with the DOCG formula, it contains a very high percentage of Sangiovese grapes and small quantities of Canaiolo. It is at least two years old before it is released and is the perfect accompaniment to all types of dishes including fish.

Badia a Coltibuono Chianti Classico Riserva is produced only in good vintage years and is aged in cellars that run deep under my kitchen. It is at least four years old before it is released. Our Riserva has the reputation of being a very elegant wine, somewhat austere; I save it for special meals. It is the perfect accompaniment for roasts of all types.

Sangioveto is the traditional Chianti area word for Sangiovese, the noble Tuscan grape variety, and the name we chose for a wine that is made only from Sangiovese grapes. They are selected from the oldest vineyards on the estate and the wine is aged for a year in small barrels of French oak, and cellared for at least another two before being released. It combines best with game and spicy foods. I serve it with wild boar, pigeon and sausage dishes.

Many of my students are wine connoisseurs and look forward to tasting some of the great Riservas from our cellars. Coltibuono is one of the few estates in Chianti with a stock of old vintages dating back to 1958. These are complex wines with aromas that are identified as pine, moss and truffles. The taste is smooth, mellow and dry with a rich and lingering aftertaste. For gradu-

ation dinner I select a fine old vintage from the seventies.

With dessert I serve Coltibuono's Vin Santo. This is a traditional Tuscan sweet wine composed of a blend of Trebbiano and Malvasia grapes. The vinification process follows an age-old method that is unique. The clusters of grapes are hung in well-aired rooms and left to dry for about two months. When the required grade of juice concentration is reached, which will give the wine its sweet taste, the raisined grapes are then pressed and the musts are put in small oak barrels that are sealed air-tight. Vin Santo ferments and ages in the same barrel for about five years, stored under the winery's roof. The seasonal temperature change also influences the fermentation process, activating it during the warm seasons and stopping it during the winter. This slow maturation gives Vin Santo its warm amber colour. It is a rich, full-bodied wine that is pleasantly, not overly, sweet. The classic way to enjoy it is with *biscotti di Prato*, the hard, finger-shaped Tuscan biscuits or cookies, which you dip into the wine.

After dinner, when we retire to the drawing room for coffee, I serve grappa, a distilled liquor produced from the lightly pressed skins of the same selected grapes used in making the Coltibuono Classico and Riserva wines. The result is a crystal clear spirit (45 percent alcohol content) that does not have any of the rough edges associated with more rustic versions of this drink. It is something of an acquired taste but often becomes a favourite night-cap for many of my students before the cooking class week is over.

Italy produces and exports (and also consumes) more wine than any other country in the world. When I travel, I have the opportunity to visit many wineries and wine-makers, from the Alps to the island of Sicily, and have tasted innumerable excellent wines. I am still discovering new ones. Those I list here are only meant to be an indication of some of the best. An American neighbour, Burton Anderson, who lives across the valley from Coltibuono, has recently written the most comprehensive book on Italian wines, entitled *The Wine Atlas of Italy*, which I highly recommend to anyone who is interested in a full treatment of this subject.

Close to home in Tuscany, south of Siena, is the production zone of Brunello di Montalcino, one of Italy's great red wines. Brunello is a particular variety of the Sangiovese grape, different from the one that is grown in Chianti. The wines produced from this strain are powerful, austere and tannic, and need a few years to develop. When it is ready, a bottle of Brunello is a fine accompaniment to all rich red meat dishes. Another famous Tuscan red is Vino Nobile di Montepulciano, from the south-eastern part of the region. It, too, is made from a variety of the Sangiovese Grosso grape, called Prugnolo Gentile, and blended with Canaiolo, Malvasia and Trebbiano. In style it is somewhat similar to Chianti.

The first wine I ever drank, at least that I can recall, came from Piemonte where I spent much of my youth. It was a good place to begin. Piemonte produces two of the most renowned of Italy's red wines, Barolo and Barbaresco. They are both made from Nebbiolo, considered the noblest of Italian grape varieties and grown in vineyards around the city of Alba. Barolo is the more celebrated of the two. It is a wine with an intense concentration of fruit that is robust when young and becomes superbly elegant with age. Perhaps Barbaresco is not as big a wine as Barolo, but the best ones I have tasted are wonderfully soft and velvety. These wines should be drunk with equally robust foods, roasted and boiled meats, stews and game. Two excellent lighter red wines are also

produced in Piemonte, Barbera and Dolcetto, both fragrant and smooth. And to finish the meal there is Moscato d'Asti, a delicious, fruity sparkling wine.

The region of Friuli-Venezia Giulia in north-eastern Italy, which borders Austria and Yugoslavia, makes world-class white wines. It has an ideal climate for growing innumerable varieties of white grapes: a pale, very dry Malvasia that is good with fish; crisp, flowery Pinot Bianco that can age into a full-bodied white; Pinot Grigio, from the Collio hills, that can be a wine of distinction; Tocai Friulano, with lovely floral and herbal aromas; and the region's excellent Chardonnay. Perhaps my favourite white wine of Friuli is the full-bodied Verduzzo from the area called Colli Orientali. It combines perfectly with seafood pasta and risotto.

Another region noted for its outstanding white wines as well as several fine reds, grassy Cabernets, the popular, dry Santa Maddalena and the grand, robust Teroldego Rotaliano, is the Trentino-Alto Adige, at the northernmost corner of Italy on the border with Austria. When I visit this area I most look forward to tasting its wonderfully perfumed whites, whose flowery aromas and delicate taste have a marvellous affinity with food. The fruity Gewürztraminer is claimed to have originated in the South Tyrolean village of Tramin where the wine is called Traminer Aromatico. These wines are often compared with Alsatian varieties, but the local crisp Müller-Thurgau, dry Chardonnay and elegant Riesling, as well as others, have distinct personalities of their own.

The neighbouring region of the Veneto is the largest producer of classified wines in Italy. Its white Soave and red Bardolino and Valpolicella, all from the area of Verona, are known the world over. Classico versions of these three from the best estates can be excellent. Recently I have particularly enjoyed a lesser-known white, Bianco di Custoza, grown in vineyards on the lovely Lake Garda. It is an interesting blend of Trebbiano, Garganega and Tocai that is dry

and crisp. My preferred red wine of the region is Amarone, from the same zone as Valpolicella. It is a soft, rich wine that has a pleasantly dry, bitter (*amaro*) taste at the end from which it gets its name.

In the south of Italy I think the best wines, both red and white, come from the region of Campania in the area of Avellino and are made by one estate, Mastroberardino. The wines to watch for are Fiano, a dry, elegant white, and Taurasi, a robust, rich red that is superb with the delicious milk-fed lamb of the region.

Italy's largest region, Sicily, also has the greatest number of vineyards in the country and is the second biggest producer of wine, after Puglia. Until recently, however, many of its fine wines were little known outside the island. I always had to bring back bottles of Moscato di Pantelleria and Malvasia delle Lipari, two superb sweet wines. Now I can find them in Milan and in fine restaurants abroad. Robust reds and dry, elegant Riservas are being made from the Nerello and Perricone grape varieties.

One of best-known names in Italian wines abroad is Marsala, especially on restaurant menus, where it is found in the names of veal dishes and desserts especially. What is not so well known is that the best of this Sicilian wine is also a fine vintage to drink. There are several types and classifications of Marsala. Marsala *vergine*, with its complex aromas and distinctively dry taste, I consider to be one of the great *aperitivo* wines as well as a fine accompaniment for cheese to finish a meal.

Index